# Free Persons
# and the
# Common Good

# Free Persons
# and the
# Common Good

*Michael Novak*

WITHDRAWN

Madison Books
Lanham • New York • London

**LIBRARY OF CONGRESS**
**Library of Congress Cataloging–in–Publication Data**

Novak, Michael.
Free persons and the common good / by Michael Novak.
p.   cm.
Bibliography: p.
Includes index.
1. Sociology, Christian (Catholic)  2. Common good.  3. Catholic
Church– –Doctrines.  I. Title.
BX1793.N59    1988    88–23602 CIP
320'.01'1– –dc19
ISBN 0–8191–6499–2 (alk. paper)

All Madison Books are produced on acid-free paper.
The paper used in this publication meets the minimum requirements of American
National Standard for Information Sciences—Permanence of Paper for Printed Library
Materials, ANSI Z39.48-1984.    ∞

*In homage to Jacques Maritain*

Man is born for citizenship.

Aristotle
*Nicomachean Ethics*

By its liberty, the human person transcends the stars and all the world of nature.

Jacques Maritain
*The Person and the Common Good*

To feel much for others and little for ourselves . . . to restrain our selfish, and indulge our benevolent affections, constitutes the perfection of human nature.

Adam Smith
*The Theory of Moral Sentiments*

Thus the most democratic country in the world now is that in which men have in our time carried to the highest perfection the art of pursuing in common the objects of common desires and have applied this new technique to the greatest number of purposes.

Alexis de Tocqueville
*Democracy in America*

# TABLE OF CONTENTS

# PREFACE AND
# ACKNOWLEDGMENTS

In the rhythms of one's own reflections there are times for brief
forays of an experimental type. In a trilogy recently completed,*
I have laid out some rather large ambitions. Meanwhile, shorter
works have proven to be necessary, in order to wrestle with
particular problems looming into view. This present essay is one
such. It has been written for the general reader. Its purpose is
not to instruct specialists—far from it—but to draw attention to a
new task.

Thus, I place the new concept of the common good introduced
into history by the liberal society (and especially by the United
States) face-to-face with the more ancient Catholic concept of the
common good. To the best of my knowledge, this has never been
done before. In *Freedom With Justice*, I outlined my prevailing
hypothesis, as follows: On matters of *institutional realism*, the
liberal tradition has made discoveries that the Catholic tradition
sorely needs; reciprocally, regarding certain philosophical-theo-
logical *conceptions*, the Catholic tradition has achieved some insights (into the nature of the human person, the human community, and mediating institutions, e.g.) in which many in the

---

*The Spirit of Democratic Capitalism* (1982), *Freedom With Justice: Catholic Social Thought and Liberal Institutions* (1984), and *Will It Liberate?
Questions about Liberation Theology* (1986).

ix

liberal intellectual tradition are now expressing interest. The two traditions need each other, each being weaker where the other is stronger.

Too often, the liberal tradition is discussed wholly in terms of the individual, the rational economic agent, self-interest, and something like the utilitarian calculus. This leaves to socialists, quite inaccurately, a monopoly of concern about the social system as a whole. On the other side, too often the Catholic view of the common good is presented as though it did not respect the freedom of the human person, the rights of the individual, and the unique properties of the many different spheres through which the common good is cumulatively realized. Yet the liberal tradition has in fact greatly expanded and enriched the concept of the common good. And the Catholic tradition—through its distinctive concepts of person, will, self-deception, virtue, practical wisdom, "the dark night of the soul," and insight itself—has thickened and enriched our understanding of the individual.

Meanwhile, all around us, writers of diverse religious and philosophical backgrounds are turning anew to the concept of the common good. On the Left, the "communitarian" critics of classical liberalism such as Michael Sandel, Robert N. Bellah, Benjamin Barber, and Michael Walzer are moving in fresh directions. So are the rather different "communitarians" on the Right such as Robert Nisbet, William A. Schambra, Peter Berger, and Richard John Neuhaus. In order to achieve the common good it is not necessary, of course, that all inquirers reach agreement. Yet this unplanned convergence upon one central parapet from many different angles is quite remarkable:

> As many arrows, loosed several ways,
> Fly to one mark . . .
>
> —*King Henry V*, Act I, Scene 2

Still, the argument of this essay is not an easy one. Say that this project is wrongheaded, if you wish, or poorly executed, but do not say that it is lacking in intellectual daring. It would certainly have been of use to me to have found someone else's work to follow. In this early foray, I have been able to accomplish little more than to drive in stakes to mark where further work promises fruitfulness. At a minimum, I have called attention to three different characteristics of the new concept of the common good, and have shown how this new common good is compatible both with the right of individuals to define the good for themselves and also with an unplanned and uncoerced social order.

I am particularly in the debt of Father Oliver Williams, C.S.C., and John W. Houck for inviting me to prepare a paper for a conference on the common good held at the University of Notre Dame in the spring of 1986. Called to serve as U.S. ambassador at the Experts Meeting on Human Contacts in Bern, Switzerland, I could not, alas, be present at Notre Dame, but did later submit a paper.* This effort persuaded me that a much longer period of reflection was called for.

Then in early 1987 Ralph McInerny, director of the Maritain Center at the University of Notre Dame, invited me to present one of the following chapters as the first annual Olin lecture. To those who participated in that crowded room, and for the many good questions raised, I am further in the debt of Notre Dame— and Jacques Maritain.

I must also thank profoundly Scott Walter, who worked so intelligently to help develop the footnotes; and also Judy Shindel, Gayle Yiotis, Janet Cannon, Roberta Dougherty, Nancy Burkhart, Philip Costopoulos, and Philip Brach for assistance along the way. Robert N. Bellah, Walter Berns, Michael Walzer, Ernest Fortin, A.A., and David Hollenbach, S.J., read drafts of the book; their comments allowed me to improve it.

Since the aim of this essay is to provoke questions rather than to settle them, and to place upon the table scouting reports on materials often overlooked, I have been bold enough to offer it now for public criticism.

I do so in homage to a thinker whose contributions to the

---

*"Free Persons and the Common Good," *Crisis*, October 1986; reprinted in Oliver F. Williams and John W. Houck, eds., *The Common Good and U.S. Capitalism* (Lanham, Maryland: University Press of America, 1987).

Universal Declaration of Human Rights, to the Christian Democratic parties of the world, and to the vision of a practical, realistic humanism, will long deserve the gratitude of those who thirst for ordered liberty.

Michael Novak
August 15, 1988

*Introduction:*

# INTERWEAVING TWO TRADITIONS

For the last two decades the concept of the common good, a notion of ancient Greek, Roman, and Catholic lineage, has been in shadow even among Catholics. As of 1986, it had not had even one entry in *The Catholic Periodical and Literature Index* in nearly twenty years. Now, quite suddenly, many world events are pushing it forward into light. Pope John Paul II, for example, has used it frequently. The U.S. Catholic Bishops returned to it prominently in their pastoral letter on the U.S. economy in 1986. Oliver F. Williams and John W. Houck edited a collection, *The Common Good and U.S. Capitalism,* in 1987.[1] Meanwhile, the liberal tradition, after a long winter of neglect, is now enjoying a second spring on several continents at once. Thus, to try to show that the liberal tradition carries within it a profound and original notion of the common good is not at all untimely.[2]

The early liberals spoke often of "the commonweal," the "general welfare," and a universal "system of natural liberty." They promised a "new order of the ages." Their gaze was fixed, not on individuals solely, but on new republics, nations, systems. They knew that the dignity of the individual has no protection in history except in social orders of certain kinds, under law, within specific institutions, and that to neglect liberty's social necessities was to imperil it.

For three reasons, it is useful to work out the liberal conception of the common good in a predominantly Catholic context. First,

1

the Catholic intellectual tradition has been one of several custodians of the ancient and medieval contributions to our civilization. From within this tradition, over long centuries, our modern concepts of the person and the common good slowly emerged. No other tradition has developed so large and detailed a body of work on the common good. (The *Dictionary of the History of Ideas,* in its four volumes, does not list the concept.) Second, nearly a fifth of the world's population is immediately affected by the Catholic intellectual tradition. Third, a marriage between the liberal tradition and the Catholic tradition is of extraordinary importance to the poor of the world. It is not easy to detect any other institutions empirically more likely to lift up and to liberate the poor than liberal institutions.

But the immediate audience for my argument is not Catholic. There is considerable confusion these days in almost all camps, from libertarian to socialist, concerning how to define such basic notions as *person, community, individual, collective, association, state, private, public.*

It is widely assumed that liberal thought is highly individualistic, whereas Catholic thought, like Jewish thought, carries forward from the mists of the past a strong (perhaps too strong) social sense. To my eyes, reality seems a little different. Tutored through many years in a classical Catholic education, I did not truly encounter liberal thinking—in the flesh, in personal interchange, in the classroom—until my twenties. At first, liberal thought offended me, seemed quite wrong. The Catholic tradition teaches one nasty things about liberalism (it almost always uses "liberal" as a pejorative term), possibly in retaliation for the nasty things some liberals have had to say about the Catholic church. On the other hand, I slowly grew to admire the liberal intellectual tradition, even though I long preferred democratic socialist and social democratic thought to the classic liberal and "Whig" tradition.

Only when (about a decade ago) I became convinced that oldtime socialism is a dead end, both in practice and in theory, did I approach the liberal intellectual tradition in an openminded way. Just the same, I did not find in the classics of the liberal tradition what most liberals do (the libertarians, for example).

What kept striking me, unexpectedly, were its social dimensions. Why were these not more commonly emphasized? Polemical reasons must have governed that oversight, since the main intellectual battlefront, first against mercantilism and aristocracy and then against socialism, called for an urgent defense of the individual.

As these brief hints suggest, I have had to find my own way into the liberal tradition. I find the liberal tradition, enlarged so as to include explicitly its original social inspirations, a natural home, as natural for me as for Alexis de Tocqueville and Lord Acton, two Catholics who have preceded me upon the path I have been climbing.

Just the same, because of my training in philosophy and theology, I early found Jacques Maritain my most helpful mentor. Finding myself commissioned to execute an essay on the common good, I was reminded that 1986 marked the fortieth anniversary of his little classic, *The Person and the Common Good*. Beginning work, I found that in order to express the whole burden of my findings I needed more than a single essay.

Maritain was in Rome on February 6, 1946, when he penned the acknowledgments for *The Person and the Common Good*, four chapters of which were to appear in *The Review of Politics* during that same year.[3] The nations of the North Atlantic had just emerged from World War II. European cities were piled with rubble, and even as he was writing the winter of 1946 was unusually severe. On what basis would the new civilization of Europe arise?

Maritain believed that ideas embodied in broad ideologies have a great effect upon history. A misconception of the individual had led the bourgeois democracies to grief. A misconception of the common good had led Communist states into totalitarianism. Maritain's aim was to clarify the two necessary fundamental notions, the person and the common good. Achieving clarity about these, Europe might shape its institutions and its practices in a more liberating manner than before.

Although his immediate focus was postwar Europe, the occasion for Maritain's publication—in English, in the United States—was an unusually bitter North American controversy.

The formidable Charles De Koninck of Laval was in many ways a friend and colleague of Maritain and his work; but he was also something of a rival. (In those days, Thomists often attacked one another fiercely for disloyalty to, or misunderstanding of, St. Thomas.) In 1943, De Koninck published a long essay on the common good, with the subtitle "Against the Personalists." Since Maritain was known internationally for his attempt to supplant "individualism" with "personalism," many readers assumed that De Koninck was attacking Maritain even without mentioning the latter's name. To make matters worse, the American Dominican I. Thomas Eschmann fired off an intemperate essay defending Maritain explicitly (while misstating Maritain's views); and he also accused De Koninck of misrepresenting St. Thomas. Picking up the gauntlet, De Koninck replied in kind and at still greater length. Maritain took note of all this in a footnote early in his book, hoping that its publication would clear the record on where he stood.[4]

In one sense, the fine points of this debate among the Thomists need not detain us; much of it was ontological, even theological, in substance, rather than political or institutional. Still, a moment spent on certain political implications (here and in chapter one) may contribute to a fuller comprehension of the terms "person" and "common good."[5]

The controversy between De Koninck and Maritain brought to light, in a Christian perspective, the ground of the dignity of persons. It showed that the radical vocation to be one with God in insight and in love is so crucial to every person that this vocation may never be lawfully obstructed by any state or society. But this same guarantee of "non-obstruction," so to speak, also opens the way for any human person who so chooses to use his liberty against or apart from that vocation. It is not for state or for society to separate the wheat from the tares. Rain must fall on the just and the unjust alike. It was along these lines that Maritain proceeded to his seminal work, *Man and the State*, concerning state and society, democracy and religious liberty.[6] His sustained reflection led him to emphasize practical cooperation among citizens whose theoretical reasons for their actions were radically diverse. Still, in a genuinely pluralistic society, it is an advantage to have each participant speak in his own proper voice, rather than to sound like every other.

One should not underestimate Maritain's influence in places where more secular North American thinkers hardly penetrate, if at all. On this small planet (especially in the Third World) there are undoubtedly more persons of Catholic background than of a merely modern secular tradition. To an underestimated extent, philosophical thinking participates in cultural traditions in which lie hid the secret codes for interpreting the meaning of words.

In the essays that follow, I have not tried to recapitulate the arguments of Maritain. Rather, in addressing forty years later the same themes he earlier took up, I have tried to express lessons forced upon us by the intervening years. The world today is not where it was in 1946. The preoccupation of peoples and governments with economic issues is especially intense. This intensity has not been reduced by a virtually universal rise in standards of productivity, income, longevity, infant mortality, and education scarcely dreamed of in 1946.[7] It is as if each step forward reveals how much more must be done, and how elastic human need is.

Since World War II, the population of the world has more than doubled and increases still (except in several nations of Western Europe, which face drastic and dangerous downward trends of depopulation). Thus, the concept of the common good invoked today is chiefly in reference to the economic order. In economics, the friends of Maritain's work will certainly agree that Maritain wrote relatively little and rather romantically.[8] Not in that dismal science lay his consuming interests. The political order absorbed him intensely, and so also the moral and cultural order (art, education, the church).

Where Maritain in a sense ended, there I begin. In *Reflections on America,* he confessed quite vividly that from afar, like many other Europeans, he had always despised American bourgeois capitalism. Indeed, he made of "bourgeois individualism" a lifelong target of attack. In living in America, however, he observed a way of life that greatly falsified his earlier opinions.[9] He still had much critical to say about America, as do Americans. (There is no point in being American if one does not criticize the country for falling short of its ideals.)

As for myself, to the civilization of the United States I owe not only the beneficial refuge given to my family but also a set of intellectual insights that justifies the bold claim inscribed upon our national seal: *Novus ordo seclorum*. Since my first book, *A New Generation: American and Catholic* (1964), I have been eager to take the measure not only of the philosophy but also of the habits, practices, and institutions of the American people, according to the twin concepts Maritain first thrust on my attention: free persons and the common good.

The political institutions of the United States—constitutional limited government; the separation of powers; checks and balances; a bicameral legislature; federalism; religious liberty; the Bill of Rights; the recognition in the Constitution itself that the ideas of authors and inventors are a form of inviolable property, and so on—are sufficiently original to have commanded the attention of revolutionaries around the world for more than two hundred years. As they still do today.

Again, the American moral and cultural order, vital and creative today as never before, not only makes many claims of historical originality but is also the object of universal imitation, not least in the writing of constitutions for new nations. One of its fundamental principles, however, *the principle of association*, which Tocqueville correctly described as the new first principle of the new science of politics, has not been as widely grasped. It is nonetheless of decisive importance to our subject:

Nothing, in my view, more deserves attention than the intellectual and moral associations in America. American political and industrial associations easily catch our eyes, but the others tend not to be noticed. And even if we do notice them we tend to misunderstand them, hardly ever having seen anything similar before. However, we should recognize that the latter are as necessary as the former to the American people; perhaps more so.

. . . Among laws controlling human societies there is one more precise and clearer, it seems to me, than all the others. If men are to remain civilized or to become civilized, the art of association must develop and improve among them at the same speed as equality of conditions spreads.[10]

Notwithstanding these claims in politics and morals, it is in its economic order that the United States has given witness to its most profound originality. Although Great Britain is often singled out as the first of the capitalist countries, many of the insights that Adam Smith intended to communicate to European nations still imprisoned by the system of mercantilism were gleaned from observations concerning the North American "colonies." Even in the midnineteenth century, it was to American practices, methods, and successes that Cobden turned for examples to move his countrymen.[11] Thus, the United States wears accurately enough its title as the first of the undeveloped countries to achieve development. After World War II, it became the model for West Germany and Japan and, later, "the four little dragons" of East Asia. Even its enemies, in denouncing the "world capitalist system," have most explicitly in mind the economy of the United States.

The economic order of the United States tested a proposition; viz., whether an economy may raise the common good of all through granting unparalleled economic liberties to free persons. Such an economy is dedicated *both* to the general welfare and to the freedom of persons. In doing so, does it embody a theory? Many hold that the American economic order is guided by pragmatism, not theory. This may well be so. Still, it would be exceedingly odd if after more than two hundred years a detached observer could not detect patterns, and thus an implicit theory, even where many who acted freely were unaware of such patterns and such theory.

In the second place, not all economic orders in history have allowed so much scope to the daily pragmatism of individual agents. The *design* of how this is done will surely be of interest, not least to those who claim that "planning" is a better way. To construct an economy of impressive productivity, efficiency, and cheerful cooperation is not easy. Few countries in history have done so.

The chapters that follow, then, deal with economic questions rather more than Maritain did. Nonetheless, Maritain himself observed, without working out the implications, that, beneath the ideology of individualism, there is operating in liberal societies, chief among them the United States, an implicit theory of the common good. This theory—as, again, Maritain insisted—deserves to be made explicit.

You are advancing in the night, bearing torches toward which mankind would be glad to turn; but you leave them enveloped in the fog of a merely experiential approach and mere practical conceptualization, with no universal ideas to communicate. For lack of adequate ideology, your lights cannot be seen.[12]

In the same context, Maritain wrote that corporations

have understood that, in order simply to exist, and to keep producing, they must become more and more socially minded and concerned with the general welfare. Thus, not by reason of any Christian love, but rather of intelligent self-interest, and of the ontological generosity, so to speak, of the stream of life, the idea of the advantage of the human being—all those who cooperate on the job, and the general public as well—is gradually taking the upper hand. I do not assume that corporations have reached a stage where they would prefer the common good to their own particular good. But they are reaching a stage where for the sake of their own particular good they realize that the superior rights of the common good must be taken into account.[13]

Among existing societies (and these are the only ones to which a mind of empirical bent can turn), not many have better achieved the common good, or more deservedly won the love and loyalty of their citizens, than this quite imperfect, restlessly progressive nation. To understand better our own working practice of the common good—a practice that embodies an often neglected theory—is, then, a project worthy of philosophical reflection.

The problem of reconciling freedom for persons with the

common good is universal. Each nation must solve in its own way the riddle of reconciling what appears to be a contradiction: respect for free persons and attainment of the common good. In practice, this riddle is best solved through studying the large variety of paths pursued by this planet's many nations. Still, the ancients said that charity begins at home, and so it is not at all improper to try to understand more clearly the practices (and hidden theories) of one's own nation.

Finally, this essay may be useful for another reason. Perhaps because the "common good" was so closely identified with the intellectual traditions of the past against which the first liberal thinkers were rebelling, it is not a term altogether prominent in liberal thought; it certainly appears, and at a basic level, but substitutes for it appear more frequently. It is, in addition, a vague term, not only large and sweeping but also derivative from an era before the differentiations that mark social history had yet occurred: such differentiations as the clear distinction between "state" and "society," "individual" and "person," "church" and "state," the separation of systems (political, economic and moral-cultural), the separation of powers, and the like. Even in its own right, though, most Catholic writers have observed that the term, while retaining some validity, transcends the structures of any one historical society, and necessarily changes its meaning from one era to another, and from one society to another. "It is simply impossible," declares *The New Catholic Encyclopedia,* "to define the common good in a final way irrespective of the changing social conditions."[14] Catholic writers, one will find, not only frequently disagree about the meaning of the term but make significant errors in discussing it.

Thus, for example, in an otherwise admirable introductory essay for *The Common Good and U.S. Capitalism,* Oliver F. Williams writes about the tension between personal autonomy and the common good: "To be sure, individual autonomy is not unimportant but this notion only has meaning in the context of a community that puts limits on *any* personal projects for the sake of common life." He then adds:

> Catholic social teaching has used the term "common good"
> to point to the challenge of building the good society. The

term takes on the concreteness specific to a historical context, but always in this view freedom is never an end in itself but rather the means to achieve the good society.[15]

But Williams draws these distinctions a little too loosely. How would his terms exclude the worst abuses of a collectivist, totalitarian society? The USSR justifies all the limits it places upon personal projects "for the sake of common life." Furthermore, to treat free persons as "means to achieve the good society" is to treat them instrumentally, to place them in the kingdom of means rather than in the kingdom of ends. Williams' intention in these passages is better than his exact wording, as is clear in his defense of Solidarity in Poland in the same passage. More than he wishes, however, the formulations cited above demean the dignity of the free person. In using the language of "means" and "ends" to define the relation of the person to the common good, he errs.

Similarly, Charles Curran has observed that "since Vatican II official Catholic social teaching has not given that significant and important a role to the concept of the common good, especially as rooted in Thomistic thought." He offers four arguments in support of this thesis:

(1) Thomistic natural law method is no longer the primary basis of Catholic social teaching and ethics.
(2) The teaching itself incorporates elements [i.e., the preferential option for the poor] that seem to be in opposition to the common good tradition.
(3) [Ecclesiastical] documents [since 1965] do not explicitly give that much attention to the common good.
(4) Catholic social thought as developed by contemporary theologians seems to have neglected the concept of the common good.[16]

Curran reminds us that from volume 13 (1965–66) to volume 33 (1985–86) there is not a single entry under "common good" in the *Catholic Periodical and Literature Index*, although in preceding volumes there had been many references.

Nonetheless, the U.S. Catholic Bishops found it difficult to develop their pastoral letter on the U.S. economy without appeal to this concept. With each successive draft (of three), the term "common good" occupied an increasingly central place—partly in opposition to excessive individualism. (The term "common good" occurred twenty-six times in the second draft, and moved even more clearly to the logical center of the third.) In addition, in response to the potential divisiveness of class conflict inherent in some versions of "liberation theology" and in "the preferential option for the poor," appeals to the common good are becoming more prominent in Catholic writing. Witness also the Williams and Houck collection, already cited, in which Curran's essay is one of eighteen. Curran himself ends by noting that "the basic realities of the common good tradition are still found in Catholic social teaching." And he raises three lively questions:

> How precisely can the recognition that human beings are by nature social and civil society is basically good be reconciled with the growing emphasis on freedom, equality and rights? How much of a role should be given to power and conflict as strategies and tactics without destroying the common fabric of society? How is distributive justice related to the contemporary emphasis on equality?[17]

Interestingly enough, the Second Vatican Council (1962–65) offered a definition of the common good that seemed to subordinate the common good to the dignity of the human person:

> [The common good is] the sum of those conditions of social life which allow social groups and their individual members relatively thorough and ready access to their own fulfillment.[18]

In Christian eyes, free persons are ordered to an end far beyond the power of earthly states, societies, collectives, associations (even the family) to obstruct: eternal communion in the love of their Creator. In this respect, the individual can never be properly thought of as less than transcendent, never as a mere instrument of earthly purposes. The good community exists to protect and to further the development of free persons, to respect their dignity, and (to borrow the words of the Declaration of Independence) to secure their rights. The Second Vatican Council approached its definition of the common good in an open, inductive manner, but what is most significant in its definition (as we shall see) is the place it assigns to the fulfillment of the human person. Individual human beings may intend by "fulfillment" many different ends, but in the Catholic tradition as in secular traditions today it is not the role of the state to define them. It is the right of persons to define them.

It is true that humans are social animals and that they realize their full possibilities (even if they choose solitude) in community with others. Thus, the relation between free persons and the community is reciprocal. In one sense, free persons are ordered to the common good. Citizenship requires attention to the common institutions that secure personal liberties and help them to flower. In another sense, common institutions are ordered to the full development of free persons. Reciprocally, communities are judged by the degree to which their members develop to their full human possibilities, and persons are judged by how they create, nourish, and develop communities and institutions worthy of free persons. The free person is ordered to the building up of the common good; the common good is ordered to the fulfillment of free persons.

Still, as the title of *The Common Good and U.S. Capitalism* suggests, many contemporary theologians (not only Catholic theologians) are quite adversarial to the liberal tradition. Charles C. West, a prominent Protestant theologian, has considerable disdain for the "mystifications" of the tradition of Thomas Malthus, David Ricardo, and Herbert Spencer, through which he interprets John Locke and Adam Smith:

Stripped of all dissembling and tendentious appeals to freedom the [liberal] argument might be stated thus: there is a mechanism in the free market by which millions of individual choices in pursuit of profit, pleasure, and power, even at the cost of their neighbors, are converted into the general progress and prosperity of the human race. Despite the amorality of the process and despite the many injustices it leaves in its trail, most attempts to achieve the same benefits by responsible human policy will end in disaster. We must depend on the science of economics to show us the way toward a common good that will emerge and be defined in the process itself.[19]

From this passage, West turns to the demystification of capitalism undertaken by Marx. West judges that the "Leninist form of Marxism" has been the most ambitious attempt to create and to enforce a common good, with results that "though they seduce many Christian idealists, have been disastrous."[20]

I can remember clearly when I would have read such passages in comfortable agreement. But now I am troubled by the impoverished understanding Professor West has of the liberal tradition. No doubt, the theoretical foundations of liberal thought need serious reconstruction. No doubt, the practices of liberal societies are now, and will ever be, also in need of serious reconstruction. Surely, though, there is more than a blind "mechanism" involved in the free market. Surely, too, in reality, the "process" is not "amoral" but, on the contrary, only possible at all when certain specific moral habits have been internalized and are regularly practiced. Market behavior requires a broad and deep moral base, and the broader and deeper the latter the better the functioning of markets. Coercion, dishonesty, false measures, hidden shoddy workmanship, incivility, sloth, rudeness and many other vices are extremely damaging to markets. Under conditions of barbarism, transactions well below the standards of civilized markets prevail.

Humanists often seem driven to trivialize or to demonize commercial activities, as if to secure their own superior moral standing. What Professor West writes is not idiosyncratic; it is altogether typical of most of what I experienced in my own education. For example, one of the thinkers who influenced me profoundly in my youth was Father Virgil Michel, a Benedictine monk at St. John's University in Collegeville, Minnesota, one of the founders of the liturgical movement in the United States. Toward liberal thought (he often called it "*laissez-faire* thinking"), capitalism, and "the bourgeois mind," he was habitually scathing. He thought these the very antithesis of a Catholic sense of order. He regularly contrasted the "modern liberal world" with the happier medieval order, in which aristocrats understood *noblesse oblige* and peasants lived in secure decency, and in which daily life with its "old refinements" and its "amenities" had not yet yielded to the "matter of fact and the practical" that "spell also crudity and vulgarity." He cited favorably a famous passage from Marx:

> The bourgeoisie, wherever it has got the upperhand, has put an end to all feudal, patriarchal, idyllic relations. It has pitilessly torn asunder the motley feudal ties that bound man to his "natural superiors," and has left remaining no other nexus between man and man than naked self-interest, than callous "cash payment." It has drowned the most heavenly ecstasies of religious fervor, of chivalrous enthusiasm, of philistine sentimentalism, in the icy water of egotistical calculation. It has resolved personal worth into exchange value, and in place of the numberless indefeasible chartered freedoms, has set up that single unconscionable freedom—Free Trade. In one word, for exploitation, veiled by religious and political illusions, it has substituted naked, shameless, direct, brutal exploitation.[21]

Against the evil "bourgeois culture," Virgil Michel called for a rebirth of "Christian culture"—antibourgeois, anticapitalist, and antiliberal. Such thinking, which once excited me, now seems to me morally blind, and somehow deliberately so. There is a will in it, and not an admirable one, despite its wide acceptance.

In the case of Charles C. West, mentioned a moment ago, such an approach is all the more surprising because, after his rejection of Marxism, he turns back on his last page to the liberal tradition:

> We must start with the liberal premise: the search for a common good must start with particular goals and values which many different persons and groups pursue, and seek, in mutual respect, some accommodation.[22]

"Is there a common good?" West asks. As a natural order common to all humanity, West rejects the concept of the common good as an illusion. And he adds:

No longer can we impose on all society the goals and values, however reasonable or good, which for one group in society seem to define the meaning of the whole. Where religious authorities attempt to do so—one might mention the diverse cases of Iran and South Africa—the consequences are monstrous.[23]

Thus, even a theologian who wishes to maintain the concept of the common good as a guide toward seeking, "in mutual respect, some accommodation," cannot get very far in defining that concept, once he has failed to grasp the originality of the liberal solution to a perennial problem. West embraces liberal conclusions, probably because of their fruits, without grasping the liberal argument.

Such encounters as these warn the reader that we are about to enter wildernesses and thickets, and need to go slowly.

Eventually, in the distant future, we will in addition have to speak of a common *international* order: a common good embracing the entire planet, with full recognition of the rights of free persons everywhere. Eventually, we will have to speak, as our forefathers would have put it, of a universal system of natural liberty. A *system*. A common good. A new order of the ages. Even though its aim will be to liberate human persons everywhere, its fundamental thrust will be social. Even though its fundamental thrust will be for the good of all, its criterion will be respect for the liberty of each. Free persons and the common good—how can they be combined?

Favorably to our purposes, several intellectual currents in our culture are converging on this problematic. From its firm, traditional social sense, the Catholic tradition has been moving toward the defense of the free person and the personal dignity of every citizen. Recent studies in the classical liberal tradition, including the American framers, emphasize anew the social perspective of those who often seemed to stress the individual against the state and even against the traditional pressures of communities. Finally, contemporary liberals are more and more painfully aware that "liberal commitments" extend to the social habits and institutions in which alone free persons can find sustenance, and individual rights secure exercise.[24] The theory of the liberal society is slowly taking on new "communitarian" shape, and attracting fresh support from many often contrary directions. Its communitarian practice has too long been far ahead of its articulated theory.

The liberal society has found an imperfect, certainly not utopian, way that works in practice, whose theory has not yet been made fully explicit. Were its requirements to be made explicit, the added clarity might help us to improve our daily practice, and thus to take further steps toward achieving a fuller common good. To take at least a few solid steps in that direction is the aim I have set myself in these few pages.

In some countries, the inhabitants . . . set too high a value upon their time to spend it on the interests of the community; and they shut themselves up in a narrow selfishness, marked out by four sunk fences and a quickset hedge. But if an American were condemned to confine his activity to his own affairs, he would feel an immense void in the life which he is accustomed to lead, and his wretchedness would be unbearable.

Alexis de Tocqueville
*Democracy in America*

The common good is all the arrangements and conditions that make it possible for the individual and for small social units to work together in an orderly fashion towards the fulfillment of their divinely willed purpose—the development of personality and the fostering of culture.

Joseph (later Cardinal) Hoeffner, S.J.
*Fundamentals of Christian Sociology*

The common good is the sum of those conditions of social life which allow social groups and their individual members relatively thorough and ready access to their own fulfillment.

Vatican Council II
"The Church in the Modern World" (1965)

*Chapter One*

# THE CONCEPTUAL BACKGROUND

## 1. Can a Pluralist Society Have a Common Good?

Among American political philosophers today, it is no longer
so farfetched as it seemed only forty years ago to see in Aristotle
and St. Thomas early forerunners of positions that might be
called in some large sense "practical," "pragmatic," and "realistic." Both attached considerable importance to the study of
human actions, intentions, and circumstances. Both stressed the
role of contingency and probability. Both gave decisive importance to observation, matters of sense, and concrete particulars.
The great painting of Raphael, showing Plato pointing to the
heavens and Aristotle pointing to the earth, illustrates the general
tendency. Theorists of human action as diverse as Maurice Blon-
del, C. S. Peirce, William James, F. A. Hayek, and John Rawls
have mentioned—from a distance—that one or both these early
masters were in some respects their predecessors.[1]

Later thinkers have expressly commended the high valuation
Aristotle and Aquinas placed upon the practical order and upon
the individual's gaining mastery of his own liberty, as well as
their penetrating analyses of habits and virtues. The views of
Aristotle and Aquinas, described as "common sense," are deeply
embedded in the traditions of Western jurisprudence. Perhaps
their most systemic achievement, however, lies in linking ethics
to politics, the individual to the common good.

19

One of the achievements of the U.S. Catholic Bishops' Economic Pastoral of 1986 is to have restored to a place of honor the classic Catholic concept of the common good. This step marks (with some ambivalence) a reconnection of Catholic social thought to its Thomistic origins.[2] It occurred at a moment in history in which certain themes of Thomistic thinking were coming back into common use: habit and virtue, character, justice, intentionality. Indeed, now that the contemporary imagination easily grasps the image of "the global village" (a metaphor widely diffused by the medieval-minded Marshall McCluhan), it has again begun to operate within the penumbra of natural law: a way of imagining all human beings related to one another under similar conditions and in mutual vulnerability. Again, the twentieth-century impact of relativism, stressed by historian Paul Johnson in *Modern Times*, appears to be diminishing.[3] It is not so much the independence of cultures and moral systems that now most fascinates humans as their *inter*dependence.

Even politically, virtually all the nations of the world struggle with ideals, concepts, and institutions derived from democracy, capitalism, socialism, and Marxism. All such ideas, although now universal in their impact, originated in the relatively small North Atlantic quarter of the world (and ultimately in Jewish and Christian inspirations). There abound those who encourage us daily to think less nationalistically, more globally. To think of "the common good" of all humankind has become almost a habit.

Just the same, the concept of the common good remains uncommonly vague. How can one square the common good with personal liberty and cultural pluralism?

The concept of the common good is often most used today with respect to economic activities. We are daily exhorted to look beyond our private aims to the common good of the whole. At least, those of us who are thought to be among the "rich" are so exhorted. Few counsel the poor, in view of the superior common good, to be content with what they have. In short, the invocation of the phrase is generally intended to have as its operative meaning: redistribution.[4] Yet redistribution is not the central problematic evoked by the term. The central problematic is whether *any* concept of the common good is consistent with the personal liberties to which Englishmen and Americans, among many others, have become accustomed. Consider ancient societies. Plato was quite explicit about the ranks of human beings, some of whom were free citizens, supported by the labor and the slavery of others. Aristotle, for all his liberating genius, never broke from the culture of slavery. And although one can say that centuries later, through the historical impulse of those first called liberals, slavery at last came to be condemned and rejected, one cannot say that the first generations of liberals broke entirely from that dreadful tradition.[5] Thus, premodern conceptions of the common good were consistent with arguments justifying fateful differences and fixed inequalities. Indeed, the common good has frequently been invoked as a justification for almost any and every internal ordering of society. This fact, no doubt, encouraged liberal thought early to hedge the notion in, while using it in fresh ways.

The new problem faced by liberal societies is whether the concept of the common good is consistent with personal liberties. Can such a free society even *have* a common good? A society of free persons, to be sure, does depend upon practical *cooperation*. But it can hardly be maintained that it depends upon *common* purposes, unless it is also maintained that free individual persons do have common purposes. On some very low level and in some very generous general way, free persons do have at least *some* common purposes. But the chances are overwhelming, at least in genuinely pluralistic societies (of internally various belief systems and perceptual grids), that in many important ways they do not. Even their bland purposes that seem, at first glance, to be held in common will nearly always be found to be held for different reasons, with yet other (quite pluralistic) ends in view; imagined differently, differently conceived, and of a different weight in rank and order of preference. Persons differ in their conceptions of the good. And this applies to their conceptions of both the common good and their own personal good.

Pluralism, in brief, seems to render the concept of the common good quite vacuous. Boldly, a theoretician might go even further: A genuinely pluralistic society of free persons is incommensurable with the concept of the common good. This would seem to be an error. But how and why it is so must be worked out slowly.

## 2. Aristotle

The good, Aristotle wrote (and he is the *fons et origo* of most traditional thinking about the common good), is what all things aim at. The difficulty, then, is obvious. Since in today's free societies individuals have different aims, they cannot have a common aim.

Aristotle conceived of nature dynamically. All natural things are in motion, coming to rest only when they attain their aim. All have natural tendencies toward *something*—and that (at first analogical and unspecified) "something" is what he calls their "good," attaining which they are (at least temporarily) at rest. Thus, in the classic tradition of speech about the common good, the mind is led to conceive of the common good as the terminus of a *tendency, purpose, aim, intention.* The common good is the fulfillment toward which human society tends. To discern that point of satisfaction is the province of wisdom. To aim at it is to live well, both for oneself and for the community.

But Aristotle erected a further principle: the *primacy* of the common good. He writes in the *Nicomachean Ethics:* "For even if the end is the same for the individual and for the state, the good of the state is manifestly a greater and more complete good, both to attain and to preserve. Though it is worthwhile to secure the good merely for one man, it is nobler and more godlike to attain it for a nation or for city states."[6] For Aristotle, the focus of the study of politics is, then, the common good. To many, perhaps, this formulation will seem intuitively correct. A soldier will give up his own life for the common good. The common good must have primacy. But does that mean that the individual is a means, an instrument, of the community?

Unlike some of the other Greeks, Aristotle was not a materialist. He had a sharp sense of the "spirit," the "divine element," in man. He had no problem stressing, simultaneously, the crucial human roles of the carnal body, the senses, and the passions.

Here as elsewhere, his underlying framework typically consists of conceptual pairings, especially those of *act* and *potency*, and *form* and *matter*. These pairs allowed him to see unities where others (even his beloved Plato) saw dualities. The human being, for example, is a "reasoning animal," an "embodied spirit." This is why Aristotle's thinking was in later centuries to become so crucial to Christian faith. He saved Christian thought from *Either/ Or*, and taught it how to express itself habitually as *Both/And*. Since Jesus is thought to be both God and man, the human being to be both spirit and flesh, and the church to be both divinely guided and quite human in its faults, such a way of thinking is critical to Christian self-understanding. It is important, indeed, to most forms of humanism.

One place at which Aristotle is especially penetrating lies in his insight into insight.[7] Aristotle saw early that in practical judgments concerning what to do and how to act, general rules are not enough. One must have a particular insight into *which* rule to apply and *how* to apply it, in each particular, contingent, unprecedented, and irrepeatable situation. Mere logic and conceptual clarity will not work. Ethical judgment (in action) is always about singulars. "Insight" or "perception"—"hitting the mark"—is necessary. "The crux," Aristotle writes in the *Nicomachean Ethics* (III, vii, 3), "lies with perception."

By insight, Aristotle does not mean some vague or inexplicable intuition. The content of an insight may be given precise conceptual clarity and it may (indeed, must) be supported by reasons showing it to be a true (not an illusory) insight. But what is an insight itself? The first point to note is that insight occurs. Each of us daily experiences insight in even the simplest matters—the patterns or meaning of someone's behavior, the answer to a puzzle, the meaning of a look. Having insights frequently marks persons as bright; less frequently, as dull. Insight is an act of spirit, going beyond the senses, but always (among humans) proceeding both through the senses and with the help of images and examples. To illustrate this last point, the need for examples, let me cite an example here of what it means to think of insight as an act of spirit. Insight into the meaning of "circle" as a radius pivoting upon a point goes beyond the given sensory data. No circle drawn with a pen, however perfectly, quite captures what insight arrives at. In similar fashion, the point of a story is not arrived at by the ears but by insight. A listener may hear perfectly every relevant sound in the telling of a joke, but still miss the point. Insight is an act of spirit.

Why is insight an important datum? Later, we will be led to see that a modern social order is too complex to be grasped by inspection. It is rooted in a set of ideas, and in processes embodying those ideas. Learning how such a system works (gaining insight into how it works) is not easy, and depends upon the acquisition of a whole series of preparatory insights, one clearing the way for another. But many of the requisite insights are embedded in particular experiences, in practices, and in traditions. In daily practice such insights, grasped in the tacit way persons of experience often grasp them, are subject to tests of considerable consequence. (Illusions can be extremely costly.) But many persons of high conceptual capacities and logical acuity sometimes fail to grasp important insights of this sort, not for want of understanding words but for want of the relevant *experiences*. Put otherwise, gaining an insight is not the same mental activity as forming a concept (putting insight into words) or ordering such concepts logically. That Aristotle had insight into insight is one of the reasons for the durability of portions of his method in so many areas of inquiry, when the passage of time has left the concepts of so many other thinkers of merely antiquarian interest.

Aristotle was less good in gaining insight into will and choice. Here later thinkers (such as Augustine and Aquinas) were able to make distinctions Aristotle did not reach, through reflecting on certain preoccupations of Jews and Christians—who, in a sense, carried heavier (or at least different) moral burdens than did pagan Greeks. For example, Jews and Christians face tests of responsibilities well known to them which, nonetheless, they fail. St. Paul confessed, "What I will, I do not," and Jesus said in an observation that has entered common speech, "The spirit is willing but the flesh is weak" (Matthew 26:41). The Greeks tended to believe that will follows light; that enlightenment leads smoothly to virtue. Jews and Christians had reason to be fascinated by the weakness of human will.

Not only is the play between insight and will quite complex in Jewish and Christian experience. So also is the experience of choice. Facing multifaceted circumstances, persons often surprise others by their choices, and on that simple fact hinges the suspense of most of the stories of the Jewish and Christian Testaments. One never knows for sure, at the beginning of an episode, whether King David will be faithful to his Lord or not.

In Jewish and Christian Testaments, then, the two differentiating capacities of humans on which extreme stress is laid are insight and choice. Even the Lord God is described as Light (Truth, Understanding, Way) and Love. And in His own image, God created humans. It is no wonder that Jewish-Christian culture is the origin of so many of the dynamic energies pulsating through the world's no longer dormant populations. An emphasis upon human capacities for insight and choice changes the person and the world.

Long before Europe felt the full impact of Jewish and Christian experience—and even for some time afterward— Aristotle's emphasis upon the common good resonated well in the actual practice of premodern societies. For centuries, no social order respected institutionally the unique responsibility of the human person. Antigone wrestled against her people and her conscience, trying to pay homage to conflicting traditions. Socrates, condemned by the community even as he recognized personal responsibility ("know thyself"), deferred to his death sentence. Among Jews, the prophets (few in number) were often rejected. For three centuries, Christians struggled against a hostile state, and thereafter the struggle to keep the state limited with respect to the church consumed many centuries. But the church, too, often erred on the side of stressing the community over the person. This error, moreover, endured for centuries, even though entrance into the community of faith had no other door than the interior consent of the person, of which God alone could be the final Judge.

Not until recent centuries has the religious liberty of the person been recognized in theology, political principle, and functioning institutions—but still not universally. Indeed, the Catholic church did not arrive formally at the full recognition of the socially effective principle of religious liberty until the Second Vatican Council (1962–65).

In the medieval period, the church was not adequately differentiated from the state. Institutions of political democracy and human rights had not yet been established. Markets were primitive and other institutions of free and dynamic economic development had not yet been put in place. Cultural and moral life had not yet been institutionally liberated from censorship and other authoritarian controls. In those days, care for the common good was invested in the authorities of church and state, ideally working in mutually respectful concert, but in practice often in deadly combat with one another. For such reasons, the practice (rather than the clearer theoretical concept) of the common good carried heavy symbolic overtones of paternalism.

The concept of the common good, in brief, is of premodern origin. This fact alone suggests a warning. The chief characteristic of premodern societies is their lack of differentiation, whereas many important institutions of modern societies have wisely been assigned their own proper autonomy. Although the church, for example, is now separated from the state, and secular disciplines such as law, philosophy, and physics are no longer subordinated to "the queen of the sciences," theology, few who write about the common good have taken account of the chief aspect of modernity—the differentiation of institutions to which it has given rise. That explains, perhaps, why the term "common good" has about it the dry scent of the attic. It has, to be sure, the aura of a venerable object; a certain piety necessarily attaches to it.

Useful for Aristotle, has the common good any conceptual utility today? Not until it absorbs within its grammatical field the concept of the free person.

### 3. St. Thomas Aquinas: Enter the Person

"The common good," writes Thomas Gilby, O.P., "bears three meanings in the *Summa*. It is applied first to a quasi-collective group or organic whole, second, to a political and juridical community, and third, to God because of his comprehensive final causality."[8]

The first, Gilby points out, is a collectivist, even totalitarian concept (it covers, e.g., power over slaves), the third is theological, not political. The second is "the proper interest of political philosophy." In this sense, the common good is "the good estate of the civil community or State, responsibly shared in by those who belong to it, who are called citizens." Aquinas treats of this meaning chiefly in his commentaries on Aristotle's *Ethics* and *Politics*, and in the First Part of the Second Volume of the *Summa*, qq. 90–97.

St. Thomas had several advantages over Aristotle, apart from the contemplation of nearly fifteen hundred years of intervening history. To limit ourselves to the subject at hand, he had available the concept of "person," quite distinct from the concept of the "individual" (about which more will be said below). He also had available important religious materials decisive for the political and ethical future of Europe, that is, the Jewish and Christian traditions. Judaism's notion of the One God and of the human side of consent to the Covenant led to its emphasis upon the human will, and this in turn led Western culture to reflect upon the sacredness of the human individual, known to God and loved by Him before history began. Moreover, Judaism's strong sense of peoplehood and of the communal relations of individuals required sustained meditation on the common good, even independently of the state (which was often enough hostile to Jews and later to Christians).

Christianity also added new materials on which reflection was necessary. The simple assertion that Jesus Christ is both God and man obliged Christian thinkers to find a language to express precisely what they meant. If Jesus has both a human nature and a divine nature, then what holds these two together? As an individual, is he really a man, with a special relation to the divine? Or is he really God, with only the outward appearance of a man? To meet such questions, theologians slowly constructed the concept of person. An individual is merely a member of a species, one single embodiment of a nature of a specific kind.

Person is a different sort of concept. It designates an individual with a capacity for insight (inquiry) and choice (liberty). This means a self-starting capacity, a seat of responsibility, a being that is responsible for understanding and directing its own activities, independently of any other.[9]

An individual tree may be unlike any other, and yet it can hardly be said to be responsible for its own identity. A human person *is* responsible for his or her own destiny—not wholly so, obviously (no one chooses his own parents), but to a decisive degree. So too (in Jewish and Christian traditions) the angels are also thought of as persons, each with a proper name: Gabriel, Raphael, Michael, Lucifer. Angels have powerful insight; angels choose. The concept of person may also be used analogically of God, the Source of all insight and love. (It is not altogether ironical, then, that this crucial humanistic concept, at the heart of modern "personalism," arose from the necessity of finding new ways of speaking about God.)

The distinction between individual and person was useful, therefore, for articulating with some clarity what Christians believe about Jesus Christ. (Others may believe this or not, but conceptual clarity helps to state what is at stake.) The one person, Jesus, responsible for his own thoughts, words, and actions, shares both a human and a divine nature. This person is fully human. This person is fully God. No other person shares both natures.

This concept of person, furthermore, sheds light upon something unique to humans. Unlike all the other animals, the human individual is not individuated from other members of his species solely by his material conditions, as a member of the species unlike every other. More than that, the human person is free and responsible. What he or she will make of life is in the hands of each. Each is *per se subsistens:* Free and independent of every other member of the species. Neither father nor mother, neither brother nor sister, can relieve any human person of that responsibility.

The danger in Thomistic thinking (and in the concept of the common good) has been thought to be twofold: (1) that it is static and nonhistorical; and (2) that it is incompatible with pluralism and liberty. These accusations have a *prima facie* validity, since the concepts of natural law and the common good were first articulated in the environment of the relatively static and undifferentiated authoritarian societies of the ancient and medieval Greco-Latin world. Yet even Aquinas and his colleagues were acutely aware of the differences between pagan Athens and Rome and Christian Europe. They were aware, too, of national differences, as the pattern of *nationes* at the University of Paris suggests.

Furthermore, in the twentieth century, leading democratic theoreticians among the Thomists, such as Jacques Maritain and Yves R. Simon (followed in the practical order by Sturzo, De Gasperi, Adenauer, Schuman, Malik, Erhard, and others) brought these medieval concepts into the conceptual networks of democracy, pluralism, and personalism. It would be unhistorical not to observe the transformations such thinkers wrought in the classic notions, which in any case were theoretically open to such development. In their hands, it became clear that human beings are historical animals, whose nature is dynamic, inquiring, and open to the new demands and possibilities of history—including error, conflict, and tragedy.

In his lectures at Cambridge on "The History of Freedom in Christianity," Lord Acton helps us to see how St. Thomas's notion of the person was bound to lead to intensely political results. When Edward Plantagenet sought dominion over Scotland and Ireland, the Scots and the Irish refused, Acton notes, choosing to support Robert Bruce even in defiance of the Vatican. They said:

> Divine Providence, the laws and customs of the country, which we will defend till death, and the choice of the people, have made him our king. If he should ever betray his principles, and consent that we should be subjects of the English king, then we shall treat him as an enemy, as the subverter of our rights and his own, and shall elect another in his place. We care not for glory or for wealth, but for that liberty which no true man will give up but with his life.[10]

Two generations earlier, St. Thomas Aquinas had articulated the rationale of such high esteem for human liberty and responsibility. Acton quotes as follows:

A king who is unfaithful to his duty forfeits his claim to obedience. It is not rebellion to depose him, for he is himself a rebel whom the nation has a right to put down. But it is better to abridge his power, that he may be unable to abuse it. For this purpose, the whole nation ought to have a share in governing itself; the Constitution ought to combine a limited and elective monarchy, with an aristocracy of merit, and such an admixture of democracy as shall admit all classes to office, by popular election. No government has a right to levy taxes beyond the limit determined by the people. All political authority is derived from popular suffrage, and all laws must be made by the people or their representatives. There is no security for us as long as we depend on the will of another man.[11]

Acton's lecture continues with this comment: "This language, which contains the earliest exposition of the Whig theory of revolution, is taken from the works of St. Thomas Aquinas, of whom Lord Bacon says that he had the largest heart of the school divines. And it is worth while to observe that he wrote at the very moment when Simon de Montfort summoned the Commons; and that the politics of the Neapolitan friar are centuries in advance of the English statesman's."[12]

### 4. When Personal Good and Communal Good Are One

In the controversy of the 1940s between De Koninck and Maritain alluded to earlier, the central point turned upon a Christian understanding of the purpose of human existence. That purpose is for every human person "to come home to" God—to be one with God in an everlasting communion of insight and love. God is the universal common good not only of humans but of all created things.

In the Christian intellectual tradition, further, God is imagined to be more like insight and choice than like anything else known to humans. Human insight and human love are poor things, compared to God. Yet God is more like those acts, and more accurately known through those acts, than like any of the other arrows of comparison, so to speak, that human intellect shoots upward toward the unknown God. On the one hand, each human person is ordered to union with infinite insight and love, fulfilling thereby the deepest quest of his or her own being. On the other hand, this communion in insight and love is the final purpose of all humans together. Communion in perfect insight and love—union with God, immediate and penetrating—is both the common good of humankind and the personal good of each. De Koninck was eager to stress the common destination of all persons, their common good, not to be forgotten in stressing the personal good of each free person. Maritain did not disagree.

The implications of this insight for *political* philosophy (of more interest to Maritain than to De Koninck) are profound. No state and no society can legitimately frustrate the drive of each person for his true destination. In this respect, all powers of state and society are radically limited. Naturally, a political philosopher need not be Jewish or Christian in order to recognize the primacy of personal conscience and the severe limits that ought to be placed upon the power of the state. Led by his own conscience, and the value he places upon it, the atheist may do as much. Yet it is not *hubris* to recognize that Jewish and Christian religious thinkers have many reasons besides the vindication of their own responsibility as persons for seeing that such a valuation is fitting, just, and preordained by the Creator. What in recent centuries we have come to call "human rights" have in Jewish and Christian vision a short, direct justification. That the political relevance of these conceptions took centuries of bloodshed and effort to emerge in conceptual and institutional form in human history goes without saying. That this struggle was often best advanced by nonbelievers, often in the teeth of opposition from Christian princes and prelates, is a matter of record. The lines of history twist and turn, even when the lines of intellectual implication are straight.

In Christian thought, the ultimate ground of the dignity of the human person has two parts: the unalienable responsibility of each person, *per se subsistens;* and also the final destination of each in the full insight and love of communion with God. This dignity, as we have seen, is at once personal and communal. It is shared by one, it is shared by all. Therefore, it is a quite radical error to separate by too far the good of the singular person and the common good of all persons together. Both Maritain and De Koninck were serious in their opposition to totalitarian collectivism at one extreme and to excessive individualism at the other.

De Koninck insisted upon the primacy of the common good because God is the common good of the universe, and because the logic of the relation of being to goodness requires such primacy. A flavor of the metaphysical depths of the discussion may be gleaned from a memo of "perfect accord" on five basic points worked out by the philosopher Yves R. Simon, together with De Koninck and Maritain:

1. Any good of a higher order is greater than any good of a lower order.
2. Within a given order, there is absolute primacy of the common good over any private good.
3. When a person is an absolute person (God) there is an absolute coincidence of common and personal good.
4. To the degree that a created person is a person there is a tendency toward a coincidence of personal good and common good.
5. There is no restriction on the primacy of the common good in its order; when this primacy disappears (3 and 4), this is not because the primacy then belongs to a private good, but that the problem of primacy disappears.[13]

Point four here is the decisive one. When a human person acts with reflection and choice—acts, that is, *as a person*—the personal good and the common good tend to coincide. In Madison's phrase, "private rights and public happiness," and in Tocqueville's description of "self-interest rightly understood," this coincidence is explicit. In such cases, "the problem of primacy" disappears.

Such cases involve only the *person*, not the *individual*. A formula Maritain liked was as follows: "Man will be fully a person, a *per se subsistens* and a *per se operans*, only in so far as the life of reason and liberty dominates that of the senses and passions in him; otherwise he will remain like the animal, a simple *individual*, the slave of events and circumstances, always led by something else, incapable of guiding himself; he will be only a part, without being able to aspire to the whole."[14] Another passage from Maritain further illustrates his distinction between person and individual:

> . . . it is because he is first an individual of a species that man, having need of the help of his fellows to perfect his specific activity, is consequently an *individual* of the city, a member of society. And on this count he is subordinated to the good of his city as to the good of the whole, the common good which as such is more *divine* and therefore better deserving the love of each than his very own life. But if it is a question of the destiny which belongs to man as a *person*, the relation is inverse, and it is the human city which is subordinate to his destiny.[15]

There is a critical difference, however, between intellectual principles on the pure level of theory and the actual embodiment of principles in political institutions in history. On the level of purely philosophical (or theological) principle, one might conclude that since in eternity the personal good of each human being and the communal good of all are as one, since all are then united in communion with God, so it should also be on earth. State and society, one might then argue, should be ordered toward producing that communion on earth. In this fashion, the City of God and the City of Man would share identical principles. But this proposal fails. For on this earth, human persons make their pilgrimage both in darkness and in liberty. Also, human persons manifestly do *not* all choose to live *either* according to insight and love *or* in union with God. Some reject God. Some reject the path of insight and love, in favor of paths of passion, self-enclosure, and even self-destruction. How, in that case, is one to respect the liberty and responsibility of each?

As every tree in the world is an individual with its unique

location in space and time, and with a shape all its own, so it is with every member of every species of plant and animal. To speak of the individual in this sense is to speak of what can be physically located, observed, seen, and touched. In this context, the common good would be either the sum of the goods of each individual member or "the greatest good of the greatest number." A purely materialistic conception of the individual is compatible with a high valuation on each individual. But it is also compatible with the view that the whole is greater than any part and ought to take precedence over any part. It is this latter view that George Orwell satirized in *Animal Farm*. In this view, the human being in the social body is like the steer in the herd, the bee in the hive, the ant in the colony—an individual whose good is subordinated to the good of the species.

A *person*, however, is more than an individual. As the concept of individual looks to what is material, so the concept of person looks to intellect and will: the capacities of insight and judgment, on the one hand, and of choice and decision, on the other. A person is an individual able to inquire and to choose, and, therefore, both free and responsible. For Aquinas, the person is in this sense made in the image of the Creator and endowed with unalienable responsibilities. The good of such a person, who participates in activities of insight and choice (God's own form of life), is to be united with God, without intermediary, face-to-face, in full light and love. The ultimate common good of persons is to be united with God's understanding and loving, the same activities of insight and choice coursing through and energizing all.

Analogously, on earth and in time, the common good of persons is to live in as close an approximation of unity in insight and love as sinful human beings might attain. Since this requires respect for the unalienable freedom and responsibility of each, and since human beings are imperfect at best and always flawed in character, it is by no means easy at any one historical moment either to ascertain the common good or to attain it. There is a serious problem in learning what the common good is. There is also a serious problem in achieving it. In order to solve both these problems, even approximately, persons need institutions suitable to the task.

## 5. Philosophy Leads to Institutions

But what sorts of institutions are likely to raise the probabilities of the success of disparate and divided humans in identifying and achieving the common good in history? Such institutions must be invented and tested amid the hazards of history. They are not given in advance. Human beings proceed toward the common good more in darkness than in light.

Two fundamental organizational concepts can be ruled out as errors, however, by an accurate judgment about the requirements of the human person *qua* person. *Neither* a self-enclosed individualism *nor* an unfree collectivism will adequately liberate human persons. The specific vitalities of the person spring from capacities for insight and choice (inquiry and love). From these derive principles of liberty and responsibility, in which human dignity is rooted. The human person is *dignus,* worthy of respect, sacred even, because he or she lives from the activities proper to God. To violate these is to denigrate the Almighty. Moreover the person is not solitary. The free person, enjoying liberty and finding justification for it in his very endowment (by the Creator) with "unalienable rights," is obliged to recognize these same rights in every human person. It is an error to define the individual without reference to God and without reference to those other persons who also share in God's life.

A self-enclosed, self-centered individualism rests upon a misapprehension of the capacities of the human person, in whose light each person is judged by God, by other persons, and by conscience itself (whose light is God's activity in the soul). The person is a sign of God in history or (to speak more accurately) participates in God's own most proper activities, insight and choice. The person is *theophanous:* a shining-through of God's life in history, created by God for union with God. This is the dynamic impulse in history, guided by Providence and discerned by the authors of the U.S. Declaration of Independence, when they spoke of human persons as "endowed by their Creator with certain unalienable rights," and strove to invent institutions worthy of human dignity. To achieve this, they saw that a new system was necessary, a new order, a social experiment, a republic. The task was social; a self-enclosed individualism would falsify the capacities of the human person.

On the other hand, so would any vision of the common good as a mere sum of individual goods (or the greatest good of the greatest number). Even if it were true that a hundred persons would experience more pleasure from torturing one person than that person would experience pain (in some dreadful utilitarian calculus), such an action would be an abomination. The person is never subordinate to the common good in an instrumental way. Persons are not means but ends, because of the God in Whom they live and Who lives in them. The common good of a society of persons consists in treating each of them as an end, never as a means. To arrange the institutions of human society in such a way that this happens without fail is by no means easy. The human race has so far only approximated the achievement of such institutions.

Over most of the planet's present surface, including most of the world's peoples, persons are still conceived of as means to the ends of the state. Their personal liberty is not respected. Every form of collectivism—in which each member is treated as a means to the good of the state—violates the dignity of the human person.

Fundamental conceptions, therefore, play a large role in the construction of systems and the invention of institutions. To be sure, the capacities of the human person incessantly reassert themselves, so that by trial and experiment human societies are driven back even despite themselves by the bitter taste of erroneous conceptions. By dint of error, conceptions that are true keep coming to light. Systems of self-enclosed individualism and of smothering collectivism choke the capacities of the human person. To attain the common good worthy of human persons, one must break out from such systems.

## 6. The Liberal Society or Socialism?

Liberalism has always had in view the good of the whole. . . . Historically, liberalism was the first political movement that aimed at promoting the welfare of all, not that of special groups. Liberalism is distinguished from socialism, which likewise professes to strive for the good of all, not by the goals at which it aims, but by the means that it chooses to attain that goal.[16]

Ludwig von Mises
*Liberalism in the Classical Tradition*

It is probably useful to point out that whereas in the rest of this inquiry I wish to concentrate on the liberal society—democratic in polity, capitalist in economy, and pluralist in culture—many others would follow the argument concerning the common good in a socialist direction. The problem with that solution, in my view, is that the concept of the common good lost its historical prestige in the first place because the paternalistic administration of state authorities had done so little to change the immemorial position of the poor. Many of the same symbolic overtones now attach to socialist schemes of the common good.

It is not my purpose here to argue further against socialism, but I should perhaps say that in every case in which it has so far appeared in history, the empirical effect of socialism has been to give historically unparallelled power and privilege to a small elite, while keeping the living standards of the poor well below those obtaining in free societies of comparable culture (North Korea, South Korea; East Germany, West Germany; Mainland China, Taiwan; Hungary, Austria; and so forth). But I will let the empirical challenge laid down by Peter Berger in *The Capitalist Revolution*—a set of fifty empirically falsifiable theses about capitalism and socialism—be taken up by readers eager to pursue the question.[17] I wish only to underline here a point about individualism.

The tendency of all socialist thought is to deprecate individualism ("bourgeois individualism"), private interests, private property, and "unbridled" markets. Still, two different types of socialism must be distinguished. Classic authoritarian socialism supplies as an alternative to individualism the authority of government over all aspects of economic life. By contrast, contemporary democratic socialism is eager to defend both democracy in political life and democratic, decentralized methods in all spheres of economic life. Classic authoritarian socialism, concerned to check the error of individualism, tends to trust the wisdom of authorities of the central state. Contemporary democratic socialism resists such trust in centralized authorities. It wishes to check the error of individualism by mandatory schemes of democratic cooperation among all participants in economic activities.

Manifestly, classic authoritarian socialism exerts a far more concentrated discipline than did the loose paternalism of the undifferentiated medieval society. But even contemporary democratic socialism seriously underestimates the chilling effect of decisions by committee and by worker sovereignty. Democratic methods are time-consuming and inflict heavy knowledge-costs. In politics, they play an indispensable (but not universal) role, while in morals, culture, and economics, their use is frequently in opposition to the common good. For example, the dynamics of political decisionmaking bring into economic calculation many political temptations (such as favoritism, special pleading, vote bargaining, and the domination of activists).[18]

These objections, of course, are pragmatic rather than principled. Based solely on them, I would wish many socialist experiments to go forward. Nonetheless, the record of socialist experiments of many kinds suggests that socialist ideals consistently founder on rude facts of human personality and aspiration. Becoming at last aware of this, many persons formerly inspired by socialist ideals have come to the conclusion that socialist ideals are, even in principle, based upon false premises. Moreover, unswerving socialists seldom acknowledge the coercion upon others implicit in all socialist schemes, however benevolent.[19] They tend to assume a unanimity of moral preferences in social philosophy, as if all others are, or ought to be, fired by the faith that burns in them. They itch to organize, and tend to despise dissenters, whom they cannot help thinking of as morally unworthy. Socialism is, before all else, a moral vision, and much tempted by intolerance.

This objection to socialism is principled but it is also compatible with patience regarding continued socialist experimentation.

Many socialists intend by that term not much more than that they are humanists, democrats, and to one degree or another dissatisfied with capitalism. They are at their best humanistic persons, who deserve a hearing and often make good points.

In any case, socialist invocations of the common good in the economic sphere are commonly aimed at "correcting" liberal individualism. J. Philip Wogaman, in a paper called "The Common Good and Economic Life: A Protestant Perspective," writes, for example, that the "common good at least means the repudiation of any purely individualistic conception of the common life."[20] Historically, as we have just seen, the common good was highly respected in history long before the individual was, and long before institutions emerged to protect the liberties of the individual. Indeed, after the eighteenth century, societies that respected individual rights came to be thought historically more advanced than those that did not. In referring his definition of the common good to the individual, however, Dr. Wogaman suggests an important point. In writings about "social justice" (especially in the churches and universities), the concept of the common good is defined *against* individualism. There are both conservative and socialist echoes in this insistence—and more than a touch of the premodern and the authoritarian in both.

In any case, concern for the common good and opposition to "any purely individualistic conception of the common life" are not confined to socialism. The liberal society has its own methods for giving preeminence to the common good—above all, in actually achieving and in progressively raising the levels of the common good. It does so, to be sure, by taking care to include within the definition of the common good the securing of human rights: that is, the rights of free persons and free associations. Because of its unique emphasis upon individual rights, the social dimension of liberal thought is often overlooked. In particular, the significance of the American experiment, as a new, original, and practical reconciliation of the common good with the free person, has been neglected. To remedy such neglect is now our task.

*Chapter Two:*

# THE NEW ORDER OF THE AGES

## 1. Private Rights and Public Happiness.

When a people determines that it shall be ruled only through its own consent, such a people takes upon itself responsibility for the common good. The people are sovereign over their own public good. In such a regime, a "purely individualistic conception of the common life" runs contrary to the principle of self-government, and would be fatal to the republic. This is how the framers of the U.S. Constitution saw the experiment they were about to launch.

This new experiment set before the world an original conception of the common good. It made central to the conception of the common good the protection of individual rights. Simultaneously, it invited history to test a new proposition; *viz.*, that a *society* so constituted would inculcate a new range of human virtues, achieve unparalleled prosperity through innovation in every field of human industry, and flourish under the blessings of unprecedented liberty. The framers could not be certain of the outcome of this social test. According to the philosophical conceptions of the past, an experiment in popular government ought to end, as all previous experiments had, in self-destruction through envy and division. This high probability was the nightmare of the framers.

Still, the framers were determined to try a new approach to

41

achieving the common good, an approach that simultaneously protected individual rights. They wished to attain two things at once, both private rights and the public good. Their own failures since the War of Independence had taught them that the problem to be solved in reconciling private rights and the common good is preeminently practical, in two senses. It is, first of all, a moral problem. Only a people practicing virtues of certain kinds can make such an experiment work. Without such virtues, their situation would be "pitiful." It is, second, an institutional problem. Virtue alone, experience had shown, can never be enough in politics, economics, or culture. Institutions need to be designed to cope with the structural diseases inherent in republican societies. Among these diseases are *self-interest, faction,* and (in Tocqueville's term of quite specific meaning) *individualism.*

The new concept of the common good, sought by the framers, included as its key priority the protection of the rights of free persons and free associations. So it is highly useful to remind ourselves how difficult the problem of realizing this new concept in practice appeared to our forebears. A few words on the ideas articulated in the *Federalist,* and on Tocqueville's commentary upon the framers' handiwork some forty years later, will therefore help to root our inquiry in actual history.

## 2. The *Federalist:* The Creative Uses of Self-Interest

In the America of 1787, it was abundantly clear to the wise that individuals alone (indeed, even the individual states) could not attain their own good without the achievement of a favorable public order. For this reason, the framers of the Constitution of the United States, meeting in Philadelphia during the hot summer of 1787, dared to conceive of a *new order.* Eleven years earlier, the Declaration of Independence had publicly announced the truths they held to be self-evident, around which they intended to build a new republic. Since then, they had fought and won the War of Independence, only to see their experiment begin to fall apart. Harsh experience showed them that the system of government that had survived the war was much too weak for their necessities.

The framers wished to build an *ordo* worthy of free persons, each endowed with "unalienable rights." No doubt, then, the rights of individuals were prominent in their minds. Still, they understood that in order to *secure* these rights, "governments are instituted among men." The life of the free individual cannot be separated from the protections afforded through social order. The framers thought quite carefully about the new requirements of such a social order. They were social thinkers, not mere individualists.

Indeed, the series of newspaper articles penned by Alexander Hamilton, James Madison, and John Jay to persuade their fellow citizens to give their consent to the new Constitution is a masterpiece of political and social philosophy. Like the Constitution itself, the *Federalist* is an attempt to sketch a new way for an entire public to realize the common good. The Preamble to the Constitution they were defending could scarcely be more explicit about the components of this common good:

> We the People of the United States, in Order to form a more perfect Union, establish Justice, insure domestic Tranquility, provide for the common defence, promote the general Welfare, and secure the Blessings of Liberty to ourselves and our Posterity, do ordain and establish this Constitution for the United States of America.

Three important features of this new approach to the common good deserve mention. These include the distinction between the society and the state, according to which the people, not the state, would be the chief agent of the common good; the tendency of public authorities to distort the common good; and the separation of the social system into three independent systems.

First, consensus about the common good must derive from the consent of the people. Thus, in the very first paragraph of the *Federalist*, Hamilton observed that the issue before the free persons of the United States hinged upon the formation of a new form of government through *reflection* and *choice*: ". . . it seems to have been reserved to the people of this country, by their conduct and example, to decide the important question, whether societies of men are really capable or not of establishing good government from *reflection and choice*, or whether they are forever destined to depend for their political constitutions on *accident and force*" (emphasis added). Hamilton boldly imagined that the choice made by the Americans of his generation would have universal, world-historical consequences.[1]

Second, the framers saw the need not only for *limited* government, but also for a government whose power is tied down and bound by a *written* constitution. Belief in limited government follows from the truth that free persons possess unalienable rights that are beyond the reach of the state, rights that come to them directly from the Creator. The effect of these two beliefs—in the limited powers of the state and in the unalienable rights of individuals—is twofold. As a first step, such beliefs separate the powers of the *state* from the powers of *society*. The former are strictly limited, the latter are far more ample. (The powers of society include, for example, civil argument, moral suasion, the raised eyebrow, shame and ridicule, the inculcation of republican virtue, sound education, and the like.) In the second instance, it follows that the common good must be achieved not solely by the state but by a vast range of social bodies beyond the reach of the state. The chief and most potent instrument of achieving the common good—in such a *novus ordo*—is not the state but the society at large, in its full range of social institutions. These include families, churches, schools, workers' associations, private enterprises, and so forth. Whereas in some earlier systems or social orders, the *government* was believed to be the chief agent of the common good, in the *novus ordo* a larger and more various set of social institutions would rightfully become the primary agents of the common good.

This original conception flows from a recognition of the potencies and rights of persons to enter into mutual covenants and associations, paired with a recognition of the fallibility of governments. A long passage from Hamilton in *Federalist* 15 conveys the full Niebuhrian flavor of their argument: "There was a time when we were told that breaches, by the States, of the regulations of the federal authority were not to be expected—that a sense of common interest would preside over the conduct of the respective members, and would beget a full compliance with all the constitutional requisitions of the Union." After so many recent experiences, "this language at the present day" would appear to Hamilton's contemporaries "wild." Indeed, such language has always "betrayed an ignorance of the true springs by which human conduct is actuated."

Hamilton can scarcely believe his ears: "Why has government been instituted at all? Because the passions of men will not conform to the dictates of reason and justice, without constraint. Has it been found that *bodies* of men act with more rectitude or greater disinterestedness than individuals? The contrary of this has been inferred by all accurate observers of the conduct of mankind." Further, Hamilton discerns that this tendency has its origin in the love of power. "Power controlled or abridged is almost always the rival and enemy of that power by which it is controlled or abridged. This simple proposition will teach us how little reason there is to expect, that the persons, entrusted with the administration of the affairs of the particular members of a confederacy, will at all times be ready, with perfect good humor, and an unbiassed regard to the public weal, to execute the resolutions or decrees of the general authority." Abuse of the common good by governments "results from the constitution of human nature."[2] To be sure, Hamilton is here criticizing abuses of "the public weal" by the states, and is arguing for an even stronger national government. Government may indeed serve "the public good." Unchecked, it has often in the past injured it.

The "best oracle of wisdom, experience," teaches that governors and administrators cannot be counted upon as perfect guardians of the common good. This lesson is so important to the framers that Madison returns to it (among other places) in *Federalist* 41. Utopia is not possible. To secure rights, a Constitution empowering a strong federal government is necessary.

But cool and candid people will at once reflect, that the purest of human blessings must have a portion of alloy in them, that the choice must always be made, if not of the lesser evil, at least of the GREATER, not the PERFECT good; and that in every political institution, a power to advance the public happiness, involves a discretion which may be misapplied and abused. They will see therefore that in all cases, where power is to be conferred, the point first to be decided is whether such a power be necessary to the public good; as the next will be, in case of an affirmative decision, to guard as effectually as possible against a perversion of the power to the public detriment.[3]

Third, after distinguishing the domain of the free society from the organs of the state, and after having expressed both their need of government and their unwillingness to trust it fully, the framers divided the "new order" into three rival social systems. In limiting the reach of the political system, as realism demanded, the framers kept other sectors of society free from state control. First, they made certain to legitimate the powers of a *moral-cultural system,* independent of the state, organized by the press, churches, universities, and other free associations. They also legitimated a new type of *economic system,* to be regulated and promoted by the political system, but free to a degree unprecedented in history from domination by the state.

The pictorial symbol of the *Novus Ordo Seclorum* placed upon the Great Seal of the United States—a heavy-stoned, deliberately uncompleted pyramid—is an apt representation of this three-sided *ordo.* This pyramid is presided over by an Eye, representing candor, honesty, and Providence, symbol of the moral-cultural order, and above it on a banner is the inscription *Annuit Coeptis: "[Providence] smiles upon our undertakings."* At the base of the pyramid (one can imagine) are the linked but opposite poles of "polity" and "economy."

In brief, the genius of the framers was a *social* genius, a *political* genius, a genius concerning the practical ordering of institutions. They wished to design a system "of the ages," designed to protect not solely the rights of Americans but *human* rights. They wished to meet the institutional requirements of "the system of *natural* liberty," the liberty primordial to humans precisely as human. One cannot properly think of the framers as preoccupied solely with the individualistic aspects of individual liberties. On the contrary, they were preoccupied with questions of social system, of social *ordo*, in all its institutional ramifications.

One inference to be drawn from the social order designed in Philadelphia affects the present meaning of the term "liberal." Is the key concept of the authentic liberal tradition the solitary individual or the communitarian individual?[4] Is the basic unit of analysis within liberalism the individual? Or is it, rather, the community that secures the rights of individuals, within which the individual comes to full self-fulfillment? Whatever the case may be if one begins from the tradition of British liberalism, from Locke through Adam Smith, Jeremy Bentham, John Stuart Mill, and others, among the Americans it seems certain that the correct answer is community.

Consider, for example, the "Mayflower Compact," which serves as an early instance of the American concern for covenants of mutual consent (learned from the Covenant that God made with His people in ancient Israel and again in Jesus Christ). On the heaving decks of the *Arbella*, John Winthrop gave his justly famous address, a pivotal passage of which reads as follows:

> We must delight in each other, make others' conditions our own, rejoice together, mourn together, labor and suffer together, always having before our eyes commission and community in the work, our community as members of the same body. So shall we keep the unity of the spirit in the bond of peace, the Lord will be our God and delight to dwell among us, as His own people, and will command a blessing upon us in all our ways, so that we shall see much more of His wisdom, power, goodness, and truth than formerly we have been acquainted with.
>
> We shall find that the God of Israel is among us, when ten of us shall be able to resist a thousand of our enemies, when He shall make us a praise and glory, that men shall say of succeeding plantations, "The Lord make it like that of New England." For we must consider that we shall be as a city upon a hill, the eyes of all people are upon us. So that if we shall deal falsely with our God in this work we have undertaken, and so cause Him to withdraw His present help from

us, we shall open the mouths of enemies to speak evil of the ways of God and all professors of God's worthy servants, and cause their prayers to be turned into curses upon us, till we be consumed out of the good land whither we are going.[5]

To be sure, from the Mayflower Compact, with its emphasis upon covenanted community, to the Declaration of Independence, with its emphasis upon securing individual rights, there remained a long road of discovery and experiment. The fear of failure was quite real. Indeed, the authors of the *Federalist* had ample reason to fear that in the light of the noble pledges they had made in the Declaration of Independence, they would soon become the laughingstock of the world. John Jay wrote bitingly of how foreign nations would come to regard a people that now rejected union in favor of petty and discordant states:

If . . . they find us either destitute of an effectual government (each State doing right or wrong, as to its rulers may seem convenient), or split into three or four independent and probably discordant republics or confederacies, one inclining to Britain, another to France, and a third to Spain, and perhaps played off against each other by the three, what a poor, pitiful figure will America make in their eyes! How liable would she become not only to their contempt, but to their outrage. . . .[6]

James Madison confronted explicitly two further dangers: Free persons, each given to his own self-interest, might veer apart from one another, thus wrecking the "public happiness." On the other side of the ship, the "public happiness" might fall under a "tyranny of the majority," thus abrogating "private rights." Against this Scylla and Charybdis, Madison held aloft the banner: *"PRIVATE RIGHTS* and *PUBLIC GOOD."* Knowing that all republican forms of government in the past had swiftly self-destructed, Madison bent his considerable talents to rescuing the republican idea from opprobrium. He pressed his own capacity for innovation to the utmost. He wanted to be so exactly practical and realistic that the republic to be established by the people of the United States would stand for ages.

To this end, Madison took special note of two enduring realities in human behavior: *self-interest* and *faction*. Like it or not, the human person is moved most by matters that affect his or her own self. Probably unknown to Madison, Thomas Aquinas had long before observed this tendency; the American insight, like that of Aquinas, derived from daily experience:

Private possession is . . . necessary for human life, for three reasons: first, because everyone is more careful to procure something that concerns himself alone than something that is common to all or to many others (for each one, escaping work, leaves for the other man any common task, as happens when there are a great many officials); second, since human affairs are handled in a more orderly fashion when each one goes about his own business, there would be complete confusion if everyone tried to do everything; third, because this leads to a more peaceful condition for man, while everyone is content with what he has. Hence we see that among those possessing something in common, disputes arise more often.[7]

As this example shows, self-interest is not always morally negative. A regime of private property, harnessing it, can be socially creative. Again, self-interest of a sort is the propellant of a mother's love even unto death for her child, as it is the propellant of love of one's own nation and the defense of the values one holds dear. Risking life, liberty, and sacred honor, the American founders followed self-interest into the War of Independence—self-interest and public interest commingled. Self-interest is a reality of human nature, good and bad, that wise men should not ignore.

Still, self-interest is a chameleon. It is sometimes noble, sometimes ignoble, more often a mixture. Self-interest may be ennobled; what it cannot be is extirpated from the human breast. Wherever there is human action, self-interest is inexorably intermixed with it. "If men were angels," Madison writes pointedly, "no government would be necessary." Yet not even government can escape the pull of self-interest upon the actions of its officials. So Madison adds: "If angels were to govern men, neither external nor internal controls on government would be necessary. In framing a government which is to be administered by men over men, the great difficulty lies in this: You must first enable the government to control the governed; and in the next place oblige it to control itself."[8] Although "dependence on the people" is "the primary control on government," experience "has taught mankind the necessity of auxiliary precautions."[9]

Some critics have taxed Madison with offering too pessimistic a view of human nature, relying too little upon virtue, too much upon the conviction that self-interest is an enduring part of human life. That this charge is not truly aimed is shown by Madison's reliance during the constitutional debate in Virginia in 1788 upon "this great republican principle, that the people will have virtue and intelligence to select men of virtue and wisdom." Defiantly, then, Madison asks:

> Is there no virtue among us? If there be not, we are in a wretched situation. No theoretical checks, no form of government, can render us secure. To suppose any form of government will secure liberty or happiness without any virtue in the people, is a chimerical idea. If there be sufficient virtue and intelligence in the community, it will be exercised in the selection of these men; so that we do not depend on their virtue, or put confidence in our rulers, but in the people who are to choose them.[10]

Madison does not deny the tug of virtue or the claim of constitutional rights and higher duties. He merely means to take the "auxiliary precautions" that human experience has shown to be necessary.

> Ambition must be made to counteract ambition. The interest of the man must be connected with the constitutional rights of the place. It may be a reflection on human nature that such devices should be necessary to control the abuses of

government. But what is government itself but the greatest
of all reflections on human nature?[11]

Relentlessly realistic about the propensities of humans both for
good and ill, Madison sought to check the less than honorable (or
even honorable, but one-sided) instincts of free persons, in order
to protect the public good. And he also sought to check public
power, so as to protect private rights. For him, these two are not
irreconcilable. On the contrary, private rights are an indispensable component of the public good.

Throughout the whole system of the "new order," not only in
its government, Madison observed that self-interest, good and
bad, is the inescapable datum. His policy was plain. He matched
to every interest, however noble, a countervailing interest. "This
policy of supplying, by opposite and rival interests, the defect of
better motives, might be traced through the whole system of
human affairs, private as well as public. We see it particularly
displayed in all the subordinate distributions of power, where the
constant aim is to divide and arrange the several offices in such a
manner as that each may be a check on the other—that the private
interest of every individual may be a sentinel over the public
rights."[12] Thus may self-interest be made to serve the public
good, and to become its very sentinel.

Just as Madison was a realist regarding the tension between
self-interest and the common good, so also he approached the
reality of faction. If humans are free, they are bound to form
factions. "Liberty is to faction what air is to fire, an element
without which it instantly expires."[13] By faction, he means a
number of citizens (minority or majority, as the case may be)
moved by "some common impulse of passion, or of interest,
adverse to the rights of other citizens, or to *the permanent and
aggregate interests of the community.*"[14]

Like self-interest, faction too may be defined as contrary to the
common good. Yet, as he did with self-interest, so now with
faction, Madison does jiujitsu. He takes what he defines as an
enemy of the common good, and contrives a way to make it a
defender of the common good. Neither self-interest nor faction
can be eliminated from the breasts of free persons, unless their

liberty be extirpated. Yet Madison discovers in them a way to protect the common good.

"As long as the reason of man continues fallible," Madison writes, "and he is at liberty to exercise it, different opinions will form." But differences of opinion are not evil in themselves; they may be fruitful. Liberty shows itself through diversity.

Not less, uniformity is also prevented by that "diversity in the faculties of men, from which the rights of property originate. *The protection of these faculties is the first object of government.* From the protection of different and *unequal* faculties of acquiring property, the possession of different degrees and kinds of property immediately results; and from the influence of these on the sentiments and views of the respective proprietors ensues a division of the society into different interests and parties."[15]

Madison saw with clarity how faction, unchecked, has normally injured the common good. Because their "latent causes" are "sown in the nature of man," factions have "divided mankind into parties, inflamed them with mutual animosity, and rendered them much more disposed to vex and oppress each other than to cooperate for their common good."[16]

Nonetheless, far from wanting to extirpate faction, a project as "impracticable" as it would be "unwise and destructive of liberty," Madison argues for the multiplication and the diversification of factions. A majority faction is, by Madison's definition, adversarial to the common good; it is a "tyranny of the majority." It is necessary, then, to multiply minor interests, even at the risk of forming minor factions. Factions are not good. But they may be set against each other, even fruitfully, drawing some good from evil. Under a regime of majority rule, a large diversity of minor factions will oblige partisans of each to place themselves in one another's shoes, to learn each other's interests, and to seek compromises that will permit the formation of shifting, coalitional majorities. In this way, minor factions will be obliged to learn to appreciate the reach of views and interests other than their own. Shifting majorities will thus come nearer to a sense of the public good, never perfectly perceived, always only approximate, "at least of the GREATER, not the PERFECT good."

Ironically, the more likely danger is not too little consensus about the common good, but too much. What worries Madison most is not the mere approximation of the common good reached by shifting coalitions but, rather, some unanimity about the common good reached by a majority that might then trample upon the rights of minorities. Majorities do not offer reliable protection of the public good. Majorities, too, may behave as tyrants. Madison argues from *both* of the two republican principles, majority rule and private rights. The principle of *majority rule* leads him to seek in a diversity of factions a means both of forming and of checking majorities. The principle of *private rights* confirms him in the necessity of such checks.

Thus, as earlier he used ambition to counter ambition, Madison counters the ills of self-interest with the benefits of self-interest. He ask us to envisage two possibilities, when a faction is only a minority, and when it is a majority. In the first case, "relief is supplied by the republican principle, which enables the majority to defeat its sinister views by regular vote." A minority faction may "clog the administration, it may convulse the society; but it will be unable to execute and mask its violence under the forms of the Constitution." In the second case, when a faction includes a majority:

> the form of popular government . . . enables it to sacrifice to its ruling passion or interest both the public good and the rights of other citizens. To secure the *public good* and *private rights* against the danger of such a faction, and at the same time to preserve the spirit and the form of popular government, is then *the great object to which our inquiries are directed.* Let me add that it is the great desideratum by which alone this form of government can be rescued from the opprobrium under which it has so long labored and be recommended to the esteem and adoption of mankind.[17]

Most republics in history have allowed themselves to become tyrannies of the majority. Against majorities, "neither moral nor religious motives can be relied on as an adequate control." Pure democracies, in which citizens meet face-to-face to reach decisions in a common forum, are especially prone to tyranny. "Hence it is that such democracies have ever been spectacles of turbulence and contention; have ever been found incompatible with personal security or the rights of property; and have in general been as short in their lives as they have been violent in their deaths. Theoretic politicians, who have patronized this species of government, have erroneously supposed that by reducing mankind to a perfect equality in their political rights, they would at the same time be perfectly equalized and assimilated in their possessions, their opinions, and their passions."[18]

No "theoretic politician" he, the practical Madison believes in no such equality at all, knowing that "liberty is to faction what air is to fire." He thinks a rage for "an equal division of property" is a "wicked project." He seeks "a republican remedy for the diseases most incident to republican government." Such diseases include the "rage" for equality and the deadly vice of envy. In a wholly original way, he finds this remedy in "the enlargement of the orbit" of the Union, where the multiplicity of interests is the most likely expedient to prevent both majoritarian tyranny and the narrow-minded self-enclosure of minorities.[19]

Madison thus takes his stand with those "most considerate and virtuous citizens, equally the friends of *public* and *private* faith, and of *public* and *private* liberty." For him, these two words belong together, *private* and *public*. If they are to go together in practice, designers of a "new order" must take the necessary precautions. They must overlook neither self-interest nor faction. To turn such enduring realities to creative purpose, Madison argues, Americans need to turn away from the old order, in which it is obvious that "the *public good* is disregarded in the conflicts of rival parties, and that measures are too often decided, not according to the rules of justice and the rights of the minor party, but by the *superior force* of an interested and overbearing *majority.*"[20] Not only individuals may be self-interested; so also public officials and, indeed, majorities. The last has been the surest destroyer of republics.

Madison's intellectual originality and the intricacy of his argument need to be reappropriated by every generation in full detail, as in excellent studies by Martin Diamond, Marvin Meyers, and others in the two decades preceding our own.[21] Evaluate it as one will, one cannot miss the realism of Madison's concern for the common good—or, as he often preferred to put it—"the public good and private rights." His achievement was a new and original solution to the reconciliation of free persons and the common good. He showed profound concern for the common good, to be realized through the institutional architecture of an *ordo* worthy of free persons. Such an order seeks the public good through building institutions and forming communities both to nourish the requisite habits of the heart and to check the excesses to which the human heart is prey.

How did this new architecture actually work? Forty-four years after the closing of the Constitutional Convention, the young French aristocrat, Alexis de Tocqueville, used his family's connections to win government financing for a nine-month tour of the United States. His remarkable testimony on what he found in America in 1831–32 brilliantly defines the novel conception of public and private good that he found thriving in this land. Tocqueville thought that, in the designs of Providence, this "new order" would be an irresistible model for all other nations.

### 3. Tocqueville: "Self-Interest Rightly Understood"

In cultures shaped by European aristocracy, self-interest was much disparaged. If the true aristocrat gives to others, he gives for no advantage of his own; he gives because it flows from his own nobility, *noblesse oblige*, almost as if like God, his goodness flows solely from his own abundance. In the first democratic nation, by contrast, the term self-interest was used in a sense Tocqueville had never heard before. Americans seemed always to have the term upon their lips. They used it even when they pointed to deeds done for the public interest, or out of generosity, or out of civic spirit. They used it as a term of modesty. Far from being embarrassed by the term, Americans seemed to use it of virtually any deed. They very nearly made a boast of it, expecting strangers to hold self-interest in the same high moral regard as they themselves held it.

This usage caught Tocqueville's attention and pricked his curiosity. He soon enough saw its reasons. In America, many citizens could compare their lot with the lot they had experienced in other lands under undemocratic regimes. They knew that, for the same efforts as they now expended in the United States, they would in their former condition have reaped far lesser benefits. They could measure quite tangibly, then, the increase to their private interest bestowed by the beneficial workings of their "new order." They, therefore, loved this new order and easily identified its growing strength with their own. The new order benefited them. To contribute to it was to contribute to themselves. To serve the public interest was to serve their own self-interest. Americans did not make a sharp distinction between their own self-interest and the public interest.

Thus, one of the revolutions in human behavior brought about by "the new order of the ages" was to alter the relation between citizens and the social order. To an unprecedented degree, the new order belonged to all the people, not only in the sense that it had been created and was sustained by their own consent, but also in the sense, demonstrated every day in countless benefactions, that its own growing prosperity was indistinguishable from their own. To be sure, this relation was also reciprocal. The prosperity of individual farmers and men of commerce (there were still in Tocqueville's time more of the former than of the latter) was the chief cause of the wealth of the nation as a whole. In a superficial sense, a nation's wealth is but the summing of individual gains. In a deeper sense, the new social order makes possible the latter.

Behind America's evident energy and enterprise lay liberty and social union. The protection of the rights of each and the multiplication of opportunities for each (the population of Southern slaves, alas, excepted), had resulted, exactly as the framers had predicted, in the growth of the wealth and the opportunity of all. At least until Tocqueville's visit, the experiment had evidently worked. Indeed, Abraham Lincoln was able to write a full thirty years after Tocqueville that the promises of the framers concerning the twin principles of union and liberty had resulted in an even more abundant prosperity than any had dared predict:

All this is not the result of accident. It has a philosophical cause. Without the *Constitution* and the *Union*, we could not have attained the result; but even these, are not the primary cause of our great prosperity. There is something back of these, entwining itself more closely about the human heart. That something, is the principle of "Liberty to all"—the principle that clears the *path* for all—gives *hope* to all—and, by consequence, *enterprize*, and *industry* to all.

The *expression* of that principle, in our Declaration of Independence, was most happy, and fortunate. *Without* this, as well as *with* it, we could have declared our independence of Great Britain; but *without* it, we could not, I think, have secured our free government, and consequent prosperity.[22]

The institutional key to this success, in Tocqueville's diagnosis, was the "equality" granted to all citizens (excepting slaves) in the new republic. Privilege, rank, and exemption in law had been abolished. Tocqueville saw in this historic breakthrough the hand of Providence guiding the tide of human events. He believed that this tide would eventually sweep Europe and all the world with it. To prepare Europeans for the coming of this tide was his chief motive for writing so lengthy a report.[23]

He saw, further, that these new institutional arrangements had called into existence new virtues. Like others educated in the Catholic tradition (and conservative liberals or Whigs more generally), Tocqueville placed a very strong emphasis upon habits. Ideas alone are quite powerful. Still, until ideas are actually embodied in the regularities and capacities for innovation inherent in actual human habits, they are thin vapors or passing fancies. Ideas alone are not enough. The habits of free persons are necessary preconditions for institutions of liberty. Conversely, institutions of liberty inculcate habits of liberty.[24]

Tocqueville recognized that the Americans of 1787 had been formed by nearly a century and a half of benign neglect on the part of English monarchs, during which the colonists had been obliged to learn to govern themselves, first in townships, then in counties, then in states, and only in the last instance in a federal system. Through a fit of English absentmindedness, the Americans had been schooled for generations in the habits of liberty, under institutions of their own devising.[25]

These habits, in turn, had convinced them of the necessities of mutual covenant, organization, and government. Long experience in trying to learn these habits had taught them, as well, the peculiar vices to which the hearts of men are prone. The weaknesses of human habits had taught them, in the activities of self-government, the necessities of checks, balances, and auxiliary precautions. Liberty is a difficult and demanding school. The sustained ability of free persons to make decisions from "reflection" and "choice," not solely from passion and ignorance, depends upon the calm possession of habits of self-mastery. "The idea of rights is nothing but the conception of virtue applied to the world of politics," Tocqueville wrote. "No man can be great without virtue, nor any nation great without respect for rights; one might almost say that without it there can be no society, for what is a combination of rational and intelligent beings held together by force alone?" The key, then, is a republic of virtue. "I keep asking myself," Tocqueville continued, "how, in our day, this conception may be taught to mankind and made, so to say, palpable to their senses; and I find one only, namely, to give them all the peaceful use of certain rights."[26]

For Tocqueville, the rights of the free depend upon the virtues of the free. And the learning of such virtues depends upon the exercising of rights. "Why is it that in America, the land par excellence of democracy, no one makes that outcry against property in general that often echoes through Europe?" Tocqueville answers: "Because there are no proletarians in America." Since almost everyone has some property, everybody benefits by the principle, and sees property as an extension of self—the instrument and the material through which the self exercises its liberty. "It is the same in the world of politics. The American man of the people has conceived a high idea of political rights because he has some; he does not attack those of others, in order that his own may not be violated."[27] Both in political and in economic matters, the virtues of liberty are taught through the experience of institutions of liberty.

Thus, the key to the institutional success of republics is

"equality of condition" before the law. But a regime under such a law requires habits of self-government. Such habits, in turn, constitute a set of virtues new to the human race. The republican virtues are rather different from those listed in the classical tables of the virtues, not in replacement of, but rather in addition to them. Tocqueville singles out two such habits for special attention: the habit of "association" and the habit of "self-interest rightly understood." It is the latter that concerns us here.

That there are forms of self-interest *wrongly* understood goes without saying. In Europe, the very term "self-interest" was nearly *always* used pejoratively. When men lack liberty, when their station is fixed for life, and when opportunity for self-advancement is lacking, how can the social order in which they live not seem to them to be an enemy, even if they allow for its necessity? It is a necessity, for "law and order," however oppressive, are normally preferable to a "war of all against all." But such a social order is also their enemy, because the yeast embedded in their natural liberty is neutralized against its natural rising. Since their natural liberty has no room in which to expand, the self-interest embedded in their natural capacities for liberty must necessarily seem to threaten social order. In such a social order the habits of citizens are driven into a relatively small and private compass. Public life is foreclosed to nearly all citizens except the aristocracy, which supplies officers and functionaries for most public sinecures, major and minor (as in the case of Tocqueville himself).

Ironically, then, the aristocratic disparagement of self-interest is accompanied by social structures that guarantee the security of the well born, allowing them to live without striving or care (sinecure), while among those of lowly birth, these inequalities of condition close the doors of public life, and shut off nearly all human energies *except* those of private self-interest. The horizons of those of "lowly birth" are narrowly compressed. Of what else may they think, let alone take responsibility, except their own familial interests? And since these interests are carefully contained within clearly bounded limits, self-interest must necessarily be "wrongly understood." For no more can be included within the term than that they must be contented with their lot, as it is given. Tocqueville expresses this point precisely: "Despotism, which by its nature is suspicious, sees in the separation among men the surest guarantee of its continuance, and it usually makes every effort to keep them separate. No vice of the human heart is so acceptable to it as selfishness: a despot easily forgives his subjects for not loving him, provided they do not love another. He does not ask them to assist him in governing the state; it is enough that they do not aspire to govern it themselves." Further, the tyrant stigmatizes as "turbulent and unruly spirits those who would combine their exertions to promote the prosperity of the community; and, perverting the natural meaning of words, he applauds as good citizens those who have no sympathy for any but themselves."[28]

Perhaps because my own family descends from the peasantry of central Europe, in the Tatra mountains of Slovakia, wherein serfdom itself did not come to an end until the childhood of my grandfather, the points adumbrated by Tocqueville validate personal experience. The difference between the "old order" of Central Europe and the "new order" of the United States, like the difference between the habits inculcated in "the old country" and those opened up by the "new," are quite vivid in family memory. Tocqueville does not misdescribe the reality; not at least for those Americans whose family memories span two cultures.

In brief, self-interest *wrongly* understood implies one of two general conceptions. In one conception, in which the station of the self is fixed, it implies that the proper and virtuous attitude of the citizen ought to be a sort of disinterested acceptance of his lot. In that context, self-interest implies a certain restlessness or even rebellion against the established order. In the other conception, in which opportunity is open, self-interest wrongly understood implies a meanness of spirit, whereby the citizen reacts against his experience of the harshness of life by seeking first (and perhaps only) such self-aggrandizement as each new circumstance in life presents to him. Here is where religion would cry out to the citizen to open up his heart, to be generous, and to act for others, no matter how poor or constrained (or even how lordly and well-off) may be his own condition. In both conceptions, self-interest names, and can only name, a vice.

From the Catholic tradition, Tocqueville has learned that self-interest wrongly understood is rooted in human nature. St. Bernard of Clairvaux, for example, once observed that self-love dies a quarter-hour after the self. Since even hermits know the terrors of battling in solitude against their own egotism, such self-interest endures even within monastery walls. If it is so in institutions expressly committed to the total love of God, what should a realist expect outside those walls? Thus, the many examples he encountered in America of self-interest *wrongly* understood would hardly have arrested Tocqueville's attention; only their total absence would have astonished him. For him the surprise—both as a practice and as a novel theory—lay in the phenomenon of "self-interest *rightly* understood."

Essential to Tocqueville's understanding of self-interest rightly understood is his sustained comparison between aristocratic nations and nations that have banished aristocracy and thus achieved "equality of condition."[29] An aristocrat himself, Tocqueville much admires the effects of aristocracy upon manners. Among these are independence of mind; financial security; secure attachments to land, lineage, and heirs; and a considerable freedom of action, including an unparalleled disdain for public opinion.[30] Aristocracy also fosters a certain type of community:

As in aristocratic communities all the citizens occupy fixed positions, one above another, the result is that each of them always sees a man above himself whose patronage is necessary to him, and below himself another man whose cooperation he may claim. Men living in aristocratic ages are therefore almost always closely attached to something placed out of their own sphere, and they are often disposed to forget themselves. It is true that in these ages the notion of human fellowship is faint and that men seldom think of sacrificing themselves for mankind; but they often sacrifice themselves for other men. . . . Aristocracy had made a chain of all the members of the community, from the peasant to the king; democracy breaks that chain and severs every link of it.[31]

Curiously, then, aristocratic structures teach human beings a communitarian way of life. The places of all (or almost all) are fixed through heredity. The notion of solitary individuality is almost unthinkable. Indeed, the very word *individualism*, a new word, fascinates Tocqueville, who immediately contrasts it with the ancient word, *selfishness*. "*Individualism* is a novel expression, to which a novel idea has given birth. Our fathers were only acquainted with *égoisme* [selfishness]. Selfishness is a passionate and exaggerated love of self, which leads a man to connect everything with himself and to prefer himself to everything in the world." By contrast, "Individualism is a mature and calm feeling, which disposes each member of the community to sever himself from the mass of his fellows and to draw apart with his family and his friends, so that after he has thus formed a little circle of his own, he willingly leaves society at large to itself."[32]

This view, although perhaps admixed with aristocratic prejudices, highlights an axial shift in conceptions of community. Selfishness is perversity of the heart. Individualism is an erroneous conception in the mind. Selfishness is as old as the world, and is found in every form of society. Individualism "is of democratic origin" and races through society (or threatens to) "in the same ratio as the equality of condition." Tocqueville's hypothesis concerning how this happens is quite precise: "As social conditions grow more equal, many persons attain sufficient education and fortune to satisfy their own wants. Neither rich nor greatly powerful, they nonetheless owe nothing to any man, they expect nothing from any man; they acquire the habit of always considering themselves as standing alone, and they are apt to imagine that their whole destiny is in their own hands." Individualism "saps the virtues of public life," in the long run weakens private virtues, too, and may degenerate into "downright selfishness."[33] Thus does individualism, in Tocqueville's sense, undermine republics.

But the American framers, Tocqueville notes, saw this danger and "have subdued it." The legislators of America "did not suppose that a general representation of the whole nation would suffice to ward off a disorder at once so natural to the frame of democratic society and so fatal; they also thought that it would be well to infuse political life into each portion of the territory in order to multiply to an infinite extent opportunities of acting in concert for all the members of the community and to make them constantly feel their mutual dependence. The plan was a wise one."[34]

In local affairs, citizens quickly see the connection between their private interests and the general interest. To instruct them on such connections, a proposal to build a road across a portion of their property will not need to be accompanied by philosophical treatises. Therefore, the federal principle at the root of the American experiment draws as many citizens as possible into the exercise of local responsibilities. Such experiences teach citizens that they constantly stand in need of one another, and instruct them that "to earn the love and respect of the population that surrounds you, a long succession of little services rendered and of obscure good deeds, a constant habit of kindness, and an established reputation for disinterestedness will be required." Thus, local freedom "perpetually brings men together and forces them to help one another in spite of the propensities that sever them."[35]

Every imagination in the United States seems to stretch "to invent means of increasing the wealth and satisfying the wants of the public." In each district, the best informed "constantly use their information to discover new truths that may augment the general prosperity; and if they have made any such discoveries, they eagerly surrender them to the mass of the people."[36] On this point, Madison had anticipated Tocqueville. To promote the innovation that is the chief cause of the wealth of nations, the prescient Madison had found an *institutional* device: the addition of the copyright and patent clause to Article I of the Constitution.

Madison's explicit purpose was to wed the private to the public good. Thus, Article I, section 8, grants to the Congress the power "to promote the progress of science and useful arts, by securing for limited times to authors and inventors the exclusive right to their respective writings and discoveries." The copyright of authors had long been recognized in Great Britain as a right in common law. But the Americans went a full step further, adjudging with equal reason that the same right belongs to inventors. Madison's comment in *Federalist* 43 is succinct: "The public good fully coincides in both cases with the claims of individuals." Thus the habit of innovation for the public as well as the private good was institutionally grounded in American law.

Observing the fruits of this law, Tocqueville marvels at the zeal with which Americans express love for the improvement of their common life. He cannot believe this zeal to be insincere without disbelieving the evidence of his senses. Through the institutions of political responsibility Americans combat individualism, and through their own exertions learn every day that to help the public is simultaneously to help themselves. From personal experience, Americans know they have what they have because of the regime of which they are a part. Even more onerous efforts elsewhere had rewarded them far less. They have thus learned to see in their own success their indebtedness to the social order, and in the common good the key to their own.

Perhaps for this reason it perfectly suits the American conviction that in the Pledge of Allegiance recited by school children at the beginning of each day, Americans do not pledge allegiance, as other citizens elsewhere do, to land or soil, to peoplehood or nationhood. In pledging allegiance to the flag, they pledge allegiance to a particular form of government: the Republic. Take away the republican form of government and the bonds of loyalty snap. In the United States, republican virtue is the deepest political virtue. America is not geography; it is a form of government, a way of life.[37] The distinctive feature of the republican form of government is that its sovereign is the people. To serve that government, then, is to serve themselves. To achieve the good of free persons, under such a regime, is the public aim, and the public good is the fecund spring of the private good of each.

The general principle of American life, Tocqueville discerns, is the truth "that man serves himself in serving his fellow creatures and that his private interest is to do good."[38] The heart of the American idea is to transform self-interest into a personal interest in the public good. In aristocratic cultures, the world was managed by a few rich and powerful individuals. Since their own rewards were already taken care of, quite apart from their own efforts, such men talked incessantly of the beauties of virtue, but thought altogether little about its utility. In the United States, a humbler and more modest view was appropriate. Americans thought it better actually to improve the common condition than to think beautiful thoughts. They encouraged effective public-spiritedness, and viewed lofty speech with caution. Every citizen ought to add to the public good, and the public good ought to be refracted in every individual good. American interest habitually sought out and focused upon practical points at which "private interest and public interest meet and amalgamate."

This American translation of the classical aristocratic virtues into the humbler but more effective republican virtues is a central theme of Tocqueville's entire work. And now he is coming close to its core:

> I have already shown, in several parts of this work, by what means the inhabitants of the United States almost always manage to combine their own advantage with that of their fellow citizens; my present purpose is to point out the general rule that enables them to do so. In the United States hardly anybody talks of the beauty of virtue, but they maintain that virtue is useful and prove it every day. The American moralists do not profess that men ought to sacrifice themselves for their fellow creatures because it is noble to make such sacrifices, but they boldly aver that such sacrifices are as necessary to him who imposes them upon himself as to him for whose sake they are made.[39]

Recognizing candidly that humans naturally attach themselves to realities that affect their own lives—that is, to interests that become self-interests—the Americans had no need to pretend that habits of self-interest would miraculously disappear from history. Realists, they hinged their hopes upon redirecting natural self-interest to the common interest. Their success in doing so was demonstrated by the tide of private human energy released for the common good. Although the existence and power of self-interest rightly understood had long been known to philosophers, among the Americans of the 1830s "you may trace it at the bottom of all their actions, you will remark it in all they say. It is as often asserted by the poor man as by the rich." It is a principle transcending class distinctions. In Europe, people were ashamed to speak of self-interest, since existing regimes had seldom arranged for self-interest and public interest to coincide. "The Americans, on the other hand, are fond of explaining almost all the actions of their lives by the principle of self-interest rightly understood; they show with complacency how an enlightened regard for themselves constantly prompts them to assist one another and inclines them willingly to sacrifice a portion of their time and property to the welfare of the state."[40]

The degree to which this is true surprises Tocqueville. Even when Americans do give way to "those disinterested and spontaneous impulses that are natural to man," the Americans persist in explaining such generosity, too, in terms of the principle of self-interest. "In this respect, I think they frequently fail to do themselves justice," Tocqueville writes. "They are more anxious to do honor to their philosophy than to themselves."[41]

Still, the principle of self-interest rightly understood is neither the summit nor the sum of republican virtue. It is not a lofty principle, only a very modest and realistic one, set to the measure of human weakness. Yet it is rooted in reason itself. As a moral principle, it "checks one personal interest by another, and uses, to direct the passions, the very same instrument that excites them." (Here Tocqueville recapitulates the views of Madison exactly.) It "suggests daily small acts of self-denial." It teaches "habits of regularity, temperance, moderation, foresight, self-command." It draws men into the good habits required by the other virtues. It makes gross depravity less common. Although its universal practice would perhaps reduce the number of men who would rise far above the common level, it raises up a multitude who would otherwise have fallen far below it. "I am not afraid to say that the principle of self-interest rightly understood appears to me the best suited of all philosophical theories to the wants of the men of our time, and that I regard it as their chief remaining security against themselves. Towards it, therefore, the minds of the moralists of our age should turn; even should they judge it to be incomplete, it must nevertheless be adopted as necessary."[42]

Christianity itself, Tocqueville points out, appeals to two motives: self-interest rightly understood, and the sacrifice of personal interests to the "consummate order of all created things," as willed by God. Like Pascal's wager, the former motive appeals to fears of damnation and to desires of everlasting bliss; the latter motive goes beyond punishment and reward to self-sacrificing love. The latter motive is nobler and deeper. The former is more persuasive and more popular. Self-interest is not the sole motive of religious men, but it is "the principal means that religions themselves employ to govern men."[43] "What doth it profit a man . . .?" the Scripture asks, speaking at times of the nobler, at times of the humbler, springs of human conduct. Both come from God.

\* \* \*

One should not of course too much "spiritualize" the reality of self-interest rightly understood. Tocqueville didn't. He recognized that one of its most common manifestations lay in commercial activities. In aristocratic and priestly times often taken to be lowly, commercial activities are the mainstay of the economic life of common lay majorities. Like the framers, who proudly bear the title "the commercial republicans," Tocqueville also recognized that commerce instructs citizens in certain virtues crucial to republican governance. Under feudal and aristocratic regimes, the martial values gain sway, together with high esteem for deeds of heroism in battle. By contrast, commercial activities are far less romantic, and they both require and teach respect for law and peace. ("Trade and peace" is the motto of Amsterdam.) Commercial activities encourage attention to small gains and small losses. They inculcate prudence. They teach as well a love for risk and innovation. They tame fanaticism. They moderate the excesses of natural glory and extreme religious passion. They teach tolerance, and respect achievement rather than the accidents of birth or station or race or class or faith.

Narrowly regarded, commercial activities are pursued with a view to private gain. Yet even this gain can be accrued on an enduring basis only if the needs of purchasers are served reliably and well. Although aimed at private gain, commercial activities oblige their agents to be in a basic and plain sense other-regarding, not perhaps according to the high mode of charity and yet nonetheless with real and practical effect. The bias of commercial activity is toward cooperation, in the sense that such activities can prosper only through voluntary and reliable relations with a multitude of others. As aristocratic cultures disdain "self-interest," so they look down on vulgar commerce. The paradox is that, as in the Thomistic discussion of the superiority of private property to collective ownership, commercial activities undertaken for private gain turn out historically to serve the common good better than regimes of collective distribution. They achieve greater productivity, result in less dissension, and spur habits of voluntary and cheerful cooperation. Such claims, by the late eighteenth century, were asserted as empirical propositions, derived from a comparison of the then existing alternatives. It is a nice irony, then, that in the humble order of economics (soon to be known as "the dismal science"), activities undertaken with a view to private gain should turn out better to serve the common good than the more highly lauded activities of princes, dukes, bishops, and "theoretic politicians."

Following Darwin later in the nineteenth century, newer generations were to look upon commercial activities as "dog eat dog" and "the survival of the fittest." That is not how either the American framers or Tocqueville looked upon the actual workings of commerce. They did not spurn private gain, but saw its possibilities as a humble instrument of service to the common good. They valued commercial activity not solely for its economic fecundity in increasing the wealth of peoples and nations, but also for the unromantic virtues it inculcated in its participants. They deemed such virtues indispensable to the republican project, and ranked them among the full panoply of "republican virtues." In a sustained way, what aristocratic cultures counted as lowly and lacking in beauty, to be despised and rejected, they looked to for solutions to perennial practical problems.

★   ★   ★

In summary, then, self-interest *wrongly* understood leads to *selfishness* as well as to the self-enclosure that Tocqueville intends by the word *individualism*. The principle of self-interest *rightly* understood is its contrary. Lowly enough in its origins, it begins with the quickening excitement that interests touching the self awaken spontaneously and naturally in the human breast. Its essence consists in attaching these instincts, neutral in themselves, to worthy and socially beneficial projects. The principle of self-interest rightly understood teaches humans that they are social animals, that they have need of one another, and that their own self-development depends upon their becoming social beings. The principle of self-interest rightly understood attaches the interests of the self to the public interest. It is the foundational principle of the human obligation to serve the common good. Without it, the common good would appear to be a good to be pursued only by angels, since if men were angels, they would need no principle of self-interest rightly understood to lead them to serve the common good. Thus, the principle of self-interest rightly understood perfectly expresses the social nature of the human person, in whose profound interest it is to exercise his liberty in free, kindly, and open cooperation with his fellows. Such use of liberty is in his own self-interest. It is in the common interest. The whole point of self-interest rightly understood is that these two should be coincident.

## 4. The Principle of Lowliness.

Oddly enough, many American intellectuals not only overlook the wisdom of Tocqueville and Madison concerning self-interest rightly understood, but quite flagrantly misunderstand it. Many distinguished scholars have seriously misapprehended their own heritage, and others have reduced the beliefs of the American framers to something like Mandeville's paradoxical formulation, "private vices, public virtues," a formulation that Adam Smith called "wholly pernicious."[44] Neither Madison nor Tocqueville took self-interest rightly understood to be a vice. Both clearly distinguished, each in his own way, self-interest wrongly understood from self-interest rightly understood. Only the latter, not the former, serves the public interest and the common good.

Indeed, the former can be prevented from harming the public interest and the common good only by strenuous efforts. Institutions and personal habits must be carefully constructed so as to make "ambition to counteract ambition," and errant interest to counteract other errant interests. Were citizens to practice self-interest wrongly understood systematically and universally, republican self-government would at that instant become impossible. The condition of free persons would become "pitiful." Men would become to each other as wolves to wolves. The jungle would replace civil community. Thus, private vices are *not* the road to public virtue. Such vices must either be corrected and painstakingly reformed into virtues or, when human weakness defeats that possibility, vigilantly checked by wisely crafted institutions and organized opposition. Richard Hofstadter sums up well the balance sought by the founders:

> Political economists of the laissez-faire school were saying that private vices could be public benefits, that an economically beneficent result would be providentially or "naturally" achieved if self-interest were left free from state interference and allowed to pursue its ends. But the Fathers were not so optimistic about politics. If, in a state that lacked constitutional balance, one class or one interest gained control, they believed, it would surely plunder the poor. Even Gouverneur Morris, who stood as close to the extreme aristocratic position as candor and intelligence would allow, told the Convention: "Wealth tends to corrupt the mind and to nourish its love of power, and to stimulate it to oppression. History proves this to be the spirit of the opulent."
>
> What the Fathers wanted was known as "balanced government," an idea at least as old as Aristotle and Polybius. . . . A properly designed state, the Fathers believed, would check interest with interest, class with class, faction with faction, and one branch of government with another in a harmonious system of mutual frustration.[45]

Still, checks and balances are not enough. They are quite a lot, and the achievement of an "order" or a "design" that would diminish vice and give incentive to securing the public weal dare not be underestimated. Virtue alone could never afford such protections to the public good and private rights as do "the extent and proper structure of the Union" to which Madison pointed at the end of *Federalist* 10. Still, if virtue needs the support of a proper institutional design, institutions need equally the support of virtue. Well-designed institutions cannot count upon angels or saints, and can indeed bear some weight of human vice, failure, and weakness (such is their design). But to believe that a republic can survive without active and widespread virtue is, as Madison also said, "chimerical."

Thus, the root of republican self-government lies ultimately in virtue, both in its lofty forms and in its more lowly form of self-interest rightly understood. The reason why is plain. Republican self-government consists in the practice of human liberty, in reflection and in considered choice. Truly free acts must break the chains of passion, ignorance, bigotry, self-enclosure, and intolerance. It is not easy for humans to free themselves of these. They are free only when acting at high levels of self-mastery. To become free is to have learned habits of liberty.

Thus, the framers in Philadelphia in 1787 were poignantly aware of how they themselves had had to rise above the normal play of passion, interest, and faction that would, unchecked, have dashed their purposes. Madison in *Federalist* 37 celebrates their high achievement, by contrast with the normal run of human history: "The history of almost all the great councils and consultations, held among mankind for reconciling their discordant opinions, assuaging their mutual jealousies, and adjusting their respective interests, is a history of factions, contentions, and disappointments; and may be classed among the most dark and degrading pictures which display the infirmities and depravities of the human character."[46]

In this melancholy history, Madison continues, in a few scattered instances a brighter aspect is presented, if only "as exceptions" and "by their luster to darken the gloom . . . to which they are contrasted." One of these bright moments occurred at the Constitutional Convention itself, from whose singular achievements Madison draws two conclusions:

The first is, that the Convention must have enjoyed in a very singular degree, an exemption from the pestilential influence of party animosities; the diseases most incident to deliberative bodies, and most apt to contaminate their proceedings. The second conclusion is, that all the deputations composing the Convention, were either satisfactorily accommodated by the final act; or were induced to accede to it, by a deep conviction of the necessity of sacrificing private opinions and partial interests to the public good, and by a despair of seeing this necessity diminished by delays or by new experiments.[47]

The Constitutional Convention could not have succeeded without a high practice of republican virtue. Self-interest—even to its own profound benefit—had of necessity to yield to the common interest.

From the foregoing, it is obvious that the task of reconciling private rights to the public good—or the free person to the common good—is not an easy one. Indeed, it is not easy for a man to be a man. Human nature, Judaism, Christianity, and common experience itself unite in teaching us, is divided against itself. "There is a war in our very members," as St. Paul put it. So it is also for a republic committed through its institutional design to being suited to human beings as we are. The framers, Tocqueville, Lincoln and a host of reflective commentators since have glimpsed the fragility of the American experiment in ordered liberty. How could it be otherwise? If even individually "we work out our salvation in fear and trembling," it is at least as likely that our public experiment in America should make us tremble and be vigilant.

How, then, can the necessities of the common good commend themselves to free persons, who are not angels but only human beings? Republican governments depend upon a practical, effective answer to that question. For they are explicitly based both upon the consent of the governed (majority rule) and the securing of personal rights (against majorities).

More than any other, although assisted by many, Madison is the architect of the "new order" that resolved that question institutionally, as an experiment. Tocqueville is the chronicler of the initial success of that experiment and the discerning analyst who uncovered its secret working principle, the principle that unites self-interest to the public interest.

This principle, I believe, is connected to one still deeper, the Jewish-Christian principle of lowliness. Instead of revealing Himself in blazing and irresistible light to all the world at once, the God of Judaism lowered Himself to accept the humble ways of human history, revealing Himself to a relatively small and unknown people at the edges of several gloried civilizations (Persian, Egyptian, Greek, and Roman). The God of Christianity lowered Himself as well, appearing in history as a humble carpenter of Nazareth (mocked for being called "a king"), who was given over by the Romans to the death of a common criminal. In both Judaism and Christianity, God turns human thoughts away from lofty schemes suited perhaps to angels, and toward the more humble and modest ways suited to human conditions. This God speaks in the concrete, within history, not in a grand universal voice from outside history. This God practices the principle of lowliness. It seems right for humans to do likewise.

If the reconciliation of the common good with free persons in their weakness and division is one of the most crucial of all human tasks, we do well to heed the principle of lowliness. The most realistic solutions are not likely to be grand or lofty, but humble and concrete.[48] Looking for them in the wrong place, or in the wrong mode, we are quite likely to miss them altogether. The principle of lowliness—what Jefferson once called "the humble wisdom"—is the most reliable of guides in political philosophy.

Indeed, our next task is to turn to one of the lowliest (and by philosophers longest neglected) set of human activities: economic activities. And yet daily acts of producing and exchanging material goods and services are inherently social. In their material needs, human beings are scarcely ever autonomous. Their economic activities are scarcely ever self-sufficient. Thus, the establishment of a social order that attains the common good regarding material necessities is one of the basic preconditions of civilization. The achievement of the economic common good is far from constituting the full human common good. The principle of lowliness suggests, though, that concern with such humble activities, a means to other goods necessary to a fully human level of life on earth, is a sound place to begin.

In constructing a *limited* government, the framers of the American system removed from government two principal tasks with which it had earlier been burdened: (1) responsibility for control over (but not from action regarding) conscience, information, and ideas—that is, from control over church, press, and intellectual and moral life; and (2) responsibility for control over (but not from the promotion and regulation of) economic activities. Of these two largely nongovernmental areas, the economic sphere is the dimension we must first address. If government is not to have the chief responsibility of designing, planning, and managing the achievement of the economic common good, how is such a common good to be attained?

# Chapter Three

# ORDER UNPLANNED

## 1. Common Good as Practical Intelligence

The *novus ordo* designed by the framers of the U.S. Constitution made free persons sovereign. In the old order, rulers and statesmen had been the ultimate guardians of the common good. In the new order, their power was significantly withdrawn from the cultural sphere and from the economic sphere. In the political sphere, it was limited to particular grants of power as *written down* in the Constitution. How, then, could political leaders (subdivided into legislative, judicial, and executive domains) take responsibility for achieving the full common good? They could not.

Government is not a completely trustworthy agent of the common good. It, too, must be restrained from trampling rights and subverting the common good. Democratic majorities may also act like tyrants, both in oppressing minorities and in preferring to the common good their own. Further, no full and concrete conception of the common good can be preplanned. Too many concrete, contingent conditions must be met for that. What then, does the term "common good" mean in practice? It points to two facets of human nature: human beings are social and political animals, who need one another; and striving, historical animals, always seeking outcomes not yet achieved. Together, the terms "common" and "good" capture both the social and the dynamic character of human life. Philosophically (as in St. Thomas Aquinas), the term operates at a high level of abstraction from particular regimes.

But even at a high level of abstraction, the term "common good" can be given specificity according to rival philosophies of human nature. The particular philosophy of man embodied in the U.S. Constitution, for example, is not devoid of practical effect. The U.S. Constitution would work neither for angels nor for the morally unscrupulous. Its very design presupposes citizens committed to the virtues that nourish reflection and choice; citizens who are not saints, but quite capable of self-government. As the *Federalist* shows, a theory both of responsibility and of sin is built into its architecture.

> As there is a degree of depravity in mankind which requires a certain degree of circumspection and distrust: So there are other qualities in human nature, which justify a certain portion of esteem and confidence. Republican government presupposes the existence of these qualities in a higher degree than any other form.[1]

> The aim of every political Constitution is or ought to be first to obtain for rulers, men who possess most wisdom to discern, and most virtue to pursue the common good of the society; and in the next place, to take the most effectual precautions for keeping them virtuous, whilst they continue to hold their public trust.[2]

Since the U.S. Constitution had been crafted in accord with *American* culture and history, Tocqueville noted, it would not be an apt constitution for France, a people shaped according to a quite different history and culture. Clearly, it would not suit a Leninist party, committed to the totalitarian power of a single party. The term "common good" in the context of the U.S. Constitution, therefore, is not devoid of practical content, even though its application remains highly abstract.

Yet when one tries to make the term "common good" much more concrete than that, one finds oneself speaking of a particular state of affairs—*a* common good of a particular community at a particular moment, but not *the* common good for all times and places. In daily life, the question about material particulars is the urgent one. [See Appendix for further distinctions.]

The framers, of course, did not wish to settle all future concrete questions. But they did wish to provide the *framework* for their answering. In doing so, they did not provide for a panel of planners. A major part of the common good in free republics is to allow citizens to exercise their own liberties. Public decisions must allow as large a scope to individual liberty as possible. "It is the business of government to provide more opportunity, not more government." To seek the general welfare means, above all, to preserve the blessings of liberty, than which there is no greater welfare. This, some people think, is a dangerous doctrine. It relies, they aver, on belief in magic: that, given liberty, everything will end up at the common good by happy chance.

What such thinkers overlook is the nature of practical intelligence itself. The framers believed that to allow free persons to use their own best intelligence in making practical decisions was the best way to maximize intelligent common outcomes. This is because practical intelligence leads humans to want to be cooperative. In making their own decisions, they carefully watch those of others. They choose social coordination freely, since their own good is much affected by the decisions of others—and, indeed, by the rise or fall of the common good. The American experiment aims for a higher level of the common good than any achieved before. Where the autocracies of the past had entrusted the common good to official hands, the Americans, by contrast, entrust as much of it as possible to the decisions of free persons. This is the new experiment.

In disputes and in conflicts, individuals would as before turn to public magistrates. In an array of public works and public projects, they would also entrust a broad range of specific tasks to government. They were not so much antigovernment as well-informed about its deficiencies. (What is most of previous history, they were inclined to ask, if not a reflection of the nature of government?) Mostly, they entrusted the common good to the workings of human liberty among such persons as themselves.

The people of the United States, in accepting the Constitution, chose an order that they believed would ensure their common good, both in a philosophically sound sense and in terms of successive concrete states of affairs. They did this without constituting a body of planners.

What sorts of convictions, what evidence from their own experience, could have led them to trust an unplanned order? How can it happen that order will emerge from unplanned, widely disparate activities? Is there something in human liberty itself that leads to order? To see why the framers thought so, we must try to think our way back to the convictions that make that view plausible.

Most of us today have been brought up within an intellectual culture that makes fun of a supposed "invisible hand" guiding all arrows to one point. We fail to see that intelligent persons act reflectively, taking account of how other persons are acting, and adapting their actions accordingly. We imagine that self-interest sets man against man, and flings individuals apart in centrifugal directions. We forget that human action is full of intelligence. Action is not random, wholly undirected. Free persons are intelligent and self-correcting. They have an interest in order. They do not achieve such an order "automatically," but they can detect when their shots in its direction go astray. They do not need an "invisible hand"[3] or a *deus ex machina*. What actually moves them is their own practical intelligence. To be reflective is to "think again"—and to adapt. Social order emerges from reflective animals, whose most social faculty is practical intellect.

## 2. Beyond the Common Good of the Tribe

The concept of the common good, F. A. Hayek wrongly says, is an atavistic concept that harks back to the primitive instincts of tribes of hunters, when collectivist impulses dominated human consciousness.[4] In order to survive, Hayek argues, individuals helped relatives and friends. In every tribe the actual hunters, few in number, shared their precious catch with all. Helping his friends, knowing that his efforts were indispensable to the common good, the hunter experienced powerful emotions, for which the human race, destined by its Creator for brotherly love, is ever nostalgic.

In those days, Hayek continues, the common good was simple to define. First of all, the common good entailed survival, by no means assured, against pitiless nature and marauding tribes. It entailed strong central authority, usually vested in the elders and in the most outstanding of the warriors chosen to be chief. For roving tribes, the "common good" was concretely defined by a succession of particular states of affairs: enough food and water for the month, for the winter, for the next period until replenishment. And it included provision for the old (although most died young) and for the children. If this common good was not attended to, one could point the finger of responsibility directly at the chief. The chief was both the symbol and decisionmaking agent of the common good. He could fairly be described from the point of view of the good of the tribe as just or unjust. In this sense, one could speak quite simply of "social justice." In Hayek's view, such is the anthropological root of modern feelings about "social justice" and the "common good."

Hayek does understand that "social order" is a construct of reflective, social intelligence. It covers not only material things, but also schemes of order and social relation. It does not suggest only the order of the tribe, but any other sort of order humans can come upon, imagine, or learn by trial and error to constitute. Hayek misses, however, the comparable philosophical power of the medieval thinkers who gave "common good" and "social justice" their modern salience. He also does less than justice to the social concerns of liberal thinkers.

The great liberal thinkers of France, Great Britain, and the United States expressly envisaged new patterns for the good of "nations," "the general welfare," and the improvement of the human condition everywhere on earth. To be sure, to talk about such matters in the frame of reference of all the nations of the world and in complex, differentiated modern societies required the early liberals to break away from earlier and simpler notions of the common good. Furthermore, the traditionalist foes of the liberal revolution used against them the claims of the common good, as traditionally understood. Thus, the phrase itself lost its salience. But the reality did not.

In order to understand the liberal notion of the common good, it is important to grasp several underlying concepts. One cannot understand modern societies simply by inspection—by looking at them with one's eyes. Modern societies are constructs of ideas. An effort of abstraction (or at least of sustained reflection) is necessary. This is why the Statue of Liberty is pictured with the upraised torch of enlightenment against surrounding darkness in one hand and, in the other, a tablet of the laws. To defend liberty is primarily to defend certain ideas, learned through much sweat, bloodshed, and bitter disappointment.

Here a word of caution. In speaking of ideas, I am not speaking of clear and distinct ideas reached by mind alone. Experience is the most subtle and astute teacher, and is often richer in insight than the human intellect of any one generation can put into words. Since ideas apart from experience are nearly always mischievous, if not pernicious, the human race does not arrive at laws, traditions, customs, and habits apart from hard-won lessons. The liberal tradition seeks progress, but is also respectful of the wisdom of the past and constantly revitalized by the study of experience. It values habits and institutions, as well as new ideas. One of its often unrecognized progenitors, Hayek affirmed, is St. Thomas Aquinas, "the first Whig."[5]

As a framework for the argument that follows, permit me to state here the new—the liberal—concept of the common good. "Human society," von Mises writes in *Liberalism in the Classical Tradition*, "is an association of persons for cooperative action."[6] As a start, I prefer to write: *In practice, the essence of the common good is to secure in social life the benefits of voluntary cooperation.* This concept does not exclude the actions of government and can be realized in more than one way. In the tribal period of the race, the common good was conceived of concretely, in terms of particular states of affairs: a tribe would move here for a season, not there; hunt in this way, not that; and particular tasks would be assigned to each. In a modern society, borne forward by immense internal dynamism, such a concept of the common good would soon prove fatal. It would produce a society as static and as threatened by change as the primitive tribe. A modern concept of the common good must be open to change, and—most of all—open to the invention, enterprise, creativity and free choices of multitudes of free persons.

In a tribal society, each member knew virtually every other member through lifelong familiarity. In a modern society such as France or the United States, citizens can know only a tiny fraction of the millions of their fellow citizens. Furthermore, the characteristic mobility of modern individuals means that most do not have lifelong familiarity even with most of their associates. So vast is the differentiation of modern trades, crafts, occupations, professions, technologies, and economic skills that no one person can have that learned experience in each that counts as knowing it "from within" and "by habit."

A central characteristic of modern societies, then, as contrasted with tribal societies, is the ignorance of each citizen regarding the lifework of other citizens. To speak of the common good of all in a modern society, therefore, is to speak without concrete experience of the worlds of a vast majority of others. Concerning the material content of the common good, it is to speak without concrete knowledge, behind a veil of considerable ignorance.

There is a further difficulty necessary to attend to. Tribal societies were not pluralistic, as modern societies are. The free persons of modern societies are expected to form their own judgments about the good, not only about their own personal and familial good but also about the common good. Whereas the common good of a tribal society is collective, universally subscribed to, relatively simple to grasp (almost by inspection), and binding upon all, the common good of a modern society must respect the pluralism of free persons. One can scarcely define the common good of modern societies, then, in substantive terms; one can scarcely command everyone: "We shall march in this direction." Or, rather, one can do so easily only in times of national emergency, under attack by alien forces. (This helps to explain why in modern societies powerful leaders who seek to unite the citizenry behind common purposes often take demagogic refuge in appeals to nationalism, xenophobia, and external aggression.) The issue runs even deeper. The common good of

pluralistic modern societies must leave space for the personal
definitions of the good cherished by free persons. In this context,
is it even conceptually possible to think of a common good that
does not do violence to the goods freely decided upon by free
persons?

The liberal solution to this dilemma has two parts. First, one
must shake the concept of the common good free from the image
of the concrete good expressed in a particular state of affairs.
Collectivist societies can bend every individual will to collective
purposes, defined by command and announced as the collective
good. Societies of free persons cannot. What free societies can
do, however, is to establish general rules designed to bring to all
the benefits of human cooperation, and to nourish the *habits* and
*institutions* that promote cooperation. Liberty in this sense can
never be conceived apart from law. Liberty in this sense rests
upon law. When general rules are framed in such a way as to
proscribe certain particular behaviors, they leave free a large field
of liberty for creativity and enterprise. Rules, wisely constructed,
empower liberty and by no means destroy it. General rules, then,
far from being inconsistent with personal liberties, secure the
conditions under which they thrive. Habits of respect for law and
civic cooperation, matched to institutions that respond quickly to
fresh initiatives, make the rule of law an object of love.

Second, one must also shake the tribal notion of the common
good free from conscious intentions, aims, and purposes. In a
homogeneous, collective, monist society, it is possible to infuse
individual wills with a common purpose, to direct all to common
aims, and to nourish in all a common intention. Not so in
pluralistic societies of free persons. What makes a person free is
a capacity to form his own life purposes, his immediate and
ultimate aims, and his personal motivations and intentions. It
does not follow, however, that free persons cannot cooperate with
one another, cannot give loyalty to common laws and rules, and
cannot achieve dynamic societies that manifestly improve the lot
of all.

A sharp distinction must be drawn, therefore, between concepts of the common good whose essence consists in common
intentions, aims, and purposes, and concepts of the common

good whose essence consists in mutual cooperation apart from common intentions, aims, and purposes. A footpath along a river or up a mountainside may have been formed cooperatively by human beings over centuries, but quite apart from the intentions of any one person, and in pursuit of aims as various as the multiple motives of the multitudes of persons who used such a path.[7] There are common goods apart from common intentions, aims, and purposes. Were it not so, societies of free persons could not exist.

Here an objection from a classical Catholic point of view may result in greater clarity. *To argue that the private pursuit of wealth results in the best outcome for the entire society is to view the common good as "merely an unintended, accidental consequence." This falls short of the Catholic concept of the common good.*[8] In order to achieve the common good, is it necessary to intend it? The Thomist philosopher Yves R. Simon, a friend of Maritain, made here a distinction too often overlooked.[9] The *material* common good is the concrete achievement. The *formal* common good is what is intended by the person of "good will." Such a person ardently desires to be open to the good, and to pursue the good, and to achieve the good, even *before* knowing what, materially, the good is. Formally, then, citizens of good will intend the common good of their society—and love that society for its order and its blessings—but, materially, they cannot foresee (or intend) the concrete shape that such a common good comprises. They love and intend its order, its arrangements, its rules, its traditions, its overarching system. They cannot know in advance the sum of the material conditions ("for better, for worse") that represent its concrete expression at any future time. (In this respect, the common good of society at large is not dissimilar from the common good of marriage.)

Thus, one reason citizens support the *system* is the belief that the highest possible achievements of the common good are likely to be attained through it. They intend the system—itself a sort of "common good"—in order to reach the common good (considered materially) in the most effective way possible. Within that system, one need not try to know concretely (since one can't), or to intend in every single choice, what that achievement will amount to materially. What each citizen can do is to maximize practical intelligence in matters within the range of his own choices. This implies the participation of all.

Another objection may also assist in clarification. In the concrete, human individuals rarely exhibit solely economic motives. A very few individuals may be more or less singleminded about pursuing wealth; most would regard such singlemindedness as fanatical and self-frustrating. What would be its point? Wealth is a means, not an end. Without pausing to smell the flowers, to enjoy great works of art, to pray, to give time to public service and community betterment, a human life would be quite empty. Even in their economic activities, the vast majority even of intense economic activists typically surround themselves with objects of beauty, interrupt their schedules for rest, exercise, recreation, and try to make their work "fun." Thus, although it was under liberal aegis that the modern science of economics arose, it is an error to understand the liberal tradition as concerned solely (or even chiefly) with economics. Religious liberty and liberty of intellect, conscience, and artistic creativity are even more basic.

In order to cooperate, the liberal tradition holds, for example, it is not necessary for atheists and theists to share common views of the purposes of human life. When institutions and rules are defined in appropriate ways, a full pluralism of intentions, aims, and purposes may be defended. Meanwhile, free participation in such institutions and under such rules may not only encourage vital cooperation, dynamic advances, and the liberation of much personal creativity, but also inspire significant love for any commonwealth that has blessedly arrived at such a design.[10]

A notion of the common good suitable for a society of free persons, therefore, abandons the tribal project of commanding a particular and concrete state of affairs. Further, it sets aside the tribal longing for common intentions, aims, and purposes that most of us also share. Naturally, the human race experiences a profound nostalgia for such tribal solidarities. Adolf Hitler traded upon these solidarities, as have all modern collectivists. Such solidarities, however, are incompatible with personal freedom. Personal freedom is such a valuable good that it is more than worth the surrender of tribal solidarities.

The liberal tradition holds that a society that protects personal freedoms will reap immense social benefits for all. Through liberating the creativity, enterprise, and inventiveness of its citizens, the free society acquires an enormous upward thrust in history. Such a society could hardly be static, even if it wished to be. More than that, in the face of rapid change it has capacities for flexible adjustment and innovation. In long repressed human capacities for invention and discovery, free societies activate the primary cause of the wealth of nations. (Japan, a densely populated island with virtually no natural resources, has laid hold upon these causes to a world-astonishing degree.)

Here another new concept must be adduced. No other order in nature is exactly like the human order. Thus, we seek in vain for an analogy from nature that would express what is distinctive about a human order. A hive? A flock? A tree with many branches? The human body itself, with head and hands and other parts (the "mystical body")? Each such metaphor fails. Since no other creature in history evinces the capacities of the human person for insight and choice, a social order worthy of human persons has no parallel. A merely mechanical or procedural order, for example, designed to treat all alike as if parts of a machine, is bound to miss the most crucial component of all, human character. Character is the bundle of acquired moral and intellectual powers through which each person slowly fashions his or her unique capacity for insight and choice. Character is the self-appropriation of one's own liberty. A person of character is a person in charge of his or her own life, moved from within, a self-mastering agent. As one forms one's own character, so one's character is the spring of one's own distinctive way of acting. Even if one lists all the observable descriptions of individuals on file cards, and even if two (or more) individuals by some chance were represented by identical sets of such file cards (however long), still, these descriptions, as Gabriel Marcel once pointed out,[11] would fail to predict the differences between such individuals that would emerge as soon as one began working with them in close colleagueship. A social order worthy of free persons must permit attention to the distinctive character of each person. The habits that define character give the personal liberty of each distinctive scope.

In this sense, each person is an *originating* source of insight and choice, irreplaceable, inexhaustible, beyond even an infinite set of descriptions. Even at the end of a long life together, husband and wife remain elusive and prove inexhaustible one to the other. A person's character, as one comes to know it, does provide grounds for predicting behavior ("in" character or "out" of it). Still, a lively sense of inquiry and liberty of choice ceaselessly allow persons to grow in character, and even to be converted, in finally unpredictable ways. No one responsible for choosing personnel for specific tasks will deny how great differences among persons can be, how unpredictable success is, and how misleading *curricula vitae* and references can be. Human persons are alive with possibility, both for good and for ill.

How, then, can we imagine a system designed according to the capacities of human persons? The most sustained treatments of this problem, approached in this way, have been advanced by F. A. Hayek in *Law, Legislation and Liberty* (3 vols.) and in *The Constitution of Liberty*. Hayek's work, both in its genius and in its errors, has been sorely neglected by Catholic social thinkers. To comment further on it here would overburden this chapter, for significant space would have to be assigned merely to exposition. But I would be delinquent if I did not at least mention that the consonance (and serious disagreements) between Hayek's work and such works of Jacques Maritain as *Man and the State* and *The Person and the Common Good* cry out for systematic attention.

One of the most admirable features of Hayek's work, in this respect, is masked by the disproportionate attention that libertarians of a severely individualistic bent have given it. Hayek is predominantly a social thinker, not a rugged individualist. He gives extended treatment to the social origin and social maintenance of habits, traditions, practical skills, and the forms of tacit wisdom drawn from the common experience of peoples. His profoundest themes do not center on individual will but on social order, law, legislation, and tradition. Whether or not one agrees with his particular conceptions (or his entire life project), one should not be unaware that he is not a philosopher of the lonely individual. It is in this respect, in fact, that Hayek's work begs to be read in the light of the political and social thought of Aristotle and Aquinas. Alas, I know of no such study. Yet there is a less essential reason for citing Hayek at this turn in our argument. He is best known for his Nobel prize in economics, and nowadays discussions of the common good arise most often in the context of economics, wherein Hayek has shed much useful light. For this reason, we will concentrate first upon the *economic system* best suited to achieving the common good of free persons. Later, then, we shall turn to achieving the common good of free persons in political systems and institutions, and in systems and institutions of the moral and cultural order (churches, universities, associations of writers and others, the media, families, civic groups, and the like). Although clarity is gained by beginning with the economic order, it is nevertheless important to recall that the first discoveries of liberalism began in arguments over the censorship of books and other moral and religious liberties. It was in that context, as we shall see, that the metaphor of the "marketplace" was first introduced. The importance of a free marketplace *for ideas* was discovered before its importance for economic creativity.

In the economic order, as elsewhere, the problem of the common good has two aspects: (1) how can free persons come to *know* it?; (2) under which order can it with highest probability (nothing in history being other than contingent and probable) be *achieved?* It is not so easy to imagine a complex of institutions that achieve order, while showing a maximal respect for human persons. Let us take up these two points in turn.

## 3. The Veil of Ignorance

It is not so easy, either, to come to know the common good of free persons. There are three reasons for this. First, even in trying to determine one's own economic good—in the full context of one's own political, moral, and cultural goals—one often feels confusion and uncertainty. Should one buy this house? Take this position? Accept this contract? All such decisions are made in ignorance of the future. Not all the relevant contingencies can be known, and many that can be to some degree predicted are not certain to fall into place. Choice falls in the realm of uncertainty and practical wisdom, not in the realm of logic and certainty. It follows that it is no easier to know the economic good even of one's best friends and nearest neighbors.

Secondly, each of us is necessarily ignorant about the economic good of those in trades, professions, industries, technologies, and circumstances of which we have no experience.

Third, the economic good of the entire nation—on a high level of abstraction from particular persons or groups—may be easy enough to sketch in a "wish list": low inflation, low unemployment, steady growth, credit available at low cost, a stable currency, gains in productivity, a proportionate improvement of the natural environment as compared with environmental damage, the steady advance of the poor out of poverty, care for those unable to care for themselves, and the like (almost ad infinitum). Yet the scholarly discipline designed to investigate the tradeoffs among these many competing goods has won the historical sobriquet of "the dismal science." One can easily imagine the reasons why this is so. The phrase "the common good" sounds simple and neat. But upon inspection this good turns out to consist of many goods and even of many spheres or domains of goods And in any one sphere, these goods are not only not in natural harmony with one another but often in direct conflict. Moreover, it is not easy to rank these goods in a preferential order. One person's set of preferences is not likely to be the set freely chosen by all others.

It is tempting to cut this Gordian knot by abolishing freedom and imposing a single view of order, according to someone's plan for the common good, in accordance with that person's scheme of social justice. Short of that, each person is free to try to persuade his fellow citizens that some scheme of preference, some vision of the common good in ordered rankings, is superior to others. Even so, however, the veil of ignorance is not ripped away. However beautiful any scheme may appear in theory, it may result in practice in declines in so many of the goods anticipated that the entire scheme falls into disrepute. The appeal of Catholic schemes of the common good would be far higher, for example, if the actual practices of Catholic nations had led to more admirable results. The prestige of socialist schemes has suffered from the deficiencies apparent in actual socialist experiments. Injuries done to the common good by capitalist practices afford the most severe objections thereto. And so forth.

However, once one introduces the good of personal liberty among the social goods to be included in the common good, it becomes clear that "the common good" is a concept of a special heuristic kind. Free persons typically have diverse visions of the common good. The scheme of one differs from the scheme of another, neighbor's from neighbor's. Free persons conceive of the good in often mutually incompatible ways. Human ignorance is such that it is virtually impossible to settle such disagreements even on the theoretical plane. And even if they could be settled on the plane of theory, it is not certain that any one settled vision would be treated kindly by historical reality.

Therefore, if we were to accept the ideal of the common good as a general ideal, and if we were even to agree upon a particular vision of the common good, we would still be operating in considerable darkness and uncertainty. Whatever the common good is materially, for our time and place, it is not easy to know.

## 4. Achieving (Not Intending) the Common Good

Those who use the older notion of the common good frequently exhort their fellows to "attend to" it, to "intend" it, and to "aim" at it. This conception no doubt goes back to Aristotle, who thought of all things in nature and history as "in motion," tending to an equilibrium that is their natural fulfillment or place of rest. Indeed, he defined "the good," in the most generic and unspecified sense, as that to which each natural thing aims. He conceived of a human person as an animal in motion toward self-realization, at whose (always incomplete) achievement such a person would be able to "act well" in such uniquely human capacities as inquiry, insight, choice, and decision.[12] In their childhood, Aristotle observed, humans are moved to action by pleasure and pain, feeling, emotion, memory, and passion.[13] The impact of these influences never fades, but gradually the self-realizing person comes to order such influences under the gentle (even "democratic") sway of persuasive insight and self-directed choice.[14] Through self-knowledge, a person slowly comes to self-mastery and fluid, easy, satisfying possession of all his (or her) powers. Since individual humans never achieve human perfection, we need patience with others and with ourselves. In the polis, Aristotle wrote, we must be satisfied with "a tincture" of virtue.[15]

Yet in Aristotle's Athens, as in the Paris, Rome, and Orvieto in which St. Thomas Aquinas reconceived Aristotle's notions to meet an entirely new context, city-states were only small towns and the many functions and institutions of modern societies had not yet been differentiated. In those ancient and medieval contexts, one leader, in effect, could paternalistically "see to" at least some of the basic lines of the common good. Often this meant little more than defending the citizenry from hostile attack, improving productive assets such as the supply of water, passing reasonable laws, and caring for the poor. "Golden ages" of prosperity and peace came properly to be celebrated.

Yet all this was not incompatible with a fairly rigid set of fixed inequalities, in which resignation to their own lot and station was thought for the lowly and underprivileged to be a high civic good. Compared to the surrounding rudeness of primitive life in the countryside, such small city-states radiated civilized beauty. Nonetheless, rivalries among the privileged nobles within them were often brutal, conspiratorial, and murderous, as one learns from Machiavelli and from Shakespeare. In addition, the *vox populi* was relatively mute; state and church controlled virtually all channels of commerce, industry, and economic advancement. It was against such *anciens régimes*, Max Weber points out, that the "free cities" and "city republics" of the early modern era began their revolt.[16]

Slowly, an important idea entered human consciousness. One did not need to think of the "common good" as a vision "aimed at" or "intended" or imposed by a singular ruler or set of rulers. One had to think of it also as something achieved through the *participation* of all citizens. On the way toward this achievement, sustained thought proceeded through three steps. First, the state had been experienced as the agent of excessive taxation, torture, censorship, and repression. Second, it came to be seen that government to be just must be based upon the consent of the governed. Third, it came also to be seen that citizens retain unalienable rights, endowed in them by their Creator, upon which the state could not by any means trespass. Made in the image of God, persons capable of insight and choice are worthy *(dignus)* of a sacred respect. In this way, the idea of the limited state, based upon the inviolability of personal rights, slowly emerged in human thought. Thus, as Maritain puts it, the long centuries of Jewish and Christian teaching about the dignity of the human person, working like yeast in the dumb dough of history, sought completion in institutions worthy of that dignity.[17]

This development posed a radical challenge to older notions of the common good. First, the freedom and dignity of human persons (made in the image of God) became primary criteria for any social order truly ordered to the common good. Second, the advent of personal liberty destroyed the simplicity of the concept of the common good. Now each human being was held responsible for forming his own conception both of his own good and of the common good. Traditionalists feared that such radical pluralism would end in anarchy. This, experience was to show, was not necessarily so. But it would have been so had the concept of the common good depended upon a unity of moral aims, intentions, and purposes. Instead, the concept of the common good was radically transformed. It no longer meant an aim, intention, or purpose. The common good came to represent, first, a liberating and cooperative *social order* or framework of institutions specifically designed to liberate free persons; second, a *concrete social achievement;* and, third, *a benchmark* (on this point, more in the next chapter). Thus, the common good came to include within its very definition respect for the dignity of free persons. Without such respect, no collective good is worthy of human beings. Each of these three parts of the new concept of the common good requires some exposition.

It is one thing to aim at, to intend, or to make one's purpose the common good. It is another thing actually to *achieve* a social order in which free persons have opportunities to pursue their own visions of the good, both personal and communal, both private and public. The liberals of the late eighteenth century set in motion an experiment with new sorts of institutions that, they hoped, would with high probability realize such an achievement. Because of the veil of ignorance mentioned above, they came to the insight that free persons could not be expected to agree in advance about common intentions, aims, or purposes. A society respectful of the freedom and dignity of persons would have to forebear any direct and conscious assault upon the common good. Under conditions of pluralism, that citadel could no longer be taken by frontal assault. On the other hand, it could with high probability be taken by an indirect, less paternalistic route.

## 5. An Order Compatible with Freedom

A social order proper to subservient humans is one thing. A social order proper to free persons is another. The former can be an order ordered by an orderer; formed in the mind of one, this prearranged order can be made to "inform" the actions of all. The latter must be allowed to emerge from the free rationality of many; arising from the intelligent decisions of many, from decisions taken in matters closest to their own hands, such an order can achieve a far higher quotient of practical intelligence than was embodied in any prior order.

How can this be so? We have already seen that it is difficult for any one person to be certain even of his own personal economic good. It is in principle impossible for any one person to comprehend all the concrete economic transactions that render the common good alive and vital in every nook and cranny of the economy. It is even impossible for any one person to comprehend all the concrete goods that must be intended by the phrase "the common good" in a modern economy, even on a high level of abstraction. Economists try their best to do so. Yet even they will be the first to insist that they can tell you, from their science, probable gains and losses from particular courses of action, but that they cannot tell you which of the many goods society might want to pursue it *ought* to pursue or how to rank them.

Yet all these testimonies to unavoidable human ignorance do not entail that a human economic order must be devoid of practical intelligence. On the contrary, under certain institutional arrangements and according to a set of rational rules derived from much experience, societies of humans that use such institutions wisely and obey their rules (amending them as experience teaches) can suffuse their own economic order with levels of practical intelligence never before attained. While we must doubt that any human economic order can be fully infused with translucent intelligence, designed as it must be for daily use by imperfect, highly fallible, and sinful persons, nonetheless, existing societies do differ markedly in the quotient of practical intelligence that infuses their daily economic life. Practical intelligence is infused into economic transactions in every corner of society by persons employing their own practical intelligence to the maximum degree possible. Social systems differ in their openness to the practical intelligence of individuals.

Through which concept of order can such openness be maximized?

The central liberal insight arose from reflection upon a fundamental human weakness: ignorance. Human beings do not literally *know* (for themselves and for all others) the purpose of individual lives nor the purpose of society as a whole. Individual human beings do have faiths and do cherish traditional moral visions of such purposes, and in such ways do *choose* how they will live, individually and in community. In this sense, they may "know" it for themselves, but not so as to impose his or her own personal vision upon others. In this vale of ignorance and tears, we do not yet see the Beatific Vision blindingly. We are seekers. From this pervasive state of ignorance, our liberal forefathers deduced three imperatives: (1) No coercion of conscience of one by the other (out of respect for the responsibility of each); (2) liberty of speech for everyone so that all may inquire, argue, and persuade; and (3) the development of institutions that nourish practical cooperation in practical activities, without requiring prior agreement about final ends or personal motivations.

Most philosophers in the past would have argued (and did argue) that such a threefold scheme would end in anarchy (and thence in tyranny). How can a *polis* survive if every individual person pursues private dreams? How will there be order? Practical cooperation without common purposes would have seemed to them impossible. One presupposition of this impossibility, of course, is the radical incommensurability of human individual with human individual: the orneriness of each will lead to Babel. Another presupposition mentioned above lies deeper. What model of order can one point to in the universe that would support the image of a human society fragmented by unreined personal liberties?

The truth is, there is no accessible model anywhere else in nature. One may begin by rejecting the order in the stars; the order of geometry; the order of the beehive, or the herd, or the colony of ants. One must also reject prior patterns of social order: primitive tribal life, the tyrannies of Egypt and the Orient, and even the small, homogeneous city-states of Greece and Rome. Rejecting all these, how might a liberal (pluralistic, conscience-respecting) society be *ordered?* The intuitive inclination is to assert that human orders require a human *orderer.* Someone must see the whole, plan for the future, direct the masses. Is this not the way all successful societies have proceeded in the past?

Put yourself in the place of the first liberals. What criteria would a "new order" have to meet? (1) It would have to allow for individual choice. (2) It should proceed "out of many, one," *e pluribus unum,* through coordinating a vast multiplicity of individual transactions in a peaceful, lawlike way. (3) It should be open both to new entrants and to innovations and discoveries that overturn existing equilibria and make economic life dynamic. (4) It should proceed "organically" through a vast array of tacit understandings and habits rooted in experience, in a way appropriate to practical intellect.

But before this problem arose in economics, it arose with regard to liberty of conscience. To deal with liberty of conscience, the first liberals were driven to a metaphor rooted in village experience: "a marketplace of ideas." Anyone could enter a marketplace; anyone could "sell" or "buy"; anyone could stroll through only to look and listen. In short, a market was a place in which practically everyone entered, a place without coercion, normally a place peaceful, bustling, and lawlike. As the first liberals did not fully trust human intellect (because of their basic maxim of ignorance), so also did they trust it. That is, intellect is never complete, instantaneous, and full; on the other hand, in most persons it is active, reasonably fair, and questing. The ignorance of human beings is such that no man should be entrusted with power over the unalienable responsibilities of others. But it is also such that most persons, most of the time (not always), are honest enough inquirers to acquit their own responsibilities. The first principle makes a marketplace of ideas necessary. The second principle makes it workable.

There was a difficulty with the model of a marketplace. Uniquely, the Christian era had been suspicious of markets and money (but not wealth). *Cupiditas radix malorum,* the Christian ages taught. It was thought noble to inherit wealth, but rather ignoble to earn and to acquire it. Christian tradition was deeply infected by an otherworldly perfectionism, which led too easily to despising money as "filthy lucre" and "thirty pieces of silver." (The Jewish tradition seems never to have been so infected; although in Karl Marx one does hear—concerning "exchange," "commodities," and "fetishism"—quite ancient echoes.)[18] Unlike the monastery or the library, the marketplace is a vulgar place, into which all sorts of people entered freely. The early liberals quite liked the fact that literacy was growing; that newspapers were being founded; and that ideas were no longer the property of a closed aristocracy of mind. The marketplace was vulgar, of the people. A marketplace of ideas was a metaphor to suit the rise of the poor in history.

## 6. From Freedom of Ideas to Economic Markets

Indeed, although previous ages had spurned markets, commerce, and industry—preferring wealth and titles that had been inherited—the first liberals (following inquiries initially launched by the Jesuits of Salamanca[19]) began to study markets rather closely. The roots of capitalism, the researches of Alan Macfarlane have shown, lie in the rise of Catholic monasteries as economic agents in early medieval Europe.[20] Still, systematic reflection on economic development awaited the late eighteenth century. Drawing on medieval works such as those of Salamanca, the first liberals detected lawlike patterns in the behavior of persons in markets, and so they invented economics. "The marketplace of ideas" had been at first a metaphor for liberty of inquiry. But sustained observation of existing economic markets gave rise to a new idea, called at first "political economy."

Human beings do not operate in markets as ants do in a colony. Markets show evidence of choice, variety, and rapid change. Simultaneously, markets engender coordination, cooperation, and (at the end of the typical day) mutual satisfaction. Sellers to be successful attend to wants, buyers to workmanship and costs. New products and devices need explanation; they excite curiosity and further inquiry. In markets, participants learn to be other-regarding even in pursuit of their own interests, since markets are essentially voluntary exchanges in which the happiest outcome is mutual satisfaction. This is especially true when market relations are long-term, and when trust between buyers and sellers is rooted in the mutal experience of exchanged knowledge and accountability. Advice and information are sought, not solely a material transaction. In markets, then, astute observers gain insight into an uncoerced social order available nowhere else in nature. The market illustrates effectively coordinated human behavior, voluntarily offered.

As a model of social order, the market has virtualities as well as limits. In the area of morals and culture, the market was a useful model in the struggle against censorship and in the battle for liberty of conscience. Since free persons bear responsibility for their own vision of the good, it seems right to guarantee freedoms of personal expression and personal inquiry, as well as of civil argument and public debate. In this sense, a "marketplace of ideas" is a protection against spiritual tyranny. It seems further necessary to guarantee religious liberty, both in conscience and in public worship. One imagines a "public square" in which individuals might seek social sustenance through expressing their own ideas while hearing arguments against them, as well as arguments on behalf of ideas they had not before encountered. Institutions such as the free press and the separation of church and state seem to be implied. On the other hand, it must not be assumed, because the marketplace of ideas is open to all, either that one idea is as good as any other or that the best idea is the one embraced by the greatest number.

In politics, the early liberals were in fact much concerned about the danger of "tyranny by the majority." Because of its openness, the marketplace served as a useful model for many purposes. But it was not necessarily either a good guarantor of minority rights or a sound test of truth or goodness or beauty or science. There was, in a sense, a certain democracy in markets; what most people wanted, they got. But there was also evident a certain aristocracy of tastes, disciplined excellence, learning, faculties of discrimination, and higher training (whether of mind, soul, or hand). Liberals were not often levellers. They appreciated standards. Therefore, one ought not to attribute to them (to Thomas Jefferson, for example, in his concern for the proper education of Virginians[21]) a preoccupation solely with the virtues of the market. They understood its limits. The mere fact of a majority—whether of consumers or of voters—was not in their eyes necessarily a guarantee of goodness or truth, let alone a sufficient protection for the rights of minorities.

Nonetheless, the market did supply them with an insight into a form of economic order that met their specifications. It gave them a metaphor for conceiving of the common good proper to free persons. No longer was it necessary to think of the common good in the traditional way, as a *purpose* that every individual should *intend*. The example of the market illustrated that human beings could invent practical institutions, run according to rules accepted by all, that bring about common benefits. In most villages or towns, people depart from markets either reasonably satisfied that they are better off than when that day dawned or determined to come back another day (or to seek a market elsewhere).

The metaphor of the village market allowed early liberals to see that the common good could be *achieved*, even though no individual agent makes decisions based upon *intending* to achieve it.[22] Behavior in the market shows that human institutions can, in fact, achieve a common good for the community, even though no agents who take part in them have consciously and specifically intended the entire range of the general good. This distance between outcomes and intentions may be quite large. The *formal* common good may be far superior, in the terms invented by Yves R. Simon, to the *material* common good actually achieved.

## 7. Order Unplanned, Maximizing Practical Intelligence

Markets, then, do not offer a full model for the social order. Yet just as markets are a distinctively human institution, found nowhere else in nature, and rooted in human interdependency, they offer several lowly insights into new ways of conceiving of social order and the common good. The liberal project could not have gone forward without the discovery of a form of order that is not ordered from above. The achievement of the common good in a genuinely pluralistic society could not occur without such an order. For many persons, the concept of such an order is counter-intuitive. If such an order did not exist, it would be hard to believe that it could exist, just as even today it is difficult for many to grasp how it works.

Many persons think that a spontaneous, undirected form of order (in which humans use their knowledge for their own purposes) is an illusion, a form of magic.[23] If they see order, they are led to infer a controlling orderer. (One is reminded of the proof for the existence of God, based upon the existence of order in the universe.) They are not entirely wrong about this. The order that one encounters in a village market—in its intricate working of supply, demand, and price—is indeed the product of intelligence. But it is not the product of *one* intelligence. It is the product of many individual acts of intelligence. For reasons of personal and common good, participants in markets typically try to meet the claims made by other participants, adjusting their behavior accordingly. They exemplify a sort of cooperative intelligence, each showing due respect for the needs of others. They adjust their own desires to the social reality. In this way, markets shift and are dynamic. But since the interests of all participants lie in making the necessary transactions, market activities seek the closest approximation of mutual satisfaction. They end in a significant degree of cooperation, given voluntarily. In a powerful sense, the social intelligence of individuals inherently seeks such cooperation.

The most important feature of a market order, then, is the maximization of *practical intelligence*. In order to be as clear about this as possible, I must now repeat some points made earlier. When free persons make transactions in free markets, no one can determine in advance what all these transactions will add up to. Prior to that, even when trying to determine his or her *own* best economic interests (let alone all the other interests he or she wishes to fulfill in life), economic agents are often uncertain and confused. Their own interests are not luminously clear to them. And those of millions of other economic agents are hardly known to them at all. Since it is not so easy to decide which are their own best economic choices, it is clearly impossible for them to decide the best economic interests of others and of the common economic good of the whole nation.

On the other hand, if each economic agent acts with the maximum practical intelligence available to him, the sum of all such actions around the nation is likely to manifest a high quotient of intelligent behavior. Indeed, a stronger proposition is in order. If each economic agent acts with maximal practical intelligence in the matter close at hand, better known to him than to anyone else, the probability of the entire economic order being suffused with maximal practical intelligence is very high. It is higher, indeed, than if only a handful of economic directors, however brilliant, were to attempt to impose an economic order upon all. For in any large society the billions of economic transactions summed up in the phrase "the common good" far exceed the intellectual capabilities of any directorate however brilliant. (To attempt to create economic order by putting order into billions of economic transactions from above, I once said to a Mexican journalist, would be like trying to govern a dinosaur with a very tiny brain. The next day's frontpage headline read:

"North American Theologian: Mexico Governed by Dinosaur Brain.") By contrast, to call upon millions of economic agents to infuse each of their transactions with all the practical intelligence each can muster is to suffuse the entire range of economic transactions with as much intelligence as human agents can supply.

But is this not to hold—some will hasten to object—a "mystical" proposition; to wit, that to seek private gains is automatically to contribute to the sum of the general welfare? Do not the private gains of some penalize others? This last may be so, but it is not necessarily (or even typically) the case. If one assumes that economic activities are a zero-sum game, so that if someone gains, someone else must lose, then in economic transactions there are always losers. But this assumption is nearly always false. True, *caveat emptor* (let the buyer beware) would have no historical force if buyers did not sometimes come to feel like losers. If this were the general rule, however, no one would ever buy. The satisfaction of buyers is a *sine qua non* of enduring and often-repeated transactions.

In markets as in everything else, to gain knowledge makes demands and carries costs. Informed consumers clearly gain higher satisfactions. The better informed purchasers are, the less frequently *caveat emptor* is neglected. That *caveat*, indeed, points to the intelligence necessary in market activities. "Maximize the practical intelligence you employ in economic transactions" is, therefore, highly practical advice. The society whose members realize it best is likely to achieve a common economic good of the highest order of intelligence.

Here a brief digression may be clarifying. In a classic passage, Adam Smith pointed out in 1776 that he had never known persons who said that they intended the common good ever to do very much to advance it. He made plain that he was speaking from observation. Such observation made him doubt the prevailing ideology, in which to seek one's own interest was held to be immoral. To the contrary, he observed—again, as a matter of observation, subject to empirical testing—that when persons diligently pursue their own interests, about which they are relatively quite knowledgeable, the sum of such actions cumulatively recorded on a national scale demonstrably raises the common good of the nation. The famous passage, so often misinterpreted, reads as follows:

> As every individual . . . endeavours as much as he can both to employ his capital in the support of domestick industry, and so to direct that industry that its produce may be of the greatest value; every individual necessarily labours to render the annual revenue of the society as great as he can. He *generally*, indeed, neither intends to promote the publick interest, nor knows how much he is promoting it. By preferring the support of domestick to that of foreign industry, he intends only his own security; and by directing that industry in such a manner as its produce may be of the greatest value, he intends only his own gain, and he is in this, as in many other cases, led by an invisible hand to promote an end which was no part of his intention. Nor is it *always* the worse for the society that it was no part of it. By pursuing his own interest he *frequently* promotes that of the society more effectually than when he really intends to promote it. I have never known much good done by those who affected to trade for the publick good.[24] [Italics added]

This is a cautiously worded passage; in the last three sentences alone one reads qualifiers such as "not always," "frequently," and "much." Its fundamental point is to distinguish real results from mere intentions. But its mainspring is the intelligence by which a man's work is "directed" in one "manner" rather than in another.

In this passage, nonetheless, Smith injured a powerful insight by confounding the idea of "interests" with that of practical intelligence. One should not merely make the claim that when each person seeks his own interests, then, as if by an invisible hand, his achieving those interests adds to the common good of all. This would not be true if he pursued his interests stupidly. The whole point hinges upon his achieving his own aims intelligently and successfully. Thus, the fuller and more accurate analysis is that when each citizen acts with the maximal practical

intelligence that he can bring to bear upon the economic activities
in which he is engaged, he adds to the sum of social intelligence
available in his environment. When all other economic activists
conduct their affairs with equivalent practical intelligence, then
the entire social texture is rendered more luminous by the cumu-
lative effect of all such acts. I would, therefore, emend a portion
of Smith's passage to read as follows [italics mark the emenda-
tions]:

> . . . every individual necessarily labours to render the annual
> revenue of the society as great as he can. He generally,
> indeed, neither intends to promote the publick interest, nor
> knows how much he is promoting it. By preferring the
> support of domestick to that of foreign industry, he intends
> only his own security; and by directing that industry in such
> a manner as its produce may be of the greatest value, he
> intends only *to follow* his own *practical intelligence,* and he is
> in this, as in many other cases, led by an invisible hand to
> promote an end, *the cumulative sum of practical intelligence in
> the nation,* which was no part of his intention. Nor is it always
> the worse for the society that it was no part of it. By pursuing
> his own *practical judgment* he frequently promotes *the cumu-
> lative sum of practical intelligence* of the society more effectu-
> ally than when he really intends to promote it. I have never
> known much good done by those who affected to trade for
> the publick good.

These small changes are reinforced by Smith's next paragraph,
usually omitted in popular citations but included here:

> What is the species of domestick industry which his capital
> can employ, and of which the produce is likely to be of the
> greatest value, every individual, it is evident, can, in his local
> situation, *judge much better* than any statesman or lawgiver
> can do for him. The statesman, who should attempt to *direct*
> private people in what manner they ought to employ their
> capitals, would not only load himself with a most unneces-
> sary attention, but assume an authority which could be safely

trusted, not only to no single person, but to no council or senate whatever, and which would nowhere be so dangerous as in the hands of a man who had folly and presumption enough to fancy himself fit to exercise it.[25] [Italics added]

For Smith, the crucial element is not the "interests" of the individual, but the "better judgment" of the individual. This is akin to Tocqueville's distinction between "self-interest rightly understood" and "self-interest wrongly understood." The latter is destructive of the common good. The former adds to it. The actual achievement of the common good depends upon intelligent performance at every location in society.

In order to attain the common good, the technique set before us by tradition was authority. *Someone* in government was charged with putting order into the economic life of the regime. This task exceeded human intellectual capacities. It also violated the pluralism of individual consciences. Economic *dirigisme* necessarily falls short of the pluralistic intelligence necessary for the achievement of the common good. Repeated historical failures should not be necessary to prove this point, since even in theory one can see that it must be so as Yves R. Simon did.[25a]

## 8. Three Other Virtues Required by Markets

Besides practical intelligence, however, there are other virtues in unplanned orders that should be mentioned, both because they are often overlooked and because they have contributed heavily to the historical success of liberal societies. (1) The market depends upon, and includes within its own constitution, a set of laws, rules, traditions, and their instructions. (2) The market is not neutral as regards virtue and vice, but depends heavily upon several specific virtues, and inculcates several others as few other institutions do. (3) The market is no respecter of persons, and is designed both to work well even for the nonvirtuous (in an older vocabulary, for such sinners as all of us are) and to bend our resistance to virtue in socially beneficial directions, despite ourselves.

1. *Laws, Rules, Traditions, Tacit Instructions.* In times of war and dislocation, markets are shattered. Yet what one notes is not so much the physical destruction as the collapse of order, laws, rules, traditions, and habits. Much that we take for granted is appreciated only when it is taken away. Implicit in markets there are laws and rules so powerful that we often cannot step outside our own historical experience sufficiently to grasp their importance. The right to dominion over property and its transferral is one condition of exchange. Another condition is the right of both parties in exchange to free, uncoerced decisions and to mutual satisfaction. In every culture, and in every market within it, there are special rules and traditions, sometimes tacit, which an apprentice needs time to learn. Such rules govern the range of bargaining discretion; the legitimate range of "mark-up"; the proper limits of disclosure; the acceptable standard of quality; the manner of conduct suitable to the transaction; considerations of time; systems of accounting; rights to return goods; arrangements for credit; and every other aspect of trade. There is so much to learn that neophytes in markets often err. Many of the requisite laws, rules, traditions, and tacit instructions have grown up over centuries, but markets for newly invented goods rapidly evolve their own lore. Since many of those active in markets are strangers to one another, rules and rule-keeping are indispensable.

It is true that many of these constraints are unwritten. It is true that it is possible to cut corners. But it is not true that the way of honor and decency in market behavior is not marked out with rather remarkable clarity. Experts in any trade know which of their members are morally the most reliable, which the least.

It is important to stress the ancient roots and conservative tendencies of markets, because their dynamism, innovativeness, and capacities for "creative destruction" occur chiefly at the margin. If conservative principles of evolutionary adaptation were suddenly to collapse, markets would collapse. Markets depend upon reliability. Reliability is rooted in the moral realm, in law, custom, and tradition.

2. *The market as moral teacher.* By contrast with coerced or directed social orders, the order of markets is spontaneous. But this order does not simply "come to be." It requires as its tacit

presupposition both rule-keeping and a range of social virtues. In this sense, a market order is the work of civilization. It depends upon favorable social traditions. Those who merely seize what they want, or force their own goods upon the unwilling, do not engage in market exchange; they conduct themselves like barbarians. Those who lie, cheat, deal with others rudely, care nothing about their purchasers' satisfaction, preserve their products badly, offer their services incompetently, and so on, tear at the social tissue that makes a market order civilized. Therefore, a market order is not simply neutral regarding virtue or vice. It positively reinforces certain social virtues, for its dependence upon them is very high. Satisfying purchasers year after year is the key to market longevity and purchaser loyalty. (In a free order, purchasers are intelligent enough to go elsewhere, and the locution "fly-by-night operators" expresses the obverse vividly.) So basic are common social virtues—courtesy, good service, quality, helpfulness, "satisfaction guaranteed"—that managers sometimes sound insufferably like preachers and moralists, reciting entire litanies of Sunday School proverbs. That it is boring to hear about such habits means that they have a daily provenance; they are as unexciting as they are of quotidian necessity.

Markets teach not only a certain decency but also a certain bravery. I know one newly married man with not a cent to his name, who in about 1958 mortgaged his house to the hilt and then borrowed $150,000 from friends in order to buy out a smalltown newspaper. He was not a journalist, and was understandably fearful—but he persisted. He has since taken similar risks, more often than not successfully. Not many persons would have the courage to assume such large risks or to stake their entire future on one such enterprise. Most seek quieter places in the market, where they learn respect for small losses and small gains, and for modest flexibility to meet changing tastes and demands.

At one end of the market, a certain heroic boldness is required; at the other end, moderation is taught and realism is the necessary rule. A commercial republic captures plenty of romantics, but is not easy on romanticism. Most of the railroad men who built East-West, in the dream of spanning the continent, lost their shirts; most of those who built locally flourished.[26]

3. *Bending the nonvirtuous.* Markets are designed to be impersonal, accepting persons as they are, in the full human range of virtue and of vice. Nonetheless, markets require that even those persons who are not particularly other-regarding in their personal lives become so in their market behavior. Since market exchanges are voluntary, and since the objects the purchaser might acquire are many, entry into the market obliges sellers to become to an important degree other-regarding. A seller should place himself in the position of a purchaser and prepare himself accordingly. The better you know your buyers, the better you serve them— and the more secure your place within the market. One may object that thus markets turn even altruism to self-interest. The correct analysis, however, is that markets *must* have other-regardingness, whether or not their participants are prepared to practice it for its own sake. The market does not look to motives (let God judge those). But in its intrinsic design free exchange means that each must look to the other's benefit. Mutuality is the rule. Both parties must be satisfied. The ideal outcome for market transactions cannot, therefore, be expressed as "win-lose"; it must be "win-win." At the end of the day, most parties must leave with a sense of satisfaction. Ideally, all should do so.

The panoply of behaviors surrounding market transactions is further driven by the fact that the decisions of others are both free and (to a significant degree) rational. The seller must give arguments. He must "sell" his case. As orators and rhetoricians well know, human rationality is not only abstract and intellectual. Imagination, story, and symbol, on the one hand, and desire, fear, and other emotions, on the other hand, play a necessary role in it. As in democratic politics, so in capitalist economic activities, persuasion is the central art. Civilized society is constituted by persuasion—by civil discourse, by argument, by respect for the rationality of others. Its methods are not coercive. They appeal to the free capacity for choice. In economic, political and moral-cultural activities, the scope for persuasive discourse—even, alas, seductive discourse—is very large, indeed.

When the necessities of life are acquired through a system of mutual regard, free choice, and a reasonably civil mode of discourse, the economic system lays the cultural groundwork for the politics of a free republic. It is a datum of empirical fact that, as Peter Berger sets forth in *The Capitalist Revolution*,[27] every functioning democratic polity on this planet is paired with a capitalist economy. There is in this no *logical* necessity. But there does seem to be some empirically founded necessity of history and culture. Both traditionalist, precapitalist societies (such as those of Latin America today) and socialist societies (such as those of Cuba, Eastern Europe, China, and others) tend to excesses of central authority both in economic *and* in political decisionmaking. It figures.

## 9. Saving Time, Raising up the Poor

In summary, it is an analytic mistake to view markets solely for their effects upon the individual; their role is social. A market is designed to bring economic activists into noncoercive institutional arrangements, through which mutual compacts can be reached. Its purpose is coordinative, to bring together parties whose needs are complementary. It is quite astonishing to walk into "convenience stores" in Japan (or any other free place) and to find there products from France, Italy, Britain, China, South Korea, Brazil, Israel, Jordan and almost every other place on earth.[28] How did all this orderliness and cooperation, normally displayed in cheerful surroundings and often at attractive prices, come about? Make of it what you will, we tend to take contemporary miracles of cooperation for granted.

Indeed, of all forms of human life, economic activities show the most penetrating human interdependence. Almost no one today can live in total self-sufficiency and self-enclosure, like Robinson Crusoe, totally independent of exchange with others. An American midwestern farmer does not build his own combine or drill for and refine his own gasoline, does not weave his clothes or build his own television set, and does not even grow the tea, coffee, spices, oranges, or other foodstuffs upon which his family relies in his own home. For this reason, exchange is the normal institutional channel through which human life may most agreeably proceed. Apart from reliable and convenient institutions of exchange, time would be consumed solely in the activities of bare subsistence; human society could not support human liberties. To gain time during which human liberty may encompass a broad range of voluntary activities, a highly flexible and rapid system of exchanges is indispensable. This is the social function on behalf of liberty that orderly, commercial, and swiftly functioning markets are designed to fulfill. Far from giving their lives to "consumerism," citizens in a free society have a solid interest in reducing the time given to economic exchanges. Each wants to shepherd as much time as possible in order to exercise a full range of liberties.

The market, then, is a social device for achieving the common good. Alone, the market cannot attain the *whole* common good. It is a device chiefly of the economic order, which is, in turn, only a part of political economy. Many constituent parts of the common good can only be supplied outside of markets. More than markets can accomplish cannot be asked of them. On the other hand, matched with institutions of invention and innovation, no economic institution has ever succeeded better in raising up so many of the poor. None has generated a higher standard of living, brought about a more regular and swifter circulation of elites, or inspired more extensive creativity. Its founders intended a market order based upon invention and patents to excel in its achievement of the common good. That was the experiment. In promoting the general welfare, measured empirically against what has been achieved by other systems, the market system based upon creative invention has no peer. In that respect, the common good has been a basic underlying criterion for measuring both its successes and its failures. The new concept of the common good does not require intentions, but it does require achievements. It does not require the perfect, but only the greater, good. Its essence is to establish an order promoting the free cooperation of all, for the benefit of all, among those who are not saints.

Here I must emphasize that even in their own domain markets are far from perfect. There are such things as "market failures," hidden costs displaced upon the public, "market imperfections," special advantages of place and "insiders' knowledge," and many other characteristics that prevent markets from functioning with full moral perfection. If we had to prove that markets are perfect instruments of the common good, we could not. But we do not have to do so. All that is required is to show that markets, however imperfect, are better social instruments for their limited purposes than any other known alternatives, traditionalist or socialist; and that their deficiencies may be made up through supplementary agencies of the polity and culture.

The empirical superiority of markets explains why even socialist states today are turning by necessity to an extension of market mechanisms. And why even traditionalist societies, such as Mario Vargas Llosa and Hernando de Soto are trying to reform in Peru, are being urged to open up their markets to all participants more fairly and with greater liberty.[29]

For a progressive society, however, there is another meaning to the common good: a full set of far-off but attainable benchmarks, by which to measure how much more there always is to do. The perfect is the enemy of good. As we saw in chapter two, Madison observed that this is true of the common good in political life; it is also true of the common good in economic life. Still, a market order cannot fulfill all social needs. Even in their own order market behaviors often fail, cause unintended consequences, or inflict unwanted costs upon others. Thus, the liberations sought by the liberal society never long permit complacence. Thomas Jefferson predicted another revolution every eighteen and one-third years. There are many such in the realm of discovery, innovation, and markets. *Semper reformanda* applies to economic orders as well as to churches.

*Chapter Four*

# BEYOND ECONOMICS, BEYOND POLITICS

## 1. The Common Good as Benchmark

Yet, if we avoid any utopian expectations, I believe that it is still important to talk about the common good or even about a good society. We need *a standard to measure where we are, even if we cannot expect to live up to it any time soon.*

—Robert N. Bellah[1]

The first purpose of this chapter is to specify another characteristic of the new concept of the common good: as a *benchmark* of progress yet to be attained. Its second purpose is to carry the argument decisively beyond the context of economics.

In the economic sphere the rulekeeping institutions of the market attempt to maximize social intelligence. In comparison with other historical systems, their practical fruits—prosperity, progress, and an orderly, cooperative spirit—are evident. So long as history lasts, however, it is unrealistic to expect any society to work well. The most that one can expect is that it work well enough.[2] Once basic problems of subsistence have been solved, and once standards of living have risen, other social problems and pathologies are bound to rise into view. There will always be persons with little or no income, the disabled, the unemployed,

111

and others too old or too young to enter into markets. The concept of the common good obliges citizens to look beyond markets, to confront the social whole, in order to discern where some citizens find themselves excluded, where needs are unmet, where fresh and unforeseen problems are arising. Robert N. Bellah expresses this point well:

> Most policy debates in the United States and abroad, in Europe, Japan, the socialist nations, and even the third world, concern the proper mix of market and state and the mechanisms best calculated to effectively relate them. If the argument goes on in terms of economic and administrative efficiency alone, however, there is something drastically missing. What is missing is what Adam Smith, the moral philosopher, had not given up, namely concern for the common good, for the kind of society in which we live and the kind of virtues it encourages. That often *missing third partner* in the discussion is not the economy nor the state but the public, in a free society the citizens, who bring their *ethical and religious insight* to bear in common discussions about the kind of economic and political decisions we ought to make and the kind of world in which we want to live.[3]

In significant measure, the modern market system itself arises from impulses of the Jewish and Christian inheritance of the West, which instructed our forefathers that the dignity of every human being is beyond price. That insight led to the liberation of economic activities from the repression common to traditionalist states. The creative economic energies of free citizens, so liberated, are now visible to the entire world. Traditionalist societies have stagnated, and the pure socialist alternative has failed. As Bellah puts it, "the experience of state-directed economies under the aegis of Marxian Communism has turned out to be so economically inefficient and politically tyrannical that most of the world agrees they are worse than the societies whose defects they were to remedy."[4]

By the same measure, a market system functioning within a Jewish, Christian, and humanist culture will always be subjected—quite properly—to claims of a transcendent sort. By their vocation, Jews, Christians and humanists are obliged to attend to the full dimensions of human life, both within and outside the economic sphere. The common good *as benchmark* reminds us that no level of the common good *as achievement* has yet met the full measure of legitimate expectation.The human race is a pilgrim race. At no point can we ever say, "We have attained sufficient liberty for all," "We have attained sufficient justice for all," and so on. The ideals to which we are bound always demand that we do still better. Therefore, it is not wrong to appeal to the *common good as benchmark* in order to find the current achievement of the common good still inadequate.

The concept of the common good is thus like a pair of pincers. One of its grips focuses our attention upon the concrete achieving now to be effected, the other upon further tasks yet to be met. The living legacy of Judaism, Christianity, and the humanism they have nourished has implanted a moral dynamism within us, in our own culture and in our souls. Our hearts are restless until the destiny that draws us is fulfilled. That destiny always measures us and levies fresh demands upon us. We come, thus, to a third specification of the new concept of the common good. It is not only a form of concrete achieving and a benchmark; it is also an *ordo*, a set of institutions.

Once we cease thinking of the common good as a substantive account of what the world ought to look like when all our work is done, and try to think of it both as a form of concrete achieving and as a benchmark, our minds are led naturally to try to imagine the institutions through which we can realize this achieving in a concrete, practical, regular, reliable, and routine way. Fresh impulses in human life come usually with passion and emotion. Abiding impulses find shape in institutions. *Politics begins in mysticism*, Charles Péguy used to say, *and mysticism always ends in politics.*

## 2. The Three Liberations of Liberalism

Those who first called themselves liberals had in mind three institutional liberations. They intended, first, to liberate humans from censorship and other oppressions of conscience, intellect, and art; second, to liberate humans from tyranny and torture; and, third, to liberate humans from poverty. For each of these three liberations, they invented appropriate institutions: *in the moral and cultural order,* religious liberty and the separation of church and state, the free press, rights and practices of free speech, and the independence of universities, the media, and other private associations from the state; *in the political order,* limited and constitutional government, institutions of human rights, representative democracy based upon checks and balances, and free political parties; *in the economic order,* the relatively free market, patent laws and copyrights, labor unions, corporations of many sorts, partnerships and unincorporated businesses, ease of credit and business formation, the stock association and the business company.

Each of these sets of institutions was designed to protect the pluralism appropriate to free persons. Each was also designed defensively, not so much to define the common good substantively for all, as to secure for all, against the encroachments of others, the right and the opportunity to pursue the good as each saw fit; and to construct checks and balances against the mighty.

In the political order, many discoveries of the first liberals have been much celebrated, especially those concerning representative democracy, constitutionalism, a limited government, checks and balances, free political parties, an independent judiciary, and other *institutional* devices. Less celebrated, but equally important, are the new "democratic" *habits* and *virtues* that the first liberals added to the "traditional" or "classic" tables of the virtues. The free person in democratic societies requires moral skills beyond those of the citizens of the *ancien régime:* enterprise more than resignation; civic virtue more than familial piety; respect for law and lawmaking rather than mere submission to command; self-improvement and self-realization more than contentment with an assigned station; skills in practical compromise and loyal opposition rather than in unbending moral absolutism; and yet others less often brought into awareness. Our self-consciousness about the necessary preconditions of democratic living, in the souls of humans, is quite underdeveloped. One notes this vividly in travels to countries that lack democratic experience, when one can hardly find words to articulate the sorts of habits that seem to be missing. The inventors of the liberal idea spoke of "political economy," and it is no betrayal of their fundamental vision to hold that the "political" part of political economy has a right and a duty to take action designed to "promote the general welfare" of all, including that significant proportion of every society that cannot be, or is not, economically active. In simpler, less mobile societies, large families were typically well placed to care for their own dependents. Nowadays states have taken on "the welfare function." The question of principle—that this intervention is proper—has been well established. The question of practice—how to do so with best effect[5]—is far from settled, but experiments proceed apace.

Yet it is in the economic order that the most profound originality of the first liberals lay, a fact that may explain why the work of many of them has remained much better known within the province of economics than within the province of the humanities, philosophy, and theology. To a remarkable degree, liberal economic insights are seldom the patrimony of well-educated persons today and, among many highly educated persons of high intelligence, economic IQ is often only double-digit.

How can this be? A great many well-educated persons today live and work in social organizations safely removed from the pressures and experiences of economic activities: in government, the universities, research institutes, and other large organizations whose daily experience is rather more that of moral, cultural, or political activities than that of specifically economic activities. F. A. Hayek writes quite truly: "An ever increasing part of the population of the Western world grows up as members of large organizations and, thus, as strangers to those rules of the market which have made the great open society possible. To them the market economy is largely incomprehensible."[6]

In the second place, economic history is both sadly neglected in the educations of most of us and treated in public discourse in a highly ideological way. Before one even reads Adam Smith, one has normally been taught to think him wrong about the "invisible hand," "self-interest," and "pure *laissez-faire*." Robert N. Bellah notes how unfair this view of Smith is. He notes "a benign, optimistic, and profoundly moral quality" in Adam Smith's notion of "the invisible hand," that was transformed "almost into its opposite in the gloomy amoral scientism of Malthus." And he adds:

> Adam Smith's economic views were part of a much larger conception of history which saw society as evolving toward a higher level of material prosperity and moral order. His defense of the free market was based on his belief in the virtues of the "system of natural liberty" that it embodied. Yet much as Smith admired the effectiveness of the self-regarding virtues in contributing to a productive economy, he never imagined that they were superior to the other-regarding virtues. It was, in fact, the effect of the invisible hand (we can almost write hand with a capital "h") to work for the general good. And where the market did not work for the general good Smith had no qualms about intervention by the state. He supported public assistance for the poor, public education, and even believed that should the division of labor reduce work to so narrow a compass as to limit the physical and mental development of the workers, here too the state must intervene.[7]

In the third place, those parts of the world deeply influenced by the socialist and/or Marxist critiques of the market economy learn first the case for the prosecution and only later, if at all, examine market theory in its own terms.

The first liberals had learned through harsh experience the bitter truth of Jewish and Christian teachings concerning the sinfulness, folly, and unreliability of humankind. They feared utopianism and fanaticism from any quarter. In a sense, they trusted reason, but not the reason of any particular man or party. They wished to assure a hearing for all, and to block a *diktat* from any.

The great liberals, and not least the authors of the *Federalist*, were in two important senses not ideologues. First, they trusted experience, observation, and experiment. Second, they were by temperament and choice conservatives concerning habits and institutions, although even in these respects decidedly not traditionalists. That is, they had great respect for the tacit knowing that accompanies experience, habit, tradition, and practical judgment. They were skeptical of "utopic theorists" and "men of ideas." They did not believe that their grandparents were less wise than they, but they did not fear to carry forward the work that their grandfathers had bequeathed to them. To their right, they opposed traditionalists, Tories, and the *ancien régime*. To their left, they opposed the Diggers, the Luddites and the socialists. While they were acutely aware that theirs was a new party, representing a profound revolution in the affairs of humankind, they gladly acknowledged their roots in ancient ways of thought from Aristotle and Cicero through Aquinas ("the first Whig"). Most were for a time identified with the Whig tradition; Thomas Jefferson, James Madison, Edmund Burke, Alexis de Tocqueville, Abraham Lincoln, Lord Acton, and others belonged to this company.

Because the liberal party is not utopian; because it does not offer a simple picture of paradise on earth; because it is preoccupied with checks and balances to shortsightedness, folly, and vice; because it patiently awaits the outcome of experiments and monitors unintended consequences—for all these reasons, the liberal party forms a view of the world more suited to the middle-aged mind than to the youthful mind. The artistic and the literary intellectuals have sought and found more dramatic materials elsewhere. In ideological combat all this proved for liberals during many decades a disadvantage. Today, however, in the closing years of our century, the harvest of forty years of frantic ideological experimentation is coming in. About this harvest, Daniel Bell has written brilliantly in the new Afterword to his book of twenty-five years ago, *The End of Ideology*.[8] It is a harvest of many bleached bones, dry fields, and the cawing of crows. No wonder the liberal party is enjoying an international rebirth. In its realism, it seems always to be an autumnal party, looking to the spring.

## 3. Projects Still Incomplete

Just the same, there are three themes still incomplete in the liberal intellectual inheritance, one in each of the three liberal orders. *In the political order,* the popular desire for security, as contrasted with the desire for liberty, has proved stronger than anticipated. Throughout the democracies, electorates have been wooed by the promise of governmental subventions, subsidies, and securities. Vigilance, the price of liberty, has not always been exercised. The story of the Grand Inquisitor suggests that, ideally, human beings want liberty but when they have it grow irked by its responsibilities and insecurities. There are belated signs that the public is beginning to awaken to the costs and dangers of Leviathan.

Yet it is natural enough that families, provident for their future, desire under modern conditions the sort of security that rural living once afforded. It is not mean of them to do so. But the provision of universal security does choke liberty, innovation, and advance. As parents who overprotect their children reap unintended consequences, so some forms of compassion reduce citizens to a dependence upon the state not altogether different from serfdom. Both Hilaire Belloc and F. A. Hayek, indeed, have warned liberal societies of this danger.[9] Thus, the liberal party today cannot speak only of liberty. It must distinguish rigorously among the legitimate and the illegitimate desires for security. The liberal state is certain to be to some extent a welfare state. The limits to that extent await defining. The balance between security and liberty needs constant attention.

*In the economic order,* the liberal party must now take up the dilemmas of the underdeveloped countries. Caught between cold-blooded traditionalist economies and hot socialist ideologies, many educated persons in the Third World hardly know of liberal ideas and institutions, except as these are reflected in Marxist and socialist literature. They do not recognize that the liberal order begins *from the bottom up,* that is, from universal property ownership, from open entry into markets, from ease in incorporating small businesses, from the extension of credit to the poor, and from the awakening of economic creativity and activism in the poorest sectors of the able-bodied population. Institutional realities that could be taken for granted in early North America and in Europe are novel to those still living in societies whose traditions and institutions antedate the modern era. Liberal ideas have often spread farther than liberal institutions and liberal habits.

The liberal party must think through the small steps, the tacit knowing, and the accumulated wisdom that, because of their own historical pilgrimage, they simply take for granted. The virtues, habits, attitudes, and aptitudes appropriate to a traditional society are not identical to those needed to make liberal political and economic institutions function as they ought. "Remembering the answers" to questions long ago resolved socially, but perhaps never personally, requires sustained empathetic work. Much blood and forgotten bitter learning went into our own habit-building and institution-building. The liberal hypothesis is that liberal institutions express a system of natural liberty, open to all cultures everywhere. This hypothesis is universal in its range. But, as for that other Kingdom, so in this world also, the gate is narrow and the road is strait. Not down every cultural path can free and creative economic development acquire momentum.

*In the moral and cultural order,* the liberal party in its youth rebelled against a repressive *ancien régime.* Now in its maturity the liberal party faces a far more deadly foe of liberty: relativism, decadence, hedonism, nihilism. In its early phase, the liberal party tended to concentrate upon the illegitimate restraints imposed by authorities. In its maturity, it must now concentrate its fire upon an illegitimate absence of all restraints within the souls of free men and women. The absence of internal restraints is barbarian, not civilized. An internally disordered liberty is not liberty at all, but nihilism.

The Statue of Liberty, presented to the United States by France a century ago, is a symbol of true liberty: a woman, not a warrior; bearing in one hand the torch of enlightenment against darkness, and carrying in her other hand a tablet of the law. This Lady, unmistakably purposive, disciplined and serious in countenance, is a proper symbol of liberty, as the neon-lit pornography shops in midtown Manhattan are not. Were moral decadence to become the symbol of liberal societies, liberty would be lost

within a generation. It is not necessary to be Puritan—there is
ample room for sensuality and pleasure in the liberal view—to
grasp that liberty is primarily an attribute of spirit, of intellect,
of light, of reasoned law.

The order of a free society is primarily an *embodied* idea. It
rests upon a body of insights, not quite communicable merely
through abstract concepts but, rather, deeply embodied in many
experiences, tacit understandings, and hard-earned habits. These
embodied insights must be rediscovered by every generation, as
each works its way through the passions and enthusiasms of
youth. How a social order can be designed simultaneously to
serve the common good and to respect the conscience and intellect
of every free person is not an insight given by unaided nature.
The institutions that make that achievement possible, and the
ideas upon which such institutions rest, must be thought through
again by every generation in a fresh environment. It is by thinking
that such ideas perish or survive. But a special kind of thinking
is required, a thinking attentive to such concrete realities as
institutions and the habits of the heart that allow institutions to
function and keep them honest to their purposes. "The revolution," Charles Péguy used to say, "is moral or not at all."

Human beings live in institutions as fish live in the sea. Only
through certain institutions can free persons exercise their liberties. To understand and to invigorate these institutions is the only
way to realize a common good worthy of free persons. As we have
seen, the essential feature of the common good is "the benefits of
cooperation." Rather than by commanding cooperation, free
societies have learned by experience how to elicit it. Human
beings are by nature cooperative animals (Aristotle said: "political
animals"). One need not coerce them into cooperation. Human
beings need one another. Their fates are interdependent. One
may design institutions so as to make it in the personal interest of
each (as it demonstrably is) to seek cooperation and to be other-
regarding, whatever the state of their own motivations. That is to
say, one may count upon the natural inclination of humans toward
cooperation, but one may also do considerably more than that.
One may add to the motives of their natural instinct other rewards

that will incline them toward cooperation, even if they are among those human beings moved best by considerations of selfishness.

This last point is important. The liberal party in history has been, if nothing else, chastened by human experience and determinedly realistic. To design a political economy for angels or for saints is futile work. To design a political economy for human beings as they are is to design the only form of political economy that has a chance to succeed, and any political economy that will work must be designed for sinners. To check the worst instincts in humans and to encourage the best (by incentives and rewards) is not the least of the arts of designing institutions that will in practice promote the common good. The task of achieving the common good is in large part a political task, since the designing of an appropriate institutional framework is a *sine qua non*. But the execution of that design, however noble in itself, carries a people far beyond politics.

## 4. Not by Politics Alone

An important book of the last few years, *Habits of the Heart*, by a team of scholars led by Robert N. Bellah,[10] reinforces this theme. It places emphasis, long overdue among social scientists, upon the "republican virtues" essential to the American experiment. And it employs the broader view of the common good (to be achieved largely through voluntary associations) that we are here describing as "the common good as benchmark." Still, there are several flaws in that much acclaimed study that would benefit by significant rethinking. Since the present inquiry by a different route largely supports the argument of *Habits of the Heart* (both inquiries draw much from Tocqueville), it may serve clarity to draw out these differences.

Like the present inquiry, *Habits of the Heart* takes up the two most central themes of the American experiment: the free person and the common good. In *Toward the Future: Catholic Social Thought and the U.S. Economy*, in a passage suggested by Harvard professor James Q. Wilson, a group of U.S. Catholic lay persons put this theme as follows:

Every human society must strike a proper balance between individual liberty and common action. The American experiment has entailed a keen struggle to find that balance. On the one side is the unique commitment of our people to personal liberty, as enshrined in and animating the federal Constitution. On the other is the central presupposition of that historical document: that our vigorous familial and communal life continue healthy and strong, a common unity. Strong families and strong communities teach those personal virtues without which the Constitution cannot be preserved, and provide care for those who are in need of help and guidance. *E pluribus unum:* One out of many.

Today, that sense of balance is sometimes lacking in the language of those who either choose individual liberty over all other concerns, and hence embrace a kind of radical individualism, or seek to enlarge the power and scope of government, and hence embrace a kind of statist meddlesomeness. Catholic social thought has from the first sought to avoid the "double danger" (Pius XI) of individualism and collectivism. It holds firm three basic principles: the sacred dignity of the person, the social nature of human life, and the obligation to assign social decisions to the level of authority best suited to take them.[11]

The evidence set forth by Bellah and his associates, particularly in their reports of personal interviews with a selection of American citizens, shows clearly enough that many American citizens are deeply involved in *practice* in communitarian and public activities, and yet that those same citizens often seem unable to articulate in theory the communitarian and public dimensions of their own actions.

Similarly, Tocqueville long ago observed that Americans in the 1830s habitually articulated even their public-spirited activities in the language of the self, and in particular in the language of self-interest. Americans, he writes, "enjoy explaining almost every act of their lives on the principle of self-interest properly understood."

It gives them pleasure to point out how an enlightened self-love continually leads them to help one another and disposes them freely to give part of their time and wealth for the good of the state. I think that in this they often do themselves less than justice, for sometimes in the United States, as elsewhere, one sees people carried away by the disinterested, spontaneous impulses natural to man. But the Americans are hardly prepared to admit that they do give way to emotions of this sort. They prefer to give the credit to their philosophy ["self-interest rightly understood"] rather than to themselves.[12]

Thus, it is not altogether surprising that, as the authors of *Habits of the Heart* point out, Americans still mask their public-spirited behavior behind the screen of an individualistic language, sometimes using the psychological or therapeutic jargon of recent decades.[13] Today as in the 1830s, American practice seems to be much more public-spirited and communitarian than American speech.

*Habits of the Heart* aims to inspire a new sense of "national" purpose and "public" community, which the authors regularly set off against "local" purpose and "private" community. The way in which the authors use these terms, however, often conveys, probably against their own intention, an atmosphere that many readers have experienced as sectarian, excessively polemical, and mildly coercive. Their study treats altogether too many Americans (including the most popular president of recent decades, Ronald Reagan) as enemies. Their own political, economic, and moral biases are evident to those who are made to feel excluded. Of course, as the French proverb puts it, "Whoever writes, writes against someone." It is virtually impossible, or at least exceedingly difficult, to articulate a new position that is not adversarial to others. Still, in a study purporting to inspire all Americans to one common, national vision, the distinct odor of exclusion is a flaw.

Thus, many conservatives and many neoconservatives, while unavoidably feeling drawn to many of the points raised by *Habits of the Heart* (having raised these points themselves), cannot but note that their own work is either ignored, at times even misrepresented, or set up as inimical. The profoundly conservative works of the distinguished social scientist Robert Nisbet, including *The Quest for Community*, are simply ignored. Also ignored are the seminal works of the distinguished political theorist, Martin Diamond, a close student of the communitarian strains in the American republican experiment, as are the brilliant essays on the two main and rival approaches to "the national community" by Diamond's student, William A. Schambra.[14] Again, the joint work of the conservative sociologist, Peter Berger, and his neoconservative colleague, Richard J. Neuhaus, on "mediating structures"—so extremely relevant to the study's emphasis on private associations—is ignored.[15] My own study, *The Spirit of Democratic Capitalism*, is misrepresented in a footnote and in the surrounding textual context. The works of Irving Kristol, both on the American experience and on the relation between economy, polity, and moral virtue, are missing. In an essay published after *Habits of the Heart*, as we have seen, Professor Bellah does draw upon Gertrude Himmelfarb's work on Adam Smith, and thus arrives at a more benign reading of the neoconservative recovery of the capitalist tradition. But the failure to do justice to the vein of thought suggested by these citations deprives Bellah and his colleagues of an important source of illumination. It is as if a prior decision had been reached simply to rule out from *Habits of the Heart* the body of work upon its central subjects that has been produced by conservative and neoconservative scholars.[16]

This is all the more striking because so many of the themes of *Habits of the Heart*—not least its emphasis upon "biblical republicanism," "the republican virtues," the tacit habits of the heart, and indeed its Tocquevillean horizon—have not been neglected by conservatives and neoconservatives. Perhaps, too, the explicitly socialist message of Professor Bellah's earlier volume, *The Broken Covenant*,[17] inappropriately highlighted those elements in *Habits of the Heart* that seem excessively anticapitalist, anticommercial, and at least lightly collectivist.

In the American political culture, in any case, as William A. Schambra lucidly points out, there are *two* traditions of "national community." In the "progressive" tradition, the controlling image is that the United States is ideally to be understood as one large community, given coherence by a strong national government, by a more or less centralized conception of national purpose, and by a vision of "public" that gives primacy to political and governmental priorities.[18] The American people, in Governor Mario Cuomo's scintillating evocation of this theme to the Democratic Party Convention in 1984, constitute one large national "family." The governing rudder in this "family" is a strong national government, buoyed by a strong national consensus in favor of "public" (i.e., governmental) projects. The lineage for this view owes much to the Progressive Movement of the early twentieth century, to the philosopher John Dewey, and to Franklin Delano Roosevelt.

But, Schambra points out, there is also a rival conception, of an older lineage, rooted in the understanding of the United States as a "community of communities," and emphasizing the communitarian virtues of neighborhoods and villages, a sense of local place and culture, and primary respect for freedoms and vitalities of great diversity and variety. In this view, public-spiritedness is rather rarely expressed in sweeping national projects (except in cases of national emergency, such as war, and even there with due regard for local control, state and local responsibilities and rights, and in general for what Catholics speak of as "the principle of subsidiarity"*).

To be sure, as Robert Nisbet points out in his 1988 Jefferson Lecture, under the pressures of the national mobilization generated by World War I, later by the Depression, and finally by World War II and its aftermath, the first of these models, although having appeared later in American history, has come to dominate the consciousness of American elites. This model won support for a time from the large majorities put together in "the Roosevelt Coalition."[19] Nonetheless, the inner contradictions inherent in this vision of "national community" have in recent

---

*According to this principle, decisions are most wisely made by the local agencies closest to the relevant daily realities, and by next-highest agencies only when beyond the capacities of actors at lower levels.

decades become visible to all. The more ancient tradition—Jeffersonian, Madisonian, perhaps even Tocquevillean—has been gaining in power both in the world of ideas and among popular majorities. In recent times, Ronald Reagan has been the most politically effective articulator of this rival model. In any case, the contestation between these two rival visions of "national community" is still, and will probably remain, the deepest philosophical-religious battleground of American public life. This contest between rival models has, then, both intellectual and political dimensions.

By never articulating this rival view in all its intellectual power—indeed, by excluding from treatment the scholars who have done most to recover it for our generation—and by trivializing its recent political proponents, the authors of *Habits of the Heart* have not gone as deeply as they might into the issues at stake. Their own political, religious, and intellectual sympathies prevent them from offering a sympathetic and fully realistic portrait of the vision of national community that they intend to demolish. Indeed, their own attempts at characterizing the latter often descend into caricature. This is doubly unfortunate, since their own argument, although by a different route, is forced to borrow many themes from their rivals. Their failure to grasp the existing alternatives fully and fairly weakens the synthesis it would seem to have been their intention (in their more generous moments) to envisage. While they clearly intended to marry certain "progressive" purposes to more ancient, more republican, even more religious and more conservative veins of thought, they could not, alas, resist many unnecessary and misleading polemical assaults.

For example, in the two crucial political chapters of *Habits of the Heart* (8 and 10), the authors trivialize the intellectual arguments in favor of the rival vision that they reject, which they at times call "the neocapitalist position." They assert that this vision was articulated by a friend of President Reagan's, Justin Dart, in a *Los Angeles Times* interview as follows: "I have never looked for a business that's going to render a service to mankind. I figure that if it employs a lot of people and makes a lot of money, it is in fact rendering a service to mankind. Greed is involved in everything we do. I find no fault with that."[20] Anyone who has been interviewed by a reporter, especially a hostile one, will be cautious in using such a source as evidence. Yet without citing any further evidence, the authors link Dart to Jerry Falwell and rush onward: "Neocapitalism . . . perceives the dynamics of the free market as the sole effective means of integrating the national society" (italics added). Since my own book, *The Spirit of Democratic Capitalism* is inappropriately cited as an example of what they call neocapitalism, I know that this claim, in my case, is untrue. But it is probably not true, either, in the case of Justin Dart.

Dart was long active far beyond the confines of the free market. He was an extraordinarily civic-minded and public-spirited activist. He was certainly a *political* activist. Although some might wish that Dart *had* spent all his time purely in markets, rather than in politics, in fact Dart has probably devoted more personal energy (not counting his financial contributions) to Republican politics in California and the nation than all the authors of *Habits of the Heart* together have devoted to vehicles of their own political life. It was Dart who first urged Ronald Reagan to run for the governorship of California and to begin (long ago) preparing himself for the presidency of the United States. Dart did not act as if economics were "the sole effective means of integrating" society. Dart's actions do not seem to fit the authors' theory about "neocapitalism."

I am particularly skeptical about the quotation from the *Los Angeles Times* that has Dart saying that "Greed is involved in everything we do." My reason for skepticism is that many journalists are inclined both to reduce all motivations of businessmen to greed and rather carelessly to suggest contempt for businessmen. By contrast, scholars have many reasons to suspect that the true contrast Dart was drawing was between self-interest wrongly understood and self-interest rightly understood. Dart may not be academically sophisticated enough to draw this distinction in the way that Tocqueville did; surely, though, his words imply it. If, as Dart says, a business "employs a lot of people and makes a lot of money," it is in fact "rendering a service to mankind"— perhaps not a sublime service but, nonetheless, a service superior to its opposites: massive unemployment and a loss of income to society. The authors quote Dart as saying: "Greed is involved in everything we do. I find no fault with that." If in these words Dart meant to say "self-interest" instead of "greed," then Dart was taking his stand with Tocqueville, Madison and, indeed, with biblical realism. Self-interest is a universal characteristic of human behavior.

If, on the other hand, Dart truly did say and mean "greed," then he was wrong and deserves to be criticized. Greed is self-destructive, and while it is found, as Max Weber pointed out, in every form of society (including socialist forms), it is by no means the mainspring of democratic capitalist societies.[21] It is, rather, a cancer to be universally opposed.

Moreover, the authors should have had reason to doubt whether the Jefferson of the first or second Inaugurals, or Madison, or Tocqueville (who all his life opposed the socialist cause in France) would give consent to such aggrandizement of state power as Paul Johnson has discerned as the main theme of the twentieth century.[22] The Founders would surely have understood the way Justin Dart expressed himself about self-interest—they had read their Bible, and watched self-interest at work in government officials and in democratic majorities. Tocqueville himself, as we have seen, shrewdly noted how Americans typically "do themselves less than justice," in "explaining almost every act of their lives on the principle of self-interest rightly understood," rather than in terms of those generous and "disinterested, spontaneous impulses natural to man" on which they act.

Similarly, the authors often cast the words "private" and "public" in a one-sided way, favorable only to their own vision, as when they write:

> Reagan has eloquently defined his mission as one of building "a new consensus with all those across the land who share a community of values embedded in these words: family, work, neighborhood, peace and freedom." In Reagan's rhetoric, however, such words, charged with moral resonance, are evocations of private, rather than public virtues.[23]

Perhaps I speak with a certain authority about Reagan's slogan, having coined it in an essay pointing out that most Americans have a communitarian sense and do not think of themselves solely as atomic individuals.[24] As members of extended families with roots overseas, sharing daily a sense of neighborhood and local community, finding friendliness and cooperation on the job, Americans are not, in fact, best addressed as isolated individuals. That is Reagan's point. (Governor Cuomo's use of "family" and "work" in his speech to the Democratic convention in 1984 also appears in this light to be the sincerest form of flattery; it imitates Reagan's earlier usage, on behalf of the rival vision.)

Note, too, that Reagan in fact spoke of "a new consensus . . . across the land" and a "community of values." These are not merely private realities, without public and political effect. A national "community of values" and a "new consensus across the land" may be the source, not the effect, of effective government, just as in the classical American vision "the people" precede "the government." Nor is it really true, as the authors complain, that in the list "family, work, neighborhood, peace, and freedom," their own favorite two concepts "nation" and "government" are missing. It is a presidential candidate who is speaking, enunciating for the whole nation a return to the Founding Fathers in "a new beginning." Reagan, like the framers, thinks that the national government is the servant of the people in their families, in their neighborhoods, and at work. Indeed, Reagan's express motivation in running for the presidency, and his central campaign pledge, was to *reduce* the role of *nation* and *government* to proportions more in keeping with the founding vision of the Republic. To what an extent he has been successful is another matter; but his vision was remarkably like that expressed in Thomas Jefferson's First Inaugural Address:

> . . . entertaining a due sense of our equal right to the use of our own faculties, to the acquisitions of our own industry, to honor and confidence from our fellow-citizens, resulting not from birth, but from our actions and their sense of them; enlightened by a benign religion, professed, indeed, and practiced in various forms, yet all of them inculcating hon-

esty, truth, temperance, gratitude, and the love of man; acknowledging and adoring an overruling Providence, which by all its dispensations proves that it delights in the happiness of man here and his greater happiness hereafter—with all these blessings, what more is necessary to make us a happy and a prosperous people? Still one thing more, fellow citizens—wise and frugal Government, which shall restrain men from injuring one another, shall leave them otherwise free to regulate their own pursuits of industry and improvement, and shall not take from the mouth of labor the bread it has earned. This is the sum of good government, and this is necessary to close the circle of our felicities.[25]

Compare these lines from Jefferson to Reagan's own First Inaugural:

So, as we begin, let us take inventory. We are a nation that has a government—not the other way around. And this makes us special among the nations of the Earth. Our government has no power except that granted it by the people. It is a time to check and reverse the growth of government, which shows signs of having grown beyond the consent of the governed.

. . . it's not my intention to do away with government. It is rather to make it work—work with us, not over us; to stand by our side, not ride on our back. Government can and must provide opportunity, not smother it; foster productivity, not stifle it.

If we look to the answer as to why for so many years we achieved so much, prospered as no other people on Earth, it was because here in this land we unleashed the energy and individual genius of man to a greater extent than has ever been done before.

. . . so, with all the creative energy at our command, let us begin an era of national renewal.[26]

For Reagan, government is the public vocation to which he has dedicated most of his energies for thirty very public years. But the President rightly objects when anyone describes government in terms of *private* virtues such as charity, caring, and compassion: "It's time to reject the notion that advocating government programs is a form of personal charity."[27] The authors of *Habits of the Heart* fail to grasp the obvious "implication of such remarks." Reagan's direct and unmistakable meaning is that the political left is confusing private feelings of virtue with the impersonal and coercive workings of government agencies. Not grasping this plain meaning, the authors accuse Reagan of proposing a quite different idea; *viz.*, that "community is a voluntary association of neighbors who personally know one another . . . an essentially private, rather than public, form of association." In the United Fund, the Red Cross, or even the Olympic Committee, "neighbors" do not "personally know each other." It is quite wrong to limit "public" to "governmental."

In fact, Reagan's text distinguishes more clearly than *Habits of the Heart* between personal virtue and public virtue, and better discerns aspects of the public good that can be better met through civic bodies other than the state, that is, publicly but not governmentally. *Habits of the Heart* has the habit of counting as "public" only what the state does. That in itself can be legitimate. (One can distinguish between "public sector" and "private sector" solutions.) But it is quite illegitimate to ascribe personal virtue to support for state activities while simultaneously denigrating Ronald Reagan's emphasis upon the contributions to the public good made by associations of public-spirited individuals on their own, apart from government. Government service (noble in itself) has no monopoly on the public good or even on civic virtue.

More deeply still, vast territories of what the authors refer to as "private" activities are, in an important sense, thoroughly public. Economic activism is a public activity; markets are public activities; advocacy (a younger Ronald Reagan speaking for GE) is public activity; civic actions (fundraising for the symphony, running children's camps, maintaining splendid universities, volunteering for the Red Cross) are in an important sense public activity, well beyond the intimacy of a merely family-centered life. It is *wrong* to think that only political action on the national level, on behalf of one particular vision of the proper role of government, constitutes public activity.[28]

In short, the common good is far larger than the political good. Moral and cultural institutions, as well as economic institutions (large or small), play immensely powerful roles in achieving it. To describe all activities in these institutions as "private" is to restrict the word too narrowly, and to overlook the originality of the American experiment. The first new law of politics, glimpsed by Tocqueville in American practice, is the forming of voluntary associations to enhance the common good.[29]

Again, *Habits of the Heart* several times claims urgently to be seeking a new equivalent to the Civil Rights Movement, a new consciousness in which "understanding becomes truly national in scope."[30] Desiring some new such national mobilization, the authors doubt whether their fellow citizens will join them. The gist of their reams of interviews is: ". . . though the nation was viewed as good, 'government' and 'politics' often had negative connotations. Americans, it would seem, are genuinely ambivalent about public life, and this ambivalence makes it difficult to address the problems confronting us as a whole."[31] Here again, "public" is taken to mean "government" and "politics."

Why are citizens ambivalent? Perhaps in part because of the historical record of governments set forth so clearly by the authors of the *Federalist*. All through history, corruption, tyranny, and disregard for the common good have characterized most governments. In America, too, politics has often been thought of as the least morally attractive profession. This is not because political leaders are morally inferior to others; politics remains, as Aristotle called it, the noblest profession, and has much attracted distinguished Americans down the centuries. But Aristotle also said that in the *polis* we must be satisfied with "a tincture of virtue." Imperfections and vices weigh down political life, because politics is inevitably about favors, preferments, and awards influenced by power. The authors express too little of the ambiguity that inheres in "government" and "politics."

In addition, *Habits of the Heart* exhibits too mean and narrow a conception, not only of capitalism, but also of commerce. This sets its vision apart from Tocqueville's, who was quite eloquent about the moral and spiritual contribution that commerce makes to democracy.[32] Here their vision also differs from the vision of the framers, whom in a brilliant essay Ralph Lerner properly describes as "the commercial republicans."[33] The public business of any political economy is to support the economic growth, the innovations, and the national betterment that steadily make life less burdensome for citizens, and that afford the public coffers sufficient revenues to promote the general welfare and to provide for the common defense.

Oddly enough, then, for a study devoted to the traditional republican virtues of the American way of life, *Habits of the Heart* neglects the distinctive spiritual temper and moral habits which the framers expected an enlarged role for commercial activities to inculcate. Better, perhaps, than contemporary social scientists, the framers knew by experience the then existing alternatives: the pursuit of power and glory on the part of princes and nobles, the fanaticism of religions wed to state power, and the sloth and passivity of an oppressed peasantry. The founders valued a distinctive moral virtue never earlier celebrated in the classical tables of the virtues: enterprise; i.e., that quality of alertness and innovativeness of mind, attuned to practical reality in virtually every sphere of human activity, that image of the Creator written into human liberty itself. Enterprise! For the framers, this was a noble virtue indeed, signifying both realism and imagination, both the stirring of native will and the acuity of the alert eye. They admired it in the ability of the Red Man to discern the slightest messages of the forests and the plains. They saw it in the frontiersmen and the pioneers who everywhere put up new barns, sawmills, and machine shops. They loved the noise of it, the bustle, and the steady practical gains from it that the eye could measure from month to month, as new lands were cleared, new buildings erected, new fences set in order. The builders of a new land had need of enterprise. And for them, indeed, enterprise was taken to be a uniquely democratic virtue, of universal provenance, as unalienable in humans as their rights to liberty, and rooted in their nature as images of the Creator.

Indeed, Pope John Paul II is the first Catholic pope to honor this virtue, first singled out for so much attention by the early

Americans (who named ships for it, and emblazoned its name upon flags), and to place it into the quiver of Catholic social thought in his encyclical of late 1987, *Sollicitudo Rei Socialis.* (The pope used the Latin words for "one's own enterprises," faithfully rendered in the German translation,[34] but also well set forth in English as "economic initiative." Thus, the word's American meaning was made clearer although the ringingly American term "enterprise" was obscured.) The pope defended the right to individual enterprise, first, as necessary to the common good; and, second, as a fundamental human right, like religious liberty, founded in the subjectivity of the person, that is, in each person's being made in the image of the Creator.

In the last chapter, we reflected on some features of the higher morality that commended a capitalist system to the framers, who had seen at first hand the moral deficiencies of the habits of the heart inculcated by precapitalist systems. But perhaps some observations gleaned from our own day may be useful. One of the reasons that General Secretary Gorbachev offers for insisting upon the necessity of *perestroika* in the USSR, that is, a "restructuring" of the twentieth century's paradigmatic socialist system, is the broadly apparent moral decline in the socialist labor force: passivity, indifference, carelessness, and listlessness. Indeed, presumably from firsthand knowledge of the Polish situation, Pope John Paul II describes the moral quality of such a system quite vividly:

> In the place of creative initiative there appears passivity, dependence and submission to the bureaucratic apparatus which, as the only "ordering" and "decisionmaking" body— if not also the "owner"—of the entire totality of goods and the means of production, puts everyone in a position of almost absolute dependence. . . . This provokes a sense of frustration or desperation and predisposes people to opt out of national life, impelling many to emigrate and also favoring a form of "psychological" emigration.[35]

Yet, even for Gorbachev, there is more to it than that.

When I represented the United States at the Bern meeting in

the Helsinki process, a Polish representative put a question to the Soviet ambassador in my presence as follows: "Isn't our socialist dilemma this: If we don't give our people word processors and open access to data banks, we will fall farther and farther behind? And if we do, how can we maintain the controlled society and the command economy? Isn't that our dilemma?" Uncomfortably, the Soviet ambassador agreed. This was two months before the announcement of *glasnost* and *perestroika*, in explaining which Secretary General Gorbachev was then to elaborate upon the same point. In an age of instant communications, computers, and electronics, the cause of the wealth of nations is more vividly than ever before seen to be the creativity of the human mind. "Openness" is the social condition for the free play of mind. To be sure, the General Secretary wants *glasnost* to be governed by the Party; he does not mean to abandon Lenin, he insists.[36] But Mr. Gorbachev is quite right to perceive, however dimly, that one of the moral virtues indispensable to the dynamism of commercial life in an open, interdependent world is enterprise. The new breakthroughs in the international capitalist economy have made plain to economists in India, China, Hungary, and now in the USSR that the gateway to the creation of new wealth is a distinctive set of moral and intellectual habits.

This is a very large theme, and space is lacking to pursue it in the necessary depth. Still, I would like to call to the attention of the authors of *Habits of the Heart* that there are moral strengths in an economic system based upon innovation, invention, enterprise, creativity, and other attendant commercial activities that they have not yet explored. Further, these moral habits spill over from economic activities into the arts, the sciences, culture, and civic and political life as well. The habits and institutions of democratic living depend upon sound commercial manners and habits. The latter are not, of course, unalloyed with coarser elements. They are, like all virtues, subject to correlative vices. Many references to commerce and to capitalism in *Habits of the Heart* are, unhappily, solely to negative features, almost never to the ways in which the new commercial order of the seventeenth and eighteenth centuries was perceived by those who fought for it to be morally superior to the traditional order that it was replacing. At the very least, perhaps, the authors may be persuaded to take another look at the crucial moral links between the habits inculcated by capitalist commerce and those republican habits that make democracy work. The framers did not neglect these links.[37] They studied their novelty and importance in such writers as Hume, Hutcheson, Montesquieu, and Smith.

Thus, there is much to admire in *Habits of the Heart*, and considerable support for the new concept of the common good I have been trying to delineate. Still, the terms "government" and "politics" are in that book made to bear, I think, more weight than they can long support. Politics and government are no doubt important; without them, our rights could not be secured. But the most distinctive feature of republican government is that it is constitutional, that is, expressly limited. The chaste limits it observes with regard to its own reach, and the moral virtues it nourishes, differentiate it sharply from other designs for achieving the common good. Rather than upon government primarily, it depends upon the virtues that lead citizens to do as much as possible on their own, apart from government, employing their own wit and their own resources, so as to maximize enterprise, initiative, creativity, and variety. Republican government sets citizens free to act for themselves. A system of government and politics that not only allows, but nourishes, such "blessings of liberty" properly evokes among its citizens a very great love. In this they form a powerful community, all the more powerful for being quite different from any collective of the past and from most others in the present.

In brief, *Habits of the Heart* is not, on the one hand, sufficiently critical of its own propensity to link the public good too substantively to "politics" and "government" and, on the other hand, sufficiently critical of the limits, ambiguities, unintended consequences, and coercions inherent in the activities of "politics" and "government." Put another way, *Habits of the Heart* does not have a sufficiently largeminded view of the multifarious ways in which activities beyond "politics" and "government" also have a "public" character and a "public" effect.

To think of economic activism, for example, as lacking in public service, public discipline, public virtue, and public cooperation is a basic error. A hundred years ago Iowa was an underdeveloped country. Yet in a relatively brief time, Iowa has experienced a vast public transformation, through *economically* inspired innovation in agriculture, transport, communications, and other instruments of common life. So it is not only politics that changes the world. It is not only politics that teaches new virtues. It is not only politics that is public. It is not only politics that makes a people cooperative, friendly, open one to another, and active in the world beyond their own hearths.

If free persons are genuinely to serve the public good, a great many among them must be taught the habits of the heart appropriate to the economic dimension of the public good. Many, that is, must embrace the creativity inherent in enterprise, pursue its disciplines, and rejoice in its cooperative patterns. And most must, alas, learn from experience a certain modesty about what may be expected from government. In these ways, they reconfirm an important legacy of the framers of our Constitution.

Twenty years ago, after I had lectured on "Toward a Theology for Radical Politics" at a university in Illinois, a windburned professor came up to me and said: "You talk about revolution. I'm working on a new fertilizer. If I'm right, it's going to put a lot more food in a lot more bellies than your revolution ever will." I thought about him years later when India, long thought to be in danger of imminent famine, became a net exporter of food.

Politics is the noblest profession. We should each serve the public through it. Through politics, however, one can reach only a small part of the common good. In politics, one must learn to be satisfied with a tincture of virtue. To subsume all of life, virtue, and community under politics is not progressive. Not by politics alone is the common good publicly promoted.

## 5. The Benchmarks of Progress

The liberal party is a party of progress, and progress implies a preexisting measure. For Jewish and Christian thought, humans have been created in the image of the Creator. They share two capacities with God: capacities for insight (inquiry) and choice (love). Theologically, as St. Thomas Aquinas put it, their common good consists in their enjoyment together of the Presence of God in eternity. In more worldly terms, their common good consists in giving witness on earth to a brotherhood of insight and choice, freedom and responsibility. This vision sets a very high standard for the common good of any earthly society.

Taken as a benchmark, then, the concept of the common good obliges the citizens of any particular society to lift up their eyes in order to see how well they are doing, by some standard that transcends present achievement. No progressive party can object to such a standard, providing only that it is applied with realism.

For this reason, arguments in favor of the common good are usually accompanied by an appeal to self-sacrifice. For example, speaking in Uruguay in May 1988, Pope John Paul II offered the vision of a new, humanistic "civilization of work." He holds that economic activities inspire in humans a new and deep spirituality. And he stresses the necessity for self-sacrifice inherent in the common good:

> The "civilization based on work" requires a thorough study of problems and should be ready to accept the truth; it asks at the same time that individual or group ambitions be left aside and that the common good be considered before all else. A "civilization based upon work" requires a spirit of sacrifice, of collaboration and of solidarity. Above all its fulfillment requires effort in order that the younger generation be educated in the virtues of work and in the practice of spirituality involved therein.[38]

The implication is that if the common good is to be attained, at least some individuals must sacrifice in its name their own personal good. Thus, speech about the common good is nearly always hortatory.

Except in one case. Those who speak nobly of the common good often reject *markets* as an instrument of the economic common good, on the grounds that markets do not produce equal goods for all, that there are "market failures," and the like. Here they do not appeal to a spirit of sacrifice, on the part of those injured or neglected by market outcomes. Such critics may not even concede that markets are suitable instruments of the common good; they may be anti-market for principled (that is to say, ideological) reasons. One can only reply, the market has its limits and its failures, all right; but compared to what?

No institution effects the common good of all without exceptions, flawlessly, and without inequalities. Planned societies and command economies have never done so. There is no such thing upon this planet as a morally perfect institution. One must speak, rather, of better and worse. One must speak of institutions that "on the whole" or "better than known alternatives" do thus and so. One must look to empirical results, and think of supplemental remedies.

Perhaps a hundred years ago, purely ideological speech was the only possibility; one could only predict the comparative outcomes of market systems versus socialist systems. Today, however, abundant evidence has been accumulated about empirical results. In this respect, I like best the name the Chinese have recently given to the journal of their Communist party, formerly called *Red Star*. The new name, in Chinese characters, is translated: *Seek Truth through Facts.*

There is no perfect system. But we must not let the brilliance of the utopian perfect blind us to the pedestrian good and the ordinary better. If the common good could be reached simply, by some sort of infallible mechanism, there would hardly be need to exhort individuals to sacrifice themselves for it. Self-sacrifice would not be necessary, since the common good and the personal good would be everywhere and always coincident. Failing such perfection, we are left to choose among imperfect instruments, selecting the proven better in preference to the worse, and seeking remedies for inevitable systemic failures.

For this reason, too, the common good can be approached only through approximations, and must ever be regarded in a clear sense as a set of benchmarks never anywhere on earth quite fulfilled, a stimulus to further efforts.

Consider some benchmarks that the economic order must meet. Is it really true that "the benefits of cooperation" are being extended to *all?* What is the condition of the poor and the disabled? What is being done for the elderly and for children? What about foreign laborers, migrants, and illegal immigrants? Is the level of employment what it ought to be? Interest rates, foreign debt, and trade policy? What about Third World debts, the openness of markets to Third World goods, and competition from foreign goods? Then there are the "externalities": do damages to the environment outweigh environmental improvements (such as irrigation, erosion control, forest management, the development of new sources of clean water, and the like)? These represent only a small fraction of the claims of perfection upon today's worldly economies. All such claims represent legitimate benchmarks. Altogether, they can be pressed as utopian claims demanding paradise on earth. One by one, though, each such benchmark has its own validity. Critical intelligence properly ferrets out the shortcomings of the present.

When one adds up the demands their pastoral letter makes upon the economy, for example, one finds that the U.S. Catholic bishops desire low inflation, low unemployment, a healthy physical environment, lower spending on defense, higher spending for the poor, creativity and innovation, progressive taxation, a higher minimum wage, greater equality of incomes, gains in savings and productivity, some form of "planning" for cooperation, some declaration of "economic rights" to income and medical care and old-age security, etc. If wishes were horses, the bishops would ride as cavalry. Yet who can object that this long list of goods is not *desirable?* The bishops recognize explicitly that, in the real order, "choices" and "trade-offs" are the best that can be hoped. Their essential exhortation seems to be: Do better. As every progressive society wishes. All societies of free persons properly dream of further progress. The concept of the common good, employed as a set of benchmarks, is a spur to progress.

What, then, about those larger issues of the "common good" not usually embraced today under the sphere of economic activities: a taste for excellence in all fields, a noble character, scholarship, the arts, research, teaching and education, the quest for the divine, worship, prayer, contemplation, and the rest? Here the accusations against the liberal society do not ordinarily take the form of protesting against the absence of liberty but, rather, of protesting against the corruptions of liberty. To their foes, liberal societies trail off too easily into relativism, libertinism, violence, decadence, and nihilism.

To some extent, one may reply that the liberal society constitutes a free and open expression of what individuals choose to do (alas) with their liberty. But the charge is actually more precise than that. The liberal society, in its youth, became accustomed to imagining itself in perpetual conflict with an ancient and unfree establishment. Liberals imagined themselves to be burning torches of light against the traditions of the darker past. Now in adulthood, it is no longer becoming for liberals to shout on *all* questions "greater liberty" and "no restrictions." For there are forms of thought, feeling, and action that are inimical to freedom.

This is because human freedom is rooted in intellect and insight. Those practices that darken the mind dim the source of liberty. In our "enlightened" age, the allegedly "darkening" powers of a repressive traditionalism have long since atrophied. The struggle for liberty is now being waged *within* every single mind and heart. Through drugs, fanaticism, violence, and the aberrations of passion, human beings can and do destroy the image of God in themselves. In free societies today, millions of persons are betraying their own inner agencies of insight and choice. Liberals, focused upon external enemies, have paid too little attention to the threat of darkness from within every human heart.

In recent decades, one of the great weaknesses of the liberal party is to have neglected the internal life of human beings: the struggle for character, the learning of moral and intellectual habits, the quest for God, and the battle against egoism, the flesh, and the demons. The roots of this weakness probably lie in complacence.[39] Far from sensing their own emptiness, many exhibit an unconscious reliance upon the spiritual capital of past ages, upon sound habits preconsciously passed from one generation to another, and upon a received body of ideas, stories, and images indispensable to the daily practice of liberty. This inheritance has been steadily squandered. The vacuity of California's "valley girls" suggests that liberty can scarcely be built up from outside-in, solely by sufficient food, drink, sunshine, and sport.

James Madison wrote that the rights of Americans are not defended by "parchment barriers" but by the habits and the institutions of our people. Thus, the single most important part of the common good of a free society is the habits of the heart developed by its citizens; and the second is its well-designed institutions. As these habits weaken, the decay of institutions follows swiftly. Institutions ("government," e.g.) are human persons acting according to formal rules derived from the accumulated wisdom and virtues of the past. The liberal idea is embodied in habits and institutions, and can be sustained only through a vigorous moral life. Its emphasis upon habits and institutions marks the philosophy of the liberal society as "realistic" or "conservative," just as its emphasis upon ideas marks it as "idealistic" or "progressive." Thus the Constitution fits the Declaration.

Such a diagnosis is hopeful. The strengthening of the moral life of each of us lies not in our stars but in ourselves. Fidelity, loyalty, bravery, honesty, enterprise, creativity, kindness, compassion, and other commonplace virtues still thrive in American families. Such virtues are not so highly visible, alas, in the media presentations of ourselves that our culture offers to the world—or even to our own families, in reinforcement.

In sum, the new concept of the common good pushes us beyond a simple reliance upon authority that defines for all the substantive good, and turns us instead toward achieving the rules that make an open society possible. It pushes us beyond its ancient meaning as a set of common aims, intentions, and purposes, and turns us instead to practices of cooperation. It reminds us, finally, to think beyond the political and economic struggles of the present, and to contemplate benchmarks farther ahead. It encourages citizens to be alert to goods not presently being attended to and to evils that are already choking the tree of common blessings.

In a free society every citizen depends upon the virtues of every other. The market that allows each to pursue his or her own private dreams is a social institution. Hence, the dreams most consonant with it entail building up thriving and virtuous communities, whose depth and vigor will nourish and inspire yet another generation. When each citizen builds up the universe around him, both moral and material, the sum of such universes measures the common good attained by all together. When institutions are designed to inspire creativity, to multiply acts of practical intelligence, and to check the evils that the human heart is prey to, the resulting common good increases the private goods of individuals far beyond what they could have hoped for under earlier regimes. When the blessings of liberty are shed upon a house united, private rights are well secured, and public good is most likely to be attained. To achieve the common good, there is always more for each of us to do.

Further benchmarks come at us relentlessly. They are rooted in our own intellect, in its unrestricted capacity to inquire, to seek, and to imagine. In this respect the common good has a utopian aspect. This is held in check by the lessons of experience. We must not expect a PERFECT good—to paraphrase Madison—but be content to achieve the GREATER good that is within our reach. Benchmarks are like a ladder's rungs. To reach too far is to raise the risk of a sudden slip and dizzying fall; a step at a time is surest.

*Chapter Five:*

# THE MARRIAGE OF TWO TRADITIONS

## 1. Historical Developments, New Opportunities

So far, we have seen that there are at least three characteristics of the new concept of the common good. First, there is *the common good as institutional framework*, articulated on a very high level of abstraction. It is given significant practical bite by a specific range of philosophies of human nature; viz., those that honor the capacities of human persons for *reflection* and *choice*, as well as the interdependence of human beings, their need of one another, and their shared stake in steady social progress.

Second, there is the *common good as concrete achievement*. This achievement is not necessarily either preplanned or fully intended in anyone's prior consciousness. It is gained through the systematic pursuit of successive states of affairs, each of which constitutes a better level of social satisfaction. This concept of the common good goes beyond simpler notions of "intending" the common good and of relying upon "public authorities" to define it. It may be achieved unplanned.

Third, there is the concept of the *common good as benchmark*, that is, as a form of concrete practical imagination concerning future steps toward the next possible concrete state of affairs, superior in at least some respects to the concrete achievement of

145

the common good now existing. Since human action is always oriented toward the future, the common good as benchmark helps to extend human social intelligence into the darkness, hazards, and ambiguities of the near-term future. In order to concentrate attention upon steps that are achievable, the common good as benchmark is best thought of, in the phrase of Jacques Maritain, as the form of practical intelligence that is "practical-practical."[1] That is, he makes a distinction between a practical aim that is merely desirable or merely utopian and a practical aim that is in fact within the realm of the achievable. He tries to make practical intelligence realistic rather than utopian, while respecting the natural orientation of human action toward the future. He offers, in this respect, the sort of measure that the human mind needs to distinguish progress from decline, reflecting the creative impulse of the human creature, made in the image of the Creator.

We have also taken care to incorporate within the concept of the common good the lessons of historical experience concerning the fallibility of government authorities and of democratic majorities. For one thing, under schemes of limited government (necessitated by human weakness and unreliability), the common good of human beings extends to realms beyond the limited powers of government alone. Good government is an indispensable ingredient of the common good, not least in securing the rights of free persons; but it is not a sufficient instrument for achieving the common good. Moreover, government is inherently fallible and must be constrained by constitutional limits, by checks and balances, by "auxiliary precautions," and by the constant vigilance of citizens. Finally, by every device possible the inveterate self-interest of human beings must be attracted away from "self-interest wrongly understood" (selfishness and egoism) and attracted toward "self-interest rightly understood" (in which it is the interest of every individual to advance the public good, by means both private and public).

We have also learned that the indispensable social agencies for achieving the common good of human beings in their full humanity go beyond political institutions, and indeed beyond economic institutions, to inspire activities concerned with the moral and cultural dimensions of human life. In this sphere especially, but also in the political and economic spheres, the chief social agencies are typically free associations of persons. These associations are of many kinds, limited only by the social intelligence of free persons in imagining them and in bringing them into existence and operation. They range from natural institutions, such as the family, to the entire range of voluntary institutions, such as political parties, advocacy groups, labor unions, schools, associations of writers or poets, neighborhood organizations, and a full spectrum of organizations that mediate between personal and social life. Indeed, such "mediating institutions," formed by the free acts of free men and women, are far more sweeping in their activities than is the state, and more basic to the achievement of the common good. The full panoply of social agencies is far more extensive than the reach of the state. To cite Maritain, the society is far larger than the state.[2]

At this point, it may be useful to add that the Catholic intellectual tradition, which has most continuously kept the concept of the common good near the center of its social ethic, has over the past one hundred years developed along an analogous path. To show how this has happened, in detail, would require a volume much larger than the present one. Moreover, many of the steps involved in this development appear to have been unselfconscious. In particular, little explicit cognizance has been taken of the impact of experiments in liberal institutions upon the developing understanding of the common good, as exemplified in the basic documents of the Catholic tradition.

Nonetheless, if one begins with the conception of the common good advanced by St. Thomas Aquinas in the *loci classici*, one will be struck not only by their rather remarkable prescience, but also by the concrete limitations understandably imposed upon his examples and his institutional applications due, of course, to the level of institutional development then available to his inspection. Thus, for example, Aquinas nearly always turns to "public authorities" as the chief guardian of the common good. In the thirteenth century, an age of massive social dislocation, territorial disputes, and considerable and widespread anarchy in rural territories, where brigandage and petty armies necessitated the fortification of castles and the building of great protective walls around civilized enclaves, the emphasis of Aquinas upon the bare achievement of political order was not unreasonable. Thus it fell to later ages, not least to the authors of the *Federalist*, to describe quite clearly the abuses of the public good to which "public authorities" are also prey (not that Aquinas was wholly silent on the subject), and to devise an institutional alternative, the *novus ordo*.

Furthermore, if one studies the first of the great modern Catholic documents on the common good, the encyclical letter *Rerum Novarum* (1891) of Leo XIII, and follows closely the usages of that term in the encyclical *Quadragesimo Anno* (1931) of Pius XI forty years later, one sees signs of unmistakable development. In effect, the chief function of the term appears to be, in a large sense, adversarial. Both popes are eager to combat theories that, in their eyes, place excessive emphasis upon the individual. They keep trying to call attention to the social dimensions of human nature and to human interdependence. Both popes have partly incorporated certain lessons learned from the experience of liberal institutions. (Leo XIII, e.g., turns to John Locke's theory of the common destination of the goods of nature, and to Locke's discussion of the right to private property.)[3] Simultaneously, however, the popes combat what they take to be a major stream of "liberal" ideology (they tend to use the term "liberal" pejoratively throughout). They understand the liberal philosophy to be atomistic and self-centered. They typically understand by "self-interest," not "self-interest rightly understood," but its opposite, selfishness.

In this largely adversarial approach, Popes Leo XIII and Pius XI use the term "common good" in a baffling variety of meanings and contexts. In virtually every case, its point is to emphasize the social dimension of the human condition. Sometimes they use the term in great and sweeping generality, in a way hard to decipher concretely or institutionally. Sometimes they use it to justify some very concrete proposal such as, for example, the need of fathers of families for a "living wage." Most often, indeed nearly always, they are trying to lift the eyes of humans from their personal concerns to the large changes in social structures that marked the nineteenth and early twentieth centuries, especially in Europe. They paid special attention to the needs of workers in the rapidly growing cities, as well as to the relative impoverishment of rural areas, in an era in which the chief source of wealth was rapidly shifting from land and agriculture to manufacturing and industry in the cities.

In the struggle against totalitarianism that marked the period of the Second World War, Pius XII began to inject into discussions of the common good a fresh emphasis upon the rights of persons. Like Leo XIII and Pius XI before him, he continued to stress the rights of free association. (The church, after all, is itself one such association, and its earthly destiny depends heavily upon the associations which it abundantly sponsors, including labor unions and above all the family.) Meanwhile, the work of Maritain on the human person ("personalism"), democracy, and state and society, as well as the rise of "solidarism" among many other Catholic thinkers in Germany and France, were changing the intellectual climate. The notion of the common good came to be used in such a way as to give prominence to the rights of free persons and free associations.

In brief, by the time of the Second Vatican Council (1961–65), the concept of the common good in Catholic social thought was gradually attaining a firmer shape. Alas, as we have already seen, this firming of the concept came to fruition just as Catholic thinkers were virtually ceasing to employ it. Perhaps its generality defeated them; its practical utility seemed less and less clear to many.

My own hypothesis as to why this was so is as follows. At the beginning of the 1960s, chiefly because of the "opening" of the Catholic church to the world that occurred at Vatican II (when a majority of the prelates in attendance was for the first time non-European), but at least symbolically because of the rise in universal expectations that the "New Frontier" of the young John F. Kennedy exemplified, Catholic thinkers suddenly had a full plate of particular issues to think about: ecumenism, East-West "detente," "the opening to the Left," the civil rights movement in the United States, urban renewal, the war in Vietnam, the "youth revolution," and much else. In this maelstrom of particular concerns, the concept of the common good fell from favor and was seldom publicly discussed.

More deeply still, many Catholic thinkers came to regard their own intellectual tradition, rooted in Thomistic concepts such as natural law and common good, as outmoded. Many began using the same concepts as everybody else. But, most deeply of all, few Catholic thinkers anywhere in the world set before themselves the task of thinking through, on a deep enough intellectual level, the connections between the liberal experiments in politics, economics, and culture and the older Catholic intellectual traditions. The American experiment in particular—including the *Federalist*, the Declaration of Independence and the Constitution, the works of Tocqueville and Lincoln, and the capitalism/socialism debate—was sorely neglected.

Consequently, the intellectual perplexities involved in reconciling the rights of free persons, a rather modern notion as worked out in institutional forms, with the ancient understanding of the common good were late in being confronted. In a sense, Jacques Maritain was addressing this problem in *The Person and the Common Good* as early as 1947, and the work on religious liberty achieved by John Courtney Murray, S.J., before and during Vatican Council II, put in place many of the necessary materials. Still, the great distance presumed to be separating the ways of thinking employed by the liberal tradition, including the framers of the U.S. Constitution, and the traditional Catholic conceptual architecture was never systematically investigated. In particular, the surprising success of liberal economic ideas following World War II, in more recent times almost universally judged to be superior to the Marxian socialist alternative, required a rethinking of the so-called "mixed economy," the contemporary version of "political economy." Recently, then, attention has focused on how to achieve the most favorable mix of relatively free economic markets and political interventions. Here, too, the question of the free person and the common good was especially pertinent. The relation between the institutional workings of the liberal society and the new Catholic conceptions of the person and the common good has, therefore, moved center stage.

By an accident of intellectual history, the need to take up this task arose at a time when liberal thinkers were reexamining the communitarian assumptions of their own tradition and its often unarticulated links to original conceptions of the public or common good. That happy development invited the belief that an investigation into some of the intellectual roots both of the liberal tradition and of the Catholic tradition might be of considerable use to both traditions. The gap that for nearly two centuries has separated these two traditions sorely needs to be narrowed. This marriage, it seems to me, was made in heaven, even if heaven's ways are not normally our ways. In any case, some further exploration of both traditions seems to be a fitting way to close this volume.

## 2. The American Catholic Bishops

During the years 1980–86, the Catholic bishops of the United States labored long to bring forth a document on Catholic social teaching and the U.S. economy. In a marvelously open way, perhaps unprecedented in ecclesiastical history, the bishops submitted their preliminary drafts for public criticism. Moreover, even when they had completed the final version of their document, they specifically noted that the more descriptive and practical sections of it, being based upon prudential reasoning, invited frank and civil disagreement among persons of good will. On these, they expressly welcomed public argument. And even in the more theoretical, earlier sections they did not expect persons not of the Christian faith to agree to all aspects of their moral reasoning or to each of the moral presuppositions.[4] As far as possible, they addressed the public in the language of reason rather than of faith.

In all, the bishops made public four drafts of their letter: the first draft in November 1984; the second in November 1985; the third in June 1986; and the fourth (hardly different from the third) that same November.[5] The greatest change, by far, occurred between the first and second drafts. Some of the organizational changes between the second and the third drafts also represented significant adjustments in the conceptual structure of the whole. But the gap between the first draft and the second was quite enormous. As much as possible was salvaged, but the entire structure shifted, and changes in major details numbered in the scores. Someday, an astute graduate student will no doubt offer a public description of how much changed, under what pressures, why, and to what effect. To record all that here would be out of place.

Concerning the *common good*, though, and perhaps especially the *free person*, the changes between the first and second drafts were especially significant. No one could have said that the concept of the common good lay at the structural center of the first draft. Of the second draft, that claim might have sounded plausible. The common good is not at the center of argument—concern for the poor is—but it is certainly given much prominence.

Not only that. By the final draft, the meaning of the term "common good" had been significantly altered. In earlier versions, the term had a vague meaning, although tied down by the formula of the Second Vatican Council: The common good is "the sum of those conditions of social life which allow social groups and their individual members relatively thorough and ready access to their own fulfillment." This brief text from Vatican II almost repeats the definition of the common good offered in *Mater et Magistra* (1961), the encyclical of the much loved Pope John XXIII: The common good "embraces the sum total of those conditions of social living, whereby men are enabled more fully and more readily to achieve their own perfection."[6]

In offering this definition, John XXIII again and again in *Mater et Magistra* went out of his way to emphasize the necessary initiatives, responsibilities, and liberties of persons and free associations, which he saw as the main agents of the common good.[7] The chief common good of the City of Man is the full development of all human individuals in the exercise of reflection and choice—that is, their appropriation of their own nature as free persons. To live as a free person is to exercise those virtues that protect and empower one's own regular practice of reflection and choice; otherwise put, one's ability to live as a free person ought to live. In this sense, the chief worldly common good is the universal practice of the virtues inherent in the practice of liberty and responsibility. In this, all participate. [See Appendix.]

The approach taken by John XXIII, which echoes the emphasis on the virtues of the free person in Aristotle, Cicero, and Aquinas, was already foreshadowed in the definition of the common good offered by Joseph (later Cardinal) Hoeffner, S.J., in his *Fundamentals of Christian Sociology* (1962): "all arrangements and conditions that make it possible *for the individual* and *for small social units* to work together in an orderly fashion towards the fulfillment of their divinely willed purpose—*the development of personality and the fostering of culture*" (italics added).[8]

One common thread in these definitions (*Mater et Magistra*, Vatican II, and Hoeffner) is their emphasis upon *the fulfillment of the human person*. This fulfillment is found, they note, both in the self (in the personal appropriation of the virtues that make humans free) and in free associations. Thus, over the years, the Catholic tradition at first raised the sights of humans to their common social nature, and then directed the attention of human communities to their true goal: the raising up of persons who practice the virtues proper to free persons. This double movement is essential to the Catholic idea. The emergence of the second movement from the first is attributable to the new institutional possibilities opened up for all citizens by free societies. In the liberal society, institutions suited to the daily exercise of the liberties proper to citizens have at last come into operation. Under such institutions, citizens have no one but themselves to blame if they do not live up to their responsibilities.

Furthermore, in liberal societies the people are sovereign. If the common good is to be achieved, citizens themselves must take responsibility for achieving it. They will sometimes do this through governmental structures and public authorities. But under limited constitutional governments, such structures and authorities do not and cannot take full responsibility for the common good. Their powers are expressly limited. Therefore, large and historically unprecedented scope must be left to free citizens, alone and in their associations, to achieve those many aspects of the common good that lie beyond the limited powers of the state.

The letter of the U.S. bishops on the economy respects this

new emphasis on nongovernmental responsibilities for the common good. It exhorts individuals and associations to take up their new responsibilities on its behalf. Still, perhaps in counterbalance to what the bishops perceive as libertarian tendencies in the American public, they seem eager at almost every mention of the common good to go out of their way to justify the use, at least as a last resort, of state power.[9] They are explicitly not statists.[10] (Criticisms of their earlier drafts had led them to great care on this point.) But they clearly believe themselves to be leaning against prevailing individualistic winds. They take pains, even, to rebut Thoreau's dictum, "That government is best which governs least."[11]

There seem to be two reasons why the bishops want most of all to justify state intervention. First, they want not only to serve the common good, but also to establish as their first priority in so doing a primary concern for the most poor and vulnerable. It is quite true that the test of any good society (and any purported common good) is how well it takes care of its most vulnerable members.[12] But is care for the poor the *first* priority of a society seeking the common good? The U.S. bishops say so. Their argument that the poor must be cared for is strong; their argument that this should be the first priority is weak. But the second reason is more important. Although the bishops in their later drafts added many new lines about the personal responsibilities of the poor themselves, and about the capacities of private associations to give the poor assistance, they also plainly believe that massive federal government programs—greater than at present—will be required to do the job, and that such government programs will do the job well.

The bishops do not call for government aid as a first, but as a last resort. They judge that this resort is clearly necessary. And no doubt it is. On this, the Lay Commission (of which the author was co-chairman) is in agreement.[13] Whereas the lay letter leans toward all the undone things that private associations can do, and do more effectively than the state, the bishops' letter plainly tilts toward emphasizing the necessity of state intervention. This argument between the political part (the state) and the economic part (the economy, as well as the moral-cultural sector) of "political economy" is a long and noble one. It is also a necessary one. To err too far in either direction would be a serious error. Still, the bishops lean one way, the Lay Commission another. The empirical test by which to decide between the two is *results*. Which emphasis is more likely actually to help the poor not to be poor, and actually to achieve the personal independence and full participation proper to free citizens? Results should rule, rather than ideological proclivities.

The bishops also lean toward describing the claims made upon the society by the poor as "economic rights" of the poor.These economic rights, the bishops say, are different from civil and political rights, in that the latter are immunities from state oppression or control, whereas the former are "empowerments" which as a last resort are to be granted by the state to the poor. This use of the language of rights is full of pitfalls.[14] Not least, it very much waters down the original sense of "rights" as protections against the power of the state. The same so-called economic "rights" whose aim is to "empower" the poor would also greatly empower the state. The force of the word "rights" is thereby rendered self-contradictory: in civil and political rights to limit the state, in economic rights further to empower it. The poor can be helped, even by the welfare state, so the Lay Commission argues, without involving this secondary, and largely mischievous, use of the precious term "rights."

Finally, the Lay Commission urges upon the bishops a fuller examination of the practice of those states that do champion economic rights. *Survey* magazine, for example, recently dedicated a full issue to the way in which the Soviet Union and Eastern European nations, the most prominent in boasting of their observance of economic rights, fall far short of serving the economic needs of their populations.[15] The distance between declaring that there are economic rights and actually meeting economic needs is quite immense, and is poorly filled by mere rhetoric. The crucial task is to raise up the poor so that they are no longer poor. That, the Lay Commission holds, is far more important than positing a largely rhetorical theory of economic rights. The poor can be brought into full participation in the common good as effectively by making opportunities available as by proclaiming rights. To provide opportunities (and highly personal and human assistance in gaining the skills required to seize these opportunities) is the crucial contribution.

To sum up, then, the most striking feature of recent Catholic definitions of the common good is their emphasis upon the fulfillment of persons and their free associations. This focus tilts heavily in the direction of the liberal society, one of whose premises is the respect owed to the dignity and rights of free persons. Indeed, the U.S. Catholic bishops' letter on the economy makes the dignity of the free person the measure of the economy: the economy is for the person, not the person for the economy, much as "the sabbath was made for man, not man for the sabbath" (Mark 2:27).[16] But the bishops recognize rightly that human beings find their own fulfillment only in community. They mean to emphasize both the liberal and the communitarian dimensions in the new concept of the common good. Is this so different from the analogous emphasis attributed to the liberal tradition by the Austrian economist, Ludwig von Mises?

> Morality consists in the regard for the necessary requirements of social existence that must be demanded of each individual member of society. A man living in isolation has no moral rules to follow. He need have no qualms about doing anything he finds it to his advantage to do, for he does not have to consider whether he is not thereby injuring others. But as a member of society, a man must take into consideration, in everything he does, not only his own immediate advantage, but also the necessity, in every action, of affirming society as such. For the life of the individual in society is possible only by virtue of social cooperation, and every individual would be most seriously harmed if the social organization of life and of production were to break down.[17]

Despite the great distance between the views of von Mises and those of the Catholic bishops, there are also surprising convergences, such as this one. We turn now to convergences from other directions.

## 3. Liberal and Communitarian

One of the architects of the U.S. Catholic Bishops' letter on the economy, David Hollenbach, S.J., has independently articulated "the coherent moral theory" embodied in that letter. Hollenbach suggests that the theory behind the pastoral incorporates both a part of the "liberal" tradition advanced by such contemporary writers as John Rawls, Ronald Dworkin, Amy Gutmann, William Galston, and Bruce Ackerman, and a part of the "communitarian" tradition advanced by such contemporary writers as Michael Sandel, Alasdair MacIntyre, Michael Walzer, and others.[18] Hollenbach summarizes the four "commitments" of each tradition as follows:

*Liberal Commitments*

1. The fundamental norm of social morality is the right of every person to equal concern and respect.

2. The basic political, economical, and social structure of society should be organized in a way that will insure that society is a fair system of cooperation between free and equal persons.

3. Under conditions of pluralism, free and equal persons hold different and sometimes conflicting philosophical, moral, and religious convictions about the full human good; therefore, any effort to implement a comprehensive vision of the good society through law or state power is excluded, since that would violate the rights of some persons to equal concern and respect. This perspective is summarized by affirming that the right is prior to the good.

4. Because persons cannot be said to deserve the circumstances of their birth, such as special talents or economic advantages, the tendency of these circumstances to lead to disproportionate outcomes must be counteracted by appropriate societal intervention, although not to the exclusion of all inequality of economic resources or political power.[19]

These four commitments of the contemporary American writers singled out by Hollenbach are quite at variance with some classical statements of the liberal tradition, as found in John Locke, Adam Smith, Thomas Jefferson, James Madison, Alexis de Tocqueville, John Stuart Mill, Abraham Lincoln, and others. Thus, the claim that such contemporary writers have to the title "liberal" is not beyond dispute. The "liberal" tradition as described in books by Ludwig von Mises, Friedrich A. Hayek, L. T. Hobhouse, and John Gray is rather different. To pursue such differences, substantive as well as terminological, would carry us rather far afield. But the reader should remark once more that the theoretical background of the bishops' letter largely ignores the classic liberating tradition, crucial to the American experiment.

## Communitarian Commitments

1. The human person is essentially a social being. A person's communal roles, commitments, and social bonds are constitutive of selfhood.

2. The determination of how persons ought to live depends on a prior determination of what kinds of social relationship and communal participation are to be valued as good in themselves. Therefore the good is prior to the right. In fact, the very notion of "rights," as it functions in liberalism, denies the constitutive role of community in forming the self.

3. Human beings do not know the good spontaneously, and they cannot learn it either by deeper and deeper introspection or by philosophical analysis of selfhood apart from the ends the self ought to pursue. Therefore, if we are to know how persons should live and how communities should be organized we must be schooled in virtue. That is, we must serve as apprentices in a community with a tradition that has taught it virtue.

4. How society as a whole ought to be organized will depend on a vision of the integral good of the whole community, that is, the common good. But because of the deep pluralism of modern social life, we lack a civic community with the traditions and virtues that are needed to teach us

what the common good is. Therefore, for the time being, we must concentrate on learning these virtues in communities that are smaller than humanity as a whole or than the nation, that is, in local and intentional groups that do share a vision of the human good.[20]

According to Hollenbach, the theory behind the pastoral letter blends both of these traditions. It employs the language of rights and freedoms associated with liberalism, but also the language of the virtues and the common good associated with communitarianism. It does so by using Aristotle and Aquinas (mediated for Hollenbach chiefly through John Courtney Murray, S.J.) in emphasizing that "Human life is life in community," and that "community is constitutive of selfhood."[21] Hollenbach cites several examples from the text of the pastoral showing how both the liberal and the communitarian strains are blended in it. This blending leads, of course, to "a liberalism of a strongly revisionist kind."[22] In parallel fashion, the bishops impose two sets of liberal constraints upon pure communitarianism. One set consists of a positive and a negative theological constraint, and the second concerns the nature of the liberal state.

Positively, the human person is created in the image of God, and thus is sacred in such a way as never to be simply subordinated to society as a whole, as a means to an end. Moreover, the covenant between God and Israel, which lies behind the American tradition of covenant or contract, requires the consent of the people. This implies the exercise of reflection and choice, the rising of humans to moral agency. To protect the common good of a covenanted community, therefore, is to secure the freedom and equality of all before the law.

Negatively, although made in the image of God, men are not gods. The first version of the bishops' letter was criticized for making too little of human finitude, ignorance, and evil; it somehow sounded as if humans, once redeemed, could reach utopia.[23] By the final draft, a strong Niebuhrian note of human sinfulness had been inserted. As an example of the "Christian realism" to which the final draft had moved, Hollenbach cites

Reinhold Niebuhr, but he might also have cited these words of Thomas Jefferson:

> Sometimes it is said that man can not be trusted with the government of himself. Can he, then, be trusted with the government of others? Or have we found angels in the forms of kings to govern him? Let history answer this question.[24]

Among the political constraints on communitarianism, Hollenbach cites the pastoral's claim that government has a limited but indispensable role to play in securing the common good. Here, though, Hollenbach cites a passage from the pastoral that seems to be announcing a limited role for government, while actually expanding its power quite dramatically:

> *Government has a moral function: protecting human rights and securing basic justice for all members of the commonwealth.* Society as a whole and in all its diversity is responsible for building up the common good. But it is government's role to guarantee the minimum conditions that make this rich social activity possible, namely, human rights and justice [para. 122, emphasis in the original].

By "minimum conditions," the pastoral goes on to guarantees for all citizens of income, medical care, shelter, and the like. For legitimation, Hollenbach here cites John Courtney Murray, S.J. Murray's first contribution, he says, was to draw a clear distinction between the society and the state (actually Maritain's work on this subject preceded Murray and complemented it). Next, Murray is said to have distinguished between the "common good" and the "public order." Public order is prior to the common good, in the sense that it represents the minimal cohesion needed if a society in all its diversity is to be able to pursue the common good. But the public order, in turn, rests upon four prerequisites: justice, public peace, public morality, and public prosperity. Justice calls for human rights; public peace is genuine civil coexistence based upon justice; public morality includes the minimum standards of public behavior established by consensus;

and public prosperity secures the material welfare of the people, enabling them to act.

Hollenbach then makes an interesting move, trying to show that Murray's concept of public order bears a "remarkable resemblance" to recent work of John Rawls on political community and political morality, beyond the strictly moral framework of his earlier *A Theory of Justice*.[25] For Rawls, Hollenbach says, the political good is "a fair system of cooperation among free and equal citizens."[26] Curiously, this definition also reminds one of Ludwig von Mises in *Liberalism in the Classical Tradition*: "What alone enables mankind to advance and distinguishes man from the animals is social cooperation."[27]

For Murray, the political community is not the whole of human social life. But while political justice cannot supply the whole common good, it represents a *very great* good. Political community is not like that of a family nor like that of a church, one bound by affection, the other by charity. Its form is civil. Its modality is "reasoned argument" about the nature, tasks, and common good of the community. For Murray, Hollenbach concludes, the liberal society does not suppose that the right is prior to the good, or that political justice can be defined from the standpoint of the autonomous individual. "Rather, the right is part of the good, and the achievement of justice is part of the quest for the common good."[28] Neither Rawls nor Murray sees liberalism and community as totally opposed.[29]

Thus, Hollenbach's work shows that at least some thinkers in the Catholic tradition are now taking the liberal tradition seriously, and stressing at last its communitarian dimension. This is evident, as well, in major essays on economic matters by Cardinals Hoeffner and Ratzinger, and others in Germany.[30] Hollenbach runs risks, however, in relying upon Rawls, Dworkin, and their colleagues as the sole interpreters of the liberal tradition, to the neglect of the classical liberal tradition, whose untapped wisdom has much to offer to Catholic social thought. It may be useful now to suggest at least a few of those resources, in a highly preliminary way.

What follows may be construed as an invitation to Catholics to explore the classical tradition in a fresh and nondefensive way, as happily some younger Catholic scholars are beginning to do.[31]

## 4. The Liberal Community

Just as in its evolution since 1891 Catholic social thought has articulated with ever growing clarity the unalienable rights of free persons, while retaining its strong communitarian sense, the liberal tradition has moved in a complementary direction, to stress community, while retaining its emphasis upon individual rights. The Catholic tradition has had from the beginning a strong sense of community, but has only slowly worked out the implications of its strong sense of personal dignity. By contrast, the liberal tradition burst upon the historical stage by giving unprecedented attention to the individual, and has only slowly worked out the implications of its early sense of social order, law, legislation, and the often tacit values of community, custom, and organic history. In both traditions, the person and the community—free persons and the common good—are like the paired poles that generate electricity.

Thus, Ludwig von Mises often stresses in *Liberalism in the Classical Tradition* that the interests of the human person and the common good inherently coincide. He offers the maxim: "Everything that serves to preserve the social order is moral; everything that is detrimental to it is immoral."[32] The observance of the moral law, he adds, "is in the ultimate interest of every individual, because everyone benefits from the preservation of social cooperation; yet it imposes on everyone a sacrifice, even though a provisional one that is more than counterbalanced by a greater gain."[33] Such passages—and there are many—recall the coincidence of self-interest and the public interest that Tocqueville discussed in "self-interest rightly understood."

So it is also with Friedrich A. Hayek's long explanation of community, custom, and tacit social knowledge in *Law, Legislation, and Liberty*, a set of three volumes that can by no means be regarded as solely concerned with the "autonomous" or "atomic" individual.[34] In volume two, Hayek is especially critical of what he calls *The Mirage of Social Justice.* This critique deals with secular and socialist invocations of "social justice," not with the classic theory that has come down from Thomas Aquinas—by the circuitous route traced by Father Calvez—to the German Catholic Solidarists and Pius XI.[35] Just the same, much light would be shed on Catholic teaching on social justice in response to Hayek's diagnosis of several theoretical pitfalls and popular misconceptions.

But there are many other works in the liberal tradition that cry out for reexamination in the light of current communitarian preoccupations. The early liberals, while understandably preoccupied with what they took to be their most original discovery, the natural rights of individuals, understood themselves to be making a revolution in social order. They thought they were advancing the common good of humankind. Perhaps the Central European liberals were more explicit about this social dimension than the Anglo-Saxons. Thus von Mises:

> Liberalism has always had in view the good of the whole, not that of any special group. It was this that the English utilitarians meant to express—although, it is true, not very aptly—in their famous formula, "the greatest happiness of the greatest number." Historically, liberalism was the first political movement that aimed at promoting the welfare of all, not that of special groups. Liberalism is distinguished from socialism, which likewise professes to strive for the good of all, not by the goal at which it aims, but by the means that it chooses to attain that goal.[36]

Nonetheless, the English liberals, more than is commonly believed, were also explicit about the claims of the common good, the social order, and the public interest.

## A. John Locke's Commonwealth

In a pregnant essay, Nathan Tarcov has shown that the concepts of community and the common good are integral to the philosophy of John Locke. It is incorrect, he says, to read Locke as a philosopher of atomistic individualism and merely private interests.

Locke's political teaching is not one of self-interest but one of rights. Argument from interest rather than rights represents a degradation of Lockean politics and of the political theory of our nation's founding. Lockean politics include a conception of the *common good* and a conception of *civil society* as more than an aggregate of atomistic individuals. His understanding of human nature exhibits a profound appreciation of human sociality, and families and churches play crucial roles in Lockean civil society. Locke teaches not a narrowly calculating selfishness but a set of decent moral virtues.[37]

Locke refers repeatedly to the common good in his *Second Treatise*.[38] For him, the body politic is to be thought of as a whole, in whose name individuals may be obliged by law to sacrifice their own interests. Individuals "make part of that Politic Body, each of those parts and members are taken care of, and directed in its peculiar Functions for the good of the whole by the Laws of the Society."[39] When humans "*make one community* or Government, they are thereby presently *incorporated* and make *one Body Politick* . . . one Body, with a Power to Act as one Body . . . *one community* . . . one Body Politick under one Government . . . *one Society*."[40] In another place Locke writes: "The members of a Commonwealth are united, and combined together into one coherent living Body. This is *the Soul that gives Form, Life and Unity* to the Commonwealth: From hence the several Members have their mutual Influence, Sympathy, and Connexion."[41]

In *Some Thoughts Concerning Education*, Locke writes of "every Man's indispensable Duty, to do all the Service he can to his Country."[42] He loves and uses frequently the term "commonwealth." He places virtue, not interests, at the heart of moral education. " 'Tis Vertue then, direct Vertue, which is the hard and valuable part to be aimed at in Education. . . . All other considerations and Accomplishments should give way and be postpaid to this."[43] Education does not belong to politics, but to other social institutions, such as strong families and churches. These other social institutions are necessary to protect the liberty of society against the state. The individual, atomic and alone, would have no defense against the state. Tarcov argues: "The fundamental separation of powers in the *Two Treatises* is between education, which Locke gives to the family but not to the government, and the power of life and death, which he gives to the government but not to the family."[44] In preceding generations, families took justice into their own hands, avenging injustices free-lance. It was thus no small thing to take the family out of the business of life and death, and to take education and morals out of the hands of the state.

Locke regards individuals as having social habitats, cohesion, and efficacy in families and churches. When he writes "public good," he does not mean only political good but also social good. For him, the public good means order by inherited rules, moral virtues, and customs, as well as laws.

In the *First Treatise*, Locke defines the public good as "the good of every particular Member of that Society, as far as by common Rules, it can be provided for."[45] This definition has two parts, defense of the particular man of flesh and blood, and defense of common rules. Thus Locke expresses concern for "every particular Member" of society, not merely the whole; it would be wrong for a revolutionary to murder individuals wantonly in the name of social justice. But Locke also thinks of the individual as under common rules, in one organized commonwealth, whose laws and institutions deserve esteem and even love.

## B. The Organic Society: L. T. Hobhouse

For the founders of liberalism, liberty is not solely freedom from coercion by the state. Von Mises puts the point vividly: "It is incorrect to represent the attitude of liberalism toward the state by saying that it wishes to restrict the latter's sphere of possible activity or that it abhors, in principle, all activity on the part of the state in relation to economic life. Such an interpretation is altogether out of the question."[46] And in his own stunning reconception of the liberal tradition (1911), L. T. Hobhouse locates John Stuart Mill "close to the heart of Liberalism." For Mill, liberty is no mere formula of law, or of the restriction of law. Mill would find a tyranny of custom, a tyranny of opinion, even a tyranny of circumstance, as real "as any tyranny of government and more pervasive." For Mill, liberty is not the raw "self-assertion of the individual," which is a sort of "illiberalism in personal conduct." Nor does Mill find liberty "opposed to discipline, to organization, to strenuous conviction as to what is true and just." Most strikingly of all, Mill does not identify liberalism "with tolerance of opposed opinions."

> The Liberal does not meet opinions which he conceives to be false with toleration, as though they did not matter. He meets them with justice, and exacts for them a fair hearing as though they mattered just as much as his own. He is always ready to put his own convictions to the proof, not because he doubts them, but because he believes in them. For, both as to that which he holds for true and as to that which he holds for false, he believes that one final test applies. Let error have free play. . . . If this thing be of man, i.e. if it is not rooted in actual verity, it will come to nought. If it be of God, let us take care that we be not found fighting against God.[47]

Hobhouse discerns at the heart of liberalism a powerful theory of character. The point of liberty is personal growth, which entails moral discipline. Moral discipline is "the real crux" of liberalism. The heart of the matter—for the person and for society—is the character of human beings.

> Liberalism is the belief that society can safely be founded on this self-directing power of personality, that it is only on this foundation that a true community can be built, and that so established its foundations are so deep and so wide that there is no limit that we can place to the extent of the building. Liberty then becomes not so much a right of the individual

as a necessity of society. It rests not on the claim of A to be let alone by B, but on the duty of B to treat A as a rational being.[48]

For Hobhouse, "it is not right to let crime alone or to let error alone, but it is imperative to treat the criminal or the mistaken or the ignorant as beings capable of right and truth, and to lead them on instead of merely beating them down." The rule of liberty is nothing but "the application of rational method. It is the opening of the door to the appeal of reason, of imagination, of social feeling; and except through the response to this appeal there is no assured progress of society."[49]

For Hobhouse, everything about a man is social. His language, the state of the sciences, his concept of character and virtue, his social dependence regarding virtually every material object he uses and every thought he thinks—all these came to the individual as part of his social inheritance. Indeed, such matters differ from generation to generation, depending upon the social progress of each time.

From such considerations, Hobhouse reaches an "organic" conception of society. If you take the individual outside his society, you lift him out from most of his own identity—not only from his possessions and daily exchanges with others, but also from his language, sciences, ideas, traditions, beliefs, and values. All of these are socially derived, testimonies to his dependency. "A thing is called organic when it is made up of parts which are quite distinct from one another, but which are destroyed or vitally altered when they are removed from the whole."[50] Cut off a hand and it withers. Take out an appendix and it falls into corruption. "Now the organic view of society is equally simple. It means that, while the life of society is nothing but the life of individuals as they act one upon another, the life of the individual in turn would be something utterly different if he could be separated from society. A great deal of him would not exist at all."[51]

Even the rights claimed by an individual have no reality outside the common good. Individuals often claim that they have "rights" violated by others. In itself, such a claim means nothing, unless it is soundly argued, well founded, and is seen to be so in the judgment of impartial observers. But an impartial observer will also consider each such claim in the light of claims by others. He will see such claims as relational. He will weigh and assess them in the light of expectable results, universally generalizable claims, or some other rational social ground. "That is to say, he must found his judgment on the common good. An individual right, then, cannot conflict with the common good, nor could any right exist apart from the common good."[52]

But this does not imply that the individual is subservient to society. "Society consists wholly of persons. It has no distinct personality separate from and superior to those of its members."[53] The British nation, Hobhouse writes, has a collective life: a common language, a common history, a common understanding of one person for another (such as they have for no other people). Still, the British nation is "not a mysterious entity over and above the forty odd millions of living souls who dwell together under a common law. Its life is their life, its well-being or ill fortune their well-being or ill fortune."[54]

> Thus, the common good to which each man's rights are subordinate is a good in which each man has a share. This share consists in realizing his capacities of feeling, of loving, of mental and physical energy, and in realizing these he plays his part in the social life, or, in Green's phrase, he finds his own good in the common good.[55]

From the reality of the free person, whose vocation is to become all that he can, comes the right to equality of opportunity. Neither state nor society may obstruct this free development of personality, which is, in turn, the ground of social progress. In contributing to social progress, however, persons are by no means equal in achievement. In a good society, the common good itself will demand inequalities of actual "treatment, income, rank, office, consideration," Hobhouse writes, grounding these not in the interest of the favored individual as such, but in the common good. If a society is to progress, it must allow its creative talents in every field to emerge, to find opportunity, and to lead the way into the future. The society that does not do so punishes all its members. If there are millionaires and paupers, "it must be because such contrasts are the result of an economic system which upon the whole works out for the common good, the good of the pauper being included therein as well as the good of the millionaire; that is to say, that when we have well weighed the good and the evil of all parties concerned we can find no alternative which would do better for the good of all."[56]

Hobhouse then puts his vision of fairness quite vividly. "If it is really just that A should be superior to B in wealth or power or position, it is only because when the good of all concerned is considered, among whom B is one, it turns out that there is a net gain in the arrangement as compared with any alternative that we can devise."[57]

## 5. Conclusion

A liberal is one who pays full respect to another free person. A similar insight, I believe, led St. Thomas Aquinas to define civilization as civil discourse: that is, as the respect for individual dignity paid by one citizen to another. A civilized society is constituted by acts of such respect—by rational persuasion, rather than by coercion. Necessarily, all societies fall short of that ideal. But each is judged according to the frequency with which such acts of mutual respect occur within it.

Thus, the common good is to be conceived of as a good of reason. "Liberalism," von Mises writes, "does not say that men always act intelligently, but rather that they ought, in their own rightly understood interest, always act intelligently."[58] The common good of free persons is an order in which critical communication—that is, with respect for the other's reason—occurs regularly. Such an order respects the dignity of each free person and the common order that is required for such communication. As Hobhouse has shown, participation in such an order is the highest good of the free person. It is also the condition for sustained social progress, in which each person shares.

But we have also seen that, besides defining the common good in terms of a good of order reached through civil discourse, it is also necessary to define it *institutionally*. To speak of the common good is to speak of institutions that achieve it routinely. One must speak of it, then, in terms of the sets of institutions that, empirically, have already protected such an order or are likely to do so with even higher frequency. Thus, neither mere ideas on paper nor enthusiastic idealism are enough. One must go on to describe the institutions most likely to achieve the common good in fact.

It seems plain that "a marketplace of ideas" is necessary for such an achievement: a free press, institutions of free speech and association, free research institutes and centers of inquiry, universal education and thriving universities, an unfettered artistic and intellectual community, and the like. Since democratic majorities may be tyrannical, some form of republican government, establishing the rights of minorities and studded with checks and balances against direct democracy, would also seem to be required. Again, an economic system consistent with powers of free speech and free inquiry must also be in place. Free speech, in particular, seems to be unworkable in practice without a system of private property. This fact probably explains why most democratic socialists, unlike Marxists, do not insist upon the public concentration of ownership in the hands of the state apparatus, but allow considerable latitude to private property.[59]

Thus, the definition of the common good cannot be merely utopian, but must also include reference to the specific institutions and arrangements through which the requisite good of order may actually be realized in history. A theological/philosophical definition may be helpful as a source of benchmarks measuring degrees of progress or decline. But it cannot be said to be practical until it designates the institutions through which it would be submitted to tests amid the ambiguities of history.

Further, human beings are creatures of narrative; they are inquiring, creative, and forward-looking. Thus, their common good is dynamic and on the move. But, how can human beings learn from experience—evaluate and reform the institutions with which they have experimented—unless those institutions are in some way open to criticism, correction, and further experimentation? Who knows, in advance, who among the citizenry will be the creative pioneers of the future? In order to meet such tests the institutions of the common good—even from a formal standpoint—must be shown in practice to have two characteristics: (1) They must have a proven capacity for fairly rapid reform and evolution; and (2) they must show evidence of a fairly rapid circulation of elites in every field, such that talented and creative persons among the poor may rise, even within their own lifetimes, to positions of responsibility. Otherwise, societies would seem to be closed.

In this respect, as Hobhouse suggested, neither an equality of outcomes nor an equality of treatment is likely to be consistent with the common good. It is to the advantage of all citizens that persons of unusual creativity and talent in their midst rise often and regularly to positions of power and eminence. Similarly, it is of high social value to all that such persons be able to acquire the wherewithal to realize new experiments in thought, activities, and institutions, such as will lead the entire community forward. Since concentrations of political power tend historically to familism, croneyism, and favoritism, it seems that an open economic system, relatively independent of the state, is a crucial component of the common good. Such an hypothesis is, of course, falsifiable. But there appears to be considerable evidence in its favor.

In brief, the liberal tradition—right or wrong, in its achievements and in its failures—offers as its legacy an unparalleled body of reflection upon institutional structures. It carries forward a rich heritage of institutional experimentation in politics, economics, and the transmission of morals and ideas.

Furthermore, the liberal tradition has been deeply concerned with methods of realizing public order, the commonweal, republican government, and a universal system of natural liberty. It has contributed to the human legacy a considerable body of explicit reflection upon the common good, community, and the social constitution of the human person. To describe liberalism as concerned solely with the atomistic individual, the possessive individual, or merely private interests is historically false. True enough, thinkers within the liberal tradition have not always pursued the full implications of their own express intentions. Many of their institutional experiments, plainly, did not fully encompass all that is required by the common good. No doubt, the same judgment will be rendered upon our own generation. And no one tradition is wholly self-sufficient.

Nonetheless, in the light of continuing reflections on free persons and the common good, the achievements of the liberal tradition—perhaps even more in building workable, reformable, open institutions than in elegant statements of critical theory— are works of genius that now belong to the patrimony of the entire human race. In particular, the concept of the common good as a good of order, characterized by institutions that bring acts of civil discourse to unprecedented social frequency, is an achievement of the first order. Those who can figure out, institutionally, how to increase such frequencies will also deserve the gratitude of the men and women of future generations. The essence of the common good, recorded near the beginning of these reflections, is "to secure in social life the benefits of voluntary cooperation." The new concept includes an arrangement of the institutions of the social system accordingly; the concrete achievement (*materialiter*) of a higher level of social good; and a set of realistic, progressively advanced benchmarks.

I, for one, am grateful that the Catholic tradition has kept alive the tradition of sustained reflection on the common good; and that its theory of the common good since the time of Aquinas has been so multifaceted, deep, penetrating, and open to new institutional possibilities. I am grateful to the classic liberal tradition, and especially to the American framers, for the institutional experiments that have made possible during my lifetime both greater scope for the freedom of the human person, and a broader and deeper achievement of the general welfare, than in any preceding age.

The task lying ahead of the Catholic tradition and the liberal tradition, of course, is an immense one. We are still only at the primitive, beginning stages of an era inspired by the new concept of the common good and the free person. It is my hope that during the next two hundred years, the Catholic tradition and the liberal tradition will work as allies rather than enemies, each correcting the other from its own proper viewpoint. They have different purposes—one focused on the City of God, the other on the City of Man—and operate within two different perspectives. But the free persons that both address, and the common good that both are called upon to serve, dwell under the light of both Cities simultaneously. Both are called upon to promote the common good of free persons. Would that they would do so together!

# A MAP OF THE USAGES OF "COMMON GOOD"

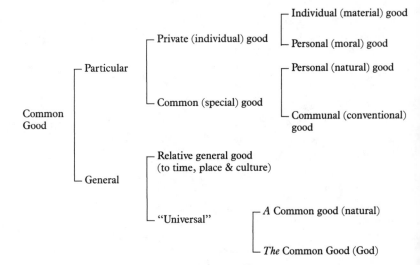

This map is based upon the work of Yves R. Simon and a chart thereof prepared by S. Iniobong Udoidem at the Catholic University of America (see p. 185).

*Appendix:*

# NOTES ON TERMINOLOGY

"The notion of the common good has been one of the most difficult concepts to clarify in the history of man's political development," writes the Nigerian S. Iniobong Udoidem in his new book on the subject.[1] Wishing to spare the reader tedious terminological discussions in the text, and intending to offer a new interpretation of the concept rather than to linger upon its history, I have saved an array of terminological points for this appendix.

The word "common" has three meanings. It may suggest "ordinary, of frequent occurrence"; it may suggest an aspect "shared" with another; and it may suggest a reference to "the whole," rather than to "the particular." When we speak of "the common good," the last two meanings predominate: the good of the whole, in which the parts share. Yet even the first meaning has some relevance. In human affairs, it is quite normal and "ordinary" that actions should be judged in reference to their effect upon the community in which they occur: the family, the village, the organization, the association, the city, the state, the world community. In "ordinary" life, we often make appeals to a common good—that of the whole family, as opposed to one child's preferences, for example.

The word "good" also has many meanings, at least as various as the many schools of philosophy. The school of thought that makes the most use of the concept of the common good is the *philosophia perennis,* the school of Aristotle, Aquinas, and in general the philosophy embodied in the common sense, common law, and common speech of Western peoples tutored by Greek and Latin culture. This includes the philosophical traditions most often (but not always) repaired to by the Catholic church since at least the time of Aquinas. Richard Hooker (1554–1600), e.g., is among the British authors who attempted to recover this concept, after some generations of neglect, for British intellectual history. The Anglo-Saxon words *commonweal* and *commonwealth* have kept the concept alive in ordinary speech.

Furthermore, as society and state became more thoroughly differentiated in the modern period, other cognate concepts have also come into frequent use, either in replacement or in modification of the ancient concept of the common good: such terms, for example, as the "public interest," the "public happiness," the "public good," and the "general welfare." These cognate usages have arisen to account for new possibilities of privacy and of public service. Thus, too, such terms as "civic spirit" and "public spirit," "civic virtue" and "public service" came to designate aspects, at least, of what in simpler and more holistic periods had been included in the concept of the common good.

Nonetheless, in looking over the abundant uses of the phrase "common good" even in any one author, St. Thomas Aquinas, e.g., not to mention in any one large patch of intellectual history, the attentive reader is struck by the multiplicity of purposes the phrase is intended to accomplish. The common good of a family may be judged to be a particular good by contrast with the common good of the city; that of the city with that of the state; that of the state with that of a confederation of states; that of a confederation with that of the entire world community of states; that of all states taken together with that of human beings, taken either as a whole (in their humanity) or even in their individual natures (with respect to their unalienable individual rights). Clearly, the many concrete meanings of "the common good" shift according to this multiplicity of contexts.

This observation has led attentive scholars such as Yves Simon to follow Aquinas in distinguishing between a "formal" meaning of the phrase "common good," which is relatively invariant across all contexts, and a "material" meaning, which designates the particular embodiments of the concept in any particular instantiation in time and place. Using a vivid example, Simon shows how these two can even be in some conflict. God wills the common good of the whole universe, for example, and may in His wisdom will my father to die tomorrow; yet God surely wants me to do all I can today to prevent my father's death. Even if the good son later accepts the will of God (the formal content of the common good of the universe), the material content such a son strains his energies to achieve (that his father not die tomorrow) runs in a contrary direction. The man of high virtue always wills "formally" the common good, but in trying to achieve the "material" content of the common good in the actual texture of his daily actions, he must proceed by a darker, more uncertain, and more limited light.

The *formal* concept of the common good is dynamic, and is always driving toward the full and ultimate development of human beings. Its aim is the highest stage of development in the personality of each, and in the most fully developed community of which they are capable. Therefore, any *material* definition of the term, designating the common good attainable at any one point in time and space, is always "under judgment" by a still higher standard, implicit in the fuller stage of human development yet to be achieved. The *formal* meaning points to the full (and future) conclusion of human development, both communal and personal. The *material* meaning points to the existing level of human development, either already achieved at any one point in time or space, or as the next proximate level of development that in practice may be realized. (That is, in its material sense, the concept of the common good may be either *empirical,* looking to what has already been achieved, or *projective,* looking to proximate, next steps, not as utopian but as realizable in near-term practice.)

Implicit in this way of imagining the common good is a vision of *liberty* and *progress.* It is assumed that humans are *responsible* for their own destiny, neither entirely trapped in unalterable circumstances nor entirely able to become magically whatever they wish to become. In their nature (in their capacities for reflection and self-criticism) lies a principle of *progress*, in whose light their actual deeds are under judgment. They themselves can judge where they are wanting; their descendants will judge them; and God will judge them. In the light of the progress that is open to them, they must make the (wise) choices that will secure it, under pain of moral failure.

Another set of assumptions implicit in this concept involves the unique nature of human *community*. Human community has no parallel in nature; it is not collectivist, in the fashion of a herd, hive, flock of birds, or school of fish. But neither are humans merely individuals, as if atomic particles (monads) entirely closed off from one another. Each is a "political animal" (Aristotle), a citizen of a city, a participant in a language, and a self-critical receiver of a tradition of thought, perception, and values. Each is a member of the human community imagined as a whole, including all ancestors, all descendants, and all contemporaries among the living; in short, the entire "family of humankind." Each is also a member of a particular historical community: a family, language, culture, city, nation, faith (or secular equivalent), etc. Each is born from the belly of one woman. Each is rooted. Yet each is also a self-conscious, self-discovering, self-defining free person.

Respect for the free person is already implicit in the Jewish scriptures (the name of each human is known to the Creator) and in the Christian scriptures (each must turn to or away from "the Light coming into the world," of his or her own free choice). But a modern conception of the human community takes explicit *institutional* account of the capacity of individual persons to make their own choices. This respect for free persons is institutionalized in republics committed to respect for the unalienable rights "endowed" in each single person by "the Creator."

In modern terms, no community can be adjudged to be good if it treats individuals as mere instruments. The purpose of *human* community is to enable each person to reach the full term of his or her personal development, in the full range of basic human skills and virtues. Each human community is to be judged in the light of how it promotes the full development of all its individual members. If it does not allow for the flowering of personal liberty, it resembles, rather, the community of the hive or herd, not the community appropriate to human beings.

Correlatively, the highest development of individual persons is not reached if those individuals remain self-enclosed, impervious to their brothers and sisters, and shut off from habits of cooperation, civic spirit, and personal contributions to the development of the human community as a whole. The answer to the primordial question: "Am I my brother's keeper?" is "yes."[2]

How to relate the fully developed human individual to the fully developed human community, both formally and (especially) materially, is not so easy to state even in theory. How to achieve both sorts of development in actual working practice, in the concrete, and through the most favorable set of functioning institutions, is even more difficult. Yet we can, at least, mark off as deficient any scheme that injuries *either* the full development of individual persons *or* the full development of the human community. Naturally, rival schemes of "full development" abound, both in rival theories and in rival programs of institutionalization.

Experience further shows that the move from theory to actual programs does not always achieve the intended results. Therefore, it is not enough to have a sound theory, if one does not also discover how to make it work in practice. In addition, it is at least conceivable that the most highly developed form of practice may be achieved incrementally, through trial and error, even without a sound overarching theory being worked out first, in all its predictive clarity. In brief, the relation between theory and practice is not a relation of deductive logic.

Yet even these distinctions are not sufficient. If we survey again the multiple occurrences of the phrase the "common good" in the classics of "the common good tradition," we will notice a great many puzzles and perplexities. Although the work of Yves Simon comes closest (see below), no complete grammar of the many usages of the term has yet been written, even from one point of view, let alone across all the many different and rival philosophies in which the term appears. Thus, we will find that "*a* common good" is not identical to "*the* common good." Again, a "particular common good" is at times distinguished from a "general common good." Indeed, we will find, further, that the deceptively simple phrase "common good" can be used to include a baffling range of particular goods, each of them quite complex in itself.

We may even be reminded that the term "good" in Aristotelian thought is convertible with the term "being," and therefore has a bearing on everything that is, across the entire range of what Aristotle calls "the categories." We may speak of the good in a thing's substance (both in the *what-is-it?* and in the *is-it?* of that thing, in its essence and in its existence).[3] But we may also speak of the good in all the "accidents" of the thing: its relations, its quantity, its quality, its place in space, its point in time, etc. In brief, the application of a term such as "common good" reaches across the whole field of all the things that are. To hold that the concept is simple, or bears only a single univocal meaning, is a grievous error.

Particular care is needed when the term "common good" is employed in the field of the practical arts, such as politics, economics, and culture. Indeed, this is the field in which, today, the term is most often invoked. The term "common good" frequently appears in hortative statements, and especially when the speaker is calling upon others to make sacrifices ("for the sake of the common good"). Here, alas, exhortation frequently replaces argument. This is especially likely when the speaker is so certain of his own image of the material content of the common good that he simply assumes that others share it. But the material content of the common good at any one point in history is among the most disputatious of subjects. To invoke the common good in this context is not to settle an argument, but to light the fuse of many arguments.

One can see how disputatious the material content of the common good must necessarily be simply by reviewing how many matters that concept embraces, and how complex each of them may be. In *The Person and the Common Good*, for example, Jacques Maritain offers a bold text, setting forth only some of the realities that are suggested in the material content of the common good. What "constitutes the common good of political society," he writes, is not only:

the collection of public commodities and services—the roads, ports, schools, etc., which the organization of common life presupposes; a sound fiscal condition of the state and its military power; the body of just laws, good customs and wise institutions, which provide the nation with its structure; the heritage of its great historical remembrances, its symbols and its glories, its living traditions and cultural treasures. The common good includes all of these and something much more besides—something more profound, more concrete and more human. For it includes also, and above all, the whole sum itself of these; a sum which is quite different from a simple collection of juxtaposed units. . . . It includes the sum or sociological integration of all the civic conscience, political virtues and sense of right and liberty, of all the activity, material prosperity and spiritual riches, of unconsciously operative hereditary wisdom, of moral rectitude, justice, friendship, happiness, virtue and heroism in the individual lives of its members. For these things all are, in a certain measure, *communicable* and so revert to each member, helping him to perfect his life and liberty of person. They all constitute the good human life of the multitude.[4]

Even after gathering in the immense sweep of this list, the reader will think of other items: the protection of forests and wildlife; the provision of public parks; care for pure waters and clean air; concerns about international trade; new possibilities of communication and transport; concern for overpopulation and the "birth dearth"; and even the sound management of change itself.

Thus, while it may be true that in a *formal* sense there are certain "outlines" of what is meant by the common good, in a *material* sense the concept includes many matters necessarily and properly subject to a broad range of often contradictory opinions. In this material sense, there may exist, indeed, terms vague and ambiguous enough to allow all to agree on "goals" (terms such as candidates for public office in democracies frequently repair to). But even these terms are chosen precisely because they disguise the programmatic, practical content that would incarnate them in reality. Moreover, of any programmatic and practical proposal claiming to be a step toward the common good, realistic minds will be inclined to ask many tough questions, and to discern many alternate possibilities. The experts will likely disagree.

In this murky field of disputation about the material common good, we confront the "veil of ignorance" mentioned above in chapter three. Many persons and parties develop *ideas* about the specifics that constitute the material content of the common good, here and now. But which of these are the truly sound ideas? Which will actually work? Answers to such inquiries are not given to us by mere introspection or luminous intuition.

Indeed, one among the points most often missed in discussing the common good is that individual persons need to participate in achieving it *where they are, at their own place* in the common order (like teammates on the playing field). Thus, while from one point of view *someone* may be thinking of the common good of the whole team, from the point of view of the individual player at any one moment each may have to concentrate upon doing perfectly his *particular* job (even while willing the common good of the team). Thus, an analyst of the common good must note that its participant parts are often *particular goods*, as seen by individuals at their particular posts. Soldiers on a battlefield may not even know, for example, how their own tactical assignment fulfills the strategic plan; they "do their job" as best, even as heroically, as they can. Moreover, participants in the common good, who are behind the veil of ignorance regarding the complete material content of the common good, do not have to *intend* the latter.

On this point, Simon uses two examples from Aquinas: *viz.*, God's will that a man's father die, and a judge's decision that a murderer be condemned to death.[5] In both cases, those most responsible for giving material content to the common good (i.e., God and the judge) have now done so. Nonetheless, God wills the son to will to do everything he can to save his father from death, and the judge expects the condemned man's wife to do everything she can to win a reduction in her husband's sentence. In such cases, Simon and Aquinas say, the individuals may in actual practice set their wills *against* what God or the empowered public official (the judge) wills as the common good; and yet even in their opposition to the common good (from that point of view) they are doing their duty to fulfill the common good proper to their station.

Indeed, by far the most powerful and subtle discussion of these points occurs in the last 35 pages of the first chapter of Yves Simon's *Philosophy of Democratic Government*. Assuming that a society wills the common good, Professor Simon recognizes the large role that the virtue of all its citizens must play in that achievement. He is by no means a utopian; he knows how little virtue is actually to be expected. Still, all our intellectual instincts lead us to notice and to criticize any falling off from the requisite virtue. Grasping this set of high expectations, Simon sets forth the six propositions of the (updated) classic theory of the common good:

1. That virtue implies love for the common good, willingness to sacrifice one's own advantage to its requirements.

2. That the common good may be intended formally without being intended materially.

3. That the virtue of the private person guarantees the intention of the common good formally considered, not the intention of the common good materially considered.

4. That society would be harmed if everyone intended the common good not only formally but also materially; that, in a material sense, particular persons and groups ought to intend particular goods.

5. That the intention of the common good, materially considered, is the business of a public reason and a public will.

6. That the intention of the common good by the public reason and will necessarily develops into a *direction* of society, by the public reason and will, toward the common good considered not only formally but also materially; which is the same as to say that the intention of the common good, materially considered, demands the operation of authority.[6]

On this last point, one must note that Simon speaks of a "direction" of society, which emerges differently in different types of political orders. (His is a "general" theory covering many possibilities). In democracies, for example, this direction emerges not only from government itself, constituted by the "consent of the governed," and operating under a system of checks and balances, but also from widespread community activities beyond the scope of "limited" government. Yet, precisely because not all citizens can know the full material content of the common good—what in particular needs to be done here and now—there emerges a natural need for organs of national decisionmaking; in short, for authorities of various types, responsible for exercises of expertise and power within a limited range. And, at some points, this veil of ignorance naturally requires the highest authority in the national community (executive or legislative or judicial, as appropriate) to make certain key decisions regarding next practical steps forward. Here, for example, the Congress established by the Articles of Confederation was failing; a sounder scheme of government needed to be constituted.

Simon holds that authority, though often abused and always characterized by human faults, is a natural and moral good. It does not result solely from human sinfulness (to restrain the worst in us). It springs from human virtue and human need. Authority is needed, for example, not only to secure individual rights, but also to give effective unity in the pursuit of such common purposes as are mentioned in the preamble to the U.S. Constitution.

Further, the six propositions set forth by Simon are in our day complicated by the liberties at the disposal of free persons, even in their development of the civic virtues. For each person is a whole universe, and in free republics each must be respected in the full range of his or her natural liberty. Each can know a portion of reality, and with infinite desire wish to master all of it. Each adds a unique and irrepeatable voice to the human chorus. Each may choose to specialize—in physics or in dance, in commerce or in sport, in politics or in journalism. Each person is a part of the human race, yet also a whole: autonomous, self-directing, seeking to know and to become joined to the whole of knowledge and the whole of human possibilities for love. No human person is other than finite; but none lacks an appetite for the infinite. How complex a task it is, then, to include within the common good respect for such diversity among persons—and to construct institutions that do so as a matter of routine!

Thus, the common good is both larger than any individual person, and incomplete unless it gathers into itself the infinite potency of every person. Each person who stunts his own development injures the common good. Any social arrangement that stunts the development of a single person injures the common good. Whether the full development of every single person has been attained is the full measure of whether the common good has been achieved. To desire such a common good formally (in will) is easier than to attain it materially (in space and time, in fact). To know its outlines formally is easier than to know its material content. That is why in its fullest sense *the* common good is held to be beyond human reach, until Paradise.

To exhort people to pursue the (formal) common good is easier than to figure out, in practice here and now, which of many material courses of action will best attain it. Pointing to their untested opinions and ill-formed prejudices, many false prophets say of the common good, "Here it is!" Those who say that they can discern what the material common good is may be well-intentioned, but they are more often foolish than wise. The wise are aware of their ignorance, fallibility, and need to try and see, before they are so sure. On earth, we must be satisfied with realizable approximations, and with steady and realistic progress.

Finally, at the risk of taxing the reader beyond endurance, it may be useful to adapt for our own purposes a map of the usage of "common good" prepared by Dr. Udoidem. [See p. 174.]

We can fill out this map with examples, beginning from its topmost lines. Since one may speak of a family's common good, one must often speak of *particular* common goods (as when parents try to persuade a reluctant child that a trip to grandma's is for the good of the family, while the child can go out with her friends any time).

But a common good may be particular in two ways: *individual* insofar as it is fulfilled through *private* members of the community, and *special* insofar as it fulfills a *part* of the whole. The good of a particular family (their virtue, their prosperity, etc.), for example, is a necessary part of the common good of all, but it is an individual and a *private* portion of the common good. Public health, on the other hand, is a particular good common to *all* citizens, though health is only a *special part* of their complete common good.

The first part of this distinction between the particular (private) common good and the general (special) common good arises because each person must do his part in contributing to the common good, and this includes taking care of individual requirements: being economically creative, providing a family home, instructing children, practicing the virtues necessary to thriving republics. Thus, these particular private goods are also indispensable contributions to the common good of the whole.

Sometimes a private particular good is in the sphere of the *individual* (material: buying a particularly suitable house), sometimes in the sphere of the *person* (moral: overcoming a nagging personal fault). "Person" and "individual" are here used in Maritain's sense.

Sometimes the common (special) good refers to widespread *personal* (natural) achievements, as when a country's citizens as a whole advance in knowledge and skills. Sometimes it is *communal* (conventional; that is, by law or other public specification), as when a public health director acts well to achieve his office's objectives.

On the lower portion of the map, the *general* common good may be looked at insofar as it is *relative* to a certain time, place, and culture, as when an authoritarian society at last sets out upon the path of democratic institutions. But it may also be looked at as meeting a *universal* common good, as when the entire human race experiences a general rise in the "awakening" of civic spirit, or invention, or enterprise, or political responsibility. In this respect, this universal common good concerns ordinary *human nature*.

In another respect, though, and in the full sense properly designated as "*the* common good," the universal common good consists in the highest possible development of human capacities for insight and choice, in union with the Creator who "draws all things to Himself." This last sense, clearly, is eschatological. *The* common good, the full "kingdom of God," never arrives within history; it is the "impossible possibility" (Reinhold Niebuhr), which nonetheless serves as the ultimate judgment upon the poor approximations to it that humans actually achieve within history.

At each level of achievement—in person, family, city, state, and humankind as a whole—the concept of the common good recognizes both an end achieved, and a new inward impulsion toward a further achievement, upon a larger and more complex plane. In this respect, the concept entails a dynamic point of view and offers "benchmarks" for new achievements, beyond any so far accomplished.

Thus, the common good is the inner dynamo of human progress, rooted in the human's capacity to *reflect* upon his or her own actions, to grasp their deficiencies and incompletenesses, and to *choose* to press onward toward the full development of the entire range of human possibilities.

In the context of social life, this concept implies that every single person has responsibilities. Each must participate in building up the human community, as well as in full self-development. The community needs every available hand and heart. And every heart is restless until it rests in the community of all with Him, Who before that heart began to beat had already extended to it His love.

Terminologically, the concept of the common good is not simple. Nor is the term univocal. On the contrary, the term is very rich and subtle. It should be used with care.

\* \* \*

Finally, we might apply these distinctions to the United States. In my view, Simon is at times too hard on the liberal society, overlooking particularly how the liberal idea was modified and intermixed with ancient classical ideas, including Jewish and Christian ideas, in the development of American institutions and ways of thought.[7]

Do the citizens of the United States will the common good— the good of the American experiment, the good of the nation? Many have willingly died for it. Lincoln led the nation through

the bloodiest civil war until that time to preserve "the Union."
And the will to pursue together the common good is fully implied
within the much loved patriotic hymn:

> *God bless America! Land that I love.*
> *Stand beside her, and guide her,*
> *Through the night with the light from above.*

This stanza expresses almost perfectly the formal content of a
properly formed commitment to the common good (the fidelity
of the commonwealth to God's will). It evokes as well the veil of
ignorance any people must face "through the night," in trying to
discern which material content best achieves that formal intention
in practice.

In addition, the Pledge of Allegiance states quite unambigu-
ously that Americans intend to purify their own intentions by
holding them under the transcendent scrutiny of God's will.
(This theme is also powerfully expressed in "The Battle Hymn of
the Republic"). Americans do not pledge allegiance to a patch of
soil, a land, a history, or a people, but rather to a form of
government: a republic. It is for republican government that the
flag stands. Moreover, it is for the constituted people as a whole,
the nation indivisible, that the flag stands. And yet more: the flag
stands for a particular type of republic, the one that stands under
God's judgment, and that is committed to the transcendent
principles "liberty and justice for all." Liberty and justice are
"transcendent" principles in the sense that they can never be
perfectly fulfilled at any point in history, but keep driving a
pilgrim race ever forward in their pursuit. In every generation,
there are always further steps in pursuit of justice and of liberty
to be taken, amid the vicissitudes of historical circumstance,
social necessity, and human fallibility.

In the history of nations, the power and purity of this nation's
*expressly stated* commitment to the formal content of the common
good may be unprecedented. In any case, "We the People of the
United States" stand expressly under God's judgment, and are
expressly committed to the pursuit of transcendent ideals of
liberty and justice for every member of the community. We invite
planetary criticism in that light.

# NOTES

## Introduction: Interweaving Two Traditions

1. Oliver F. Williams and John Houck, eds., *The Common Good and U.S. Capitalism* (Lanham, Maryland: University Press of America, 1987).

2. Evidence of the trend toward liberalism may be found in the reforms in countries such as China and the USSR, as well as in the growth of such groups as Club de l'Horloge in France and Centro de Estudios Publicos in Chile. See Le Club de l'Horloge, *Socialisme et Religion: Sont-Ils Compatibles?* (Paris: Editions Albatros, 1986); and Eliodoro Matte Larrain, ed., *Christianismo, Sociedad Libre y Opcion por los Pobres: Una Selección de Articulos y Ensayos* (Santiago: Centro de Estudios Publicos, 1988).

3. See Jacques Maritain, *The Person and the Common Good*, trans. John J. FitzGerald (New York: Charles Scribner's Sons, 1947; Notre Dame, Indiana: University of Notre Dame Press, 1972), p. 5. Chapters 1 through 4 appeared in the *Review of Politics*, October 1946.

4. See Maritain, *The Person and the Common Good*, p. 16, n. 6; Charles De Koninck, *De la primauté du bien commun* (Quebec: Editions de l'Université Laval and Montreal: Fides, 1943); I. Thomas Eschmann, "In Defense of Jacques Maritain," *The Modern Schoolman*, May 1945; De Koninck, "In Defense of St. Thomas: A Reply to Father Eschmann's Attack on the Primacy of the Common Good," *Laval théologique et philosophique* 1 (1945):9–109. For a brief history of this dispute, see Ralph McInerny, "The Primacy of the Common Good," in Williams and Houck, eds., *The Common Good and U.S. Capitalism*, pp. 70–83.

5. Maritain writes: "The human being is caught between two poles; a material pole, which, in reality, does not concern the true person but

189

rather the shadow of personality or what, in the strict sense, is called *individuality*, and a spiritual pole, which does concern *true personality*. . . .

". . . Outside of the mind, only individual realities exist. . . . Individuality is opposed to the state of universality which things have in the mind. . . .

". . . As an individual, each of us is a fragment of a species, a part of the universe, a unique point in the immense web of cosmic, ethnical, historical forces and influences—and bound by their laws. . . . Nonetheless, each of us is also a person and, as such, is not controlled by the stars. Our whole being subsists in virtue of the subsistence of the spiritual soul which is in us a principle of creative unity, independence, and liberty. . . .

". . . the metaphysical tradition of the West defines the person in terms of independence, as a reality which, subsisting spiritually, constitutes a universe unto itself, a relatively independent whole within the great whole of the universe. . . . Unlike the concept of the individuality of corporeal things, the concept of personality is related not to matter but to the deepest and highest dimensions of being. Its roots are in the spirit. . . .

". . . they are not two separate things. There is not in me one reality, called my individual, and another reality, called my person. One and the same reality is, in a certain sense an individual, and, in another sense, a person. Our whole being is an individual by reason of that in us which derives from matter, and a person by reason of that in us which derives from spirit." Maritain, *The Person and the Common Good*, chap. 3, "Individuality and Personality," pp. 33, 34, 38, 40, 43.

6. In addition to *The Person and the Common Good*, see Maritain, *Christianity and Democracy & The Rights of Man and Natural Law*, trans. Doris C. Anson (San Francisco: Ignatius Press, 1986); *Man and the State* (Chicago: University of Chicago Press, 1951); and *Integral Humanism*, trans. Joseph W. Evans (New York: Charles Scribner's Sons, 1968). In *Man and the State* (p. 13), Maritain says that "man is by no means for the State. The State is for man." This is obviously a play on Mark 2:27.

7. Nick Eberstadt supplies abundant figures in an essay that outlines the near-universal improvement in standards of living in the Third World; see "Progress against Poverty in Communist and Non-Communist Countries in the Postwar Era," in Peter Berger, ed., *Modern Capitalism*, vol. 2: *Capitalism and Equality in the Third World* (Lanham, Maryland: University Press of America, 1986).

8. Perhaps the best source for Maritain's economic views is *Reflections on America* (New York: Charles Scribner's Sons, 1958). See also Michael Novak, "The Economic System: The Evangelical Basis of a Social Market Economy," *The Review of Politics* 43 (July 1981):355–380.

9. Somewhat to his surprise, Maritain found Americans to be persons for whom "the supreme value . . . is goodness; human reliability, good

will, devotion, helpfulness. Hence, that American kindness which is so striking a feature to foreign visitors. Americans are ready to help, and happy to help. They are on equal terms of comradeship with everybody. And why? Simply because everybody is a human being. A fellow man. That's enough for him to be supposed worthy of assistance and sympathy—sometimes of exceedingly thoughtful and generous attention. When you arrive in this country you experience in this connection a strange, unforgettable sense of relief. You breathe more easily." Maritain, *Reflections on America*, pp. 67–68 (emphasis in original). Tocqueville explained this phenomenon: "The free institutions and the political rights enjoyed there provide a thousand continual reminders to every citizen that he lives in society. At every moment they bring his mind back to this idea, that it is the duty as well as the interest of men to be useful to their fellows. Having no particular reason to hate others, since he is neither their slave nor their master, the American's heart easily inclines toward benevolence. At first it is of necessity that men attend to the public interest, afterward by choice. What had been calculation becomes instinct. By dint of working for the good of his fellow citizens, he in the end acquires a habit and taste for serving them." Alexis de Tocqueville, *Democracy in America*, ed. J. P. Mayer, trans. George Lawrence (Garden City, New York: Doubleday, 1969), pp. 512–513.

10. Tocqueville, *Democracy in America*, p. 517.

11. In one of his earliest pamphlets (1835), Cobden called upon the British to pay more attention to their coming rival. He presented a barrage of statistics showing how the people of the U.S., even though fewer in number than the British, were already proportionately drawing ahead. He viewed the American system as a kind of ideal toward which the British ought to aim. Cobden believed from his observations that politics tends to corrupt, and that commercial relations, being voluntary and free, tend to be far deeper, more humane and more lawlike. Thus, the frontispiece of his pamphlet on England, Ireland, and America bore the following quotation from George Washington's Farewell Address: "The great rule of conduct for us in regard to foreign nations is, in extending our commercial relations, to have with them as little political connection as possible." Cobden, "England, Ireland, and America," in Francis W. Hirst, ed., *Free Trade and Other Fundamental Doctrines of the Manchester School Set Forth in Selections from the Speeches and Writings of Its Founders and Followers* (London: Harper & Bros., 1903; reprint ed., New York: Augustus M. Kelley, 1968), p. 1. In the same essay Cobden wrote: "It is to the industry, economy, and peaceful policy of America, and not to the growth of Russia, that our statesmen and politicians, of whatever creed, ought to direct their anxious study. . . ." Again: "We believe the Government of the United States to be at this moment the best in the world; but then the Americans are the best people. . . ." Cobden's reasons for this judgment are detailed in a long footnote. Ibid., pp. 73, 96–97.

12. Maritain, *Reflections on America*, p. 118.

13. Ibid., p. 107.

14. *New Catholic Encyclopedia*, s.v. "Common Good," by A. Nemetz.

15. Oliver F. Williams, "To Enhance the Common Good: An Introduction," in Williams and Houck, eds., *The Common Good and U.S. Capitalism*, p. 3.

16. Charles E. Curran, "The Common Good and Official Catholic Social Teaching," in Williams and Houck, eds., *The Common Good and U.S. Capitalism*, p. 113.

17. Ibid., p. 128.

18. *Gaudium et Spes*, 26.

19. Charles C. West, "The Common Good and the Participation of the Poor," in Williams and Houck, eds., *The Common Good and U.S. Capitalism*, p. 29.

20. Ibid., p. 46.

21. Quoted in Virgil Michel, "The Bourgeois Spirit and the Christian Renewal," in Robert L. Spaeth, ed., *The Social Question: Essays on Capitalism and Christianity by Fr. Virgil Michel, O.S.B.* (Collegeville, Minnesota: Office of Academic Affairs, St. John's University, 1987), p. 83.

22. West, "The Common Good and the Participation of the Poor," pp. 46–47.

23. Ibid., p. 46.

24. Writing of teenagers found out in a party where drugs were in evidence and the host's parents were not, Robert Kuttner observed honestly: "We good liberals sounded like Cotton Mather. Few parents are very liberal where 13–year–olds are concerned." He added: "The idea that children ought to obey their parents and their teachers is a conservative idea. And for that matter, navigating a family through the vicissitudes of modern life is an essentially conservative enterprise." Kuttner, "The Democrats' Family Problem," *Washington Post*, 6 March 1988.

## Chapter One: The Conceptual Background

1. See Michael Novak, "The Traditional Pragmatism," *A Time to Build* (New York: Macmillan, 1967). William James, e.g., wrote that "There is absolutely nothing new in the pragmatic method. Socrates was an adept at it. Aristotle used it methodically. Locke, Berkeley, and Hume made momentous contributions to truth by its means. . . ." James, "Pragmatism," in *Pragmatism and Other Essays* (New York: Washington Square Press, 1963), p. 25.

2. Charles E. Curran outlines this unexpected return to Thomistic thought in "The Common Good and Official Catholic Social Teaching,"

in Oliver F. Williams and John W. Houck, eds., *The Common Good and U.S. Capitalism* (Lanham, Maryland: University Press of America, 1987). See also William Gooley, "Shared Visions: Human Nature and Human Work in *Rerum Novarum* and *Laborem Exercens*" (Ph.D. dissertation, Syracuse University, 1986).

3. See Paul Johnson, *Modern Times: The World from the Twenties to the Eighties* (New York: Harper & Row, 1983), esp. chap. 1, "A Relativistic World." Johnson writes: "In the six decades which followed the First World War, knowledge expanded more rapidly than ever before. Yet in many ways an educated man in the 1980s was less equipped with certitudes than an ancient Egyptian in 2500 BC" (p. 697).

4. Several themes of recent Catholic social thought point toward redistribution. Charles Curran sees in church teaching since Pope John XXIII "a greater role for the state . . . these later documents still refer to the principle of subsidiarity, but this principle is now used to justify a greater role for the state than in the past." In addition, "The obligations of the first world vis-à-vis the Third World are very significant." "Equality and participation" have also been stressed, though Curran points out that this emphasis "raises some problems for the Catholic tradition. . . . A flat equalitarianism seems opposed to the communal and social nature of human existence which has been a hallmark of the Catholic and Thomistic traditions. *Octogesima Adveniens* recognizes the problem: '. . . an overemphasis on equality can give rise to an individualism in which each one claims one's own rights without wishing to be answerable for the common good' (par. 23)." In short, "more work needs to be done to indicate how the acceptance of equality will not ultimately destroy the solidarity and communal nature of human social existence." Curran, "The Common Good and Official Catholic Social Teaching," pp. 122–4.

5. "Popular agitation against slavery and the slave trade began in Britain late in the eighteenth century on the basis of the new [liberal] philosophic ideas about human rights. This effort achieved notable success by the first decade of the next century. . . . In a very short time Britain had been transformed from the biggest slave trader of the eighteenth century into a tremendous force to end the slave trade. This transformation was the direct consequence of new philosophic ideas about the rights of man which had influenced the evolution of British politics during the eighteenth century and shaped the American and French revolutions." Charles H. Fairbanks, Jr., "Britain and the Slave Trade: A Human Rights Policy That Worked," *This World*, Fall 1982, p. 42. Walter Berns argues that American slavery might have ended sooner and less painfully than it eventually did, had the national government encouraged more North-South commerce and thus spread the (liberal) manners and laws that commerce brings. See his "The Constitution and the Migration of Slaves," *Yale Law Journal*, 78:198–228; reprinted in Berns, *In Defense of Liberal Democracy* (Chicago: Regnery Gateway, 1984).

6. *Nicomachean Ethics*, I, ii.

7. ". . . the good man judges everything correctly: what things truly are, that they seem to him to be . . . what chiefly distinguishes the good man is that he sees the truth in each kind, being himself as it were the standard and measure of the noble and pleasant." Ibid., III, iv. ". . . one must be born with an eye, as it were, by which to judge rightly and choose what is truly good. . . ." Ibid., III, v. Whether an act is blameworthy depends "on particular facts, and the decision rests with perception." Ibid., II, ix. Aristotle values insight more than theory and mere courses in philosophy. To become a just man, one must do just acts, "but most people do not do these, but take refuge in theory and think they are being philosophers and will become good in this way, behaving somewhat like patients who listen attentively to their doctors, but do none of the things they are ordered to do. As the latter will not be made well in body by such a course of treatment, the former will not be made well in soul by such a course in philosophy." Ibid., II, iv. See also Bernard J. F. Lonergan's masterful *Insight: A Study of Human Understanding*, rev. ed. (New York: Philosophical Library, 1958).

8. St. Thomas Aquinas, *Summa Theologiae*, trans. and ed. Thomas Gilby, 60 vols. (New York: McGrawHill, 1963), 28:172 (appendix 4, "Common and Public Good").

9. Maritain writes that a being with a personality "must be endowed with a spiritual existence, capable of containing itself thanks to the operations of the intellect and freedom, capable of superexisting by way of knowledge and of love. For this reason, the metaphysical tradition of the West defines the person in terms of independence, as a reality which, subsisting spiritually, constitutes a universe unto itself, a relatively independent whole within the great whole of the universe, facing the transcendent whole which is God. . . . Unlike the concept of the individuality of corporeal things, the concept of personality is related not to matter but to the deepest and highest dimensions of being. Its roots are in the spirit inasmuch as the spirit holds itself in existence and superabounds in existence. Metaphysically considered, personality is, as the Thomistic School rightly asserts, 'subsistence,' the ultimate achievement by which the creative influx seals, within itself, a nature face to face with the whole order of existence so that the existence which it receives is *its own* existence and *its own* perfection. Personality is the subsistence of the spiritual soul communicated to the human composite . . . it is an imprint or seal which enables it to possess its existence, to perfect and give itself freely. . . ." Jacques Maritain, *The Person and the Common Good*, trans. John J. FitzGerald (New York: Charles Scribner's Sons, 1947; Notre Dame, Indiana: University of Notre Dame Press, 1972), pp. 40–41 (emphasis in original).

10. Lord Acton, "The History of Freedom in Antiquity," in *Essays on Freedom and Power*, ed. Gertrude Himmelfarb (Cleveland and New York: World Publishing Co., 1955), pp. 87–88.

11. Quoted at ibid., p. 88. Cf. *Summa Theologiae*, I–II, q. 105, a. 1.
12. Ibid.
13. Yves R. Simon to Jacques Maritain, 11 December 1945, quoted by Ralph McInerny, "The Primacy of the Common Good," in Williams and Houck, eds., *The Common Good and U.S. Capitalism*, p. 82, n. 19.
14. Jacques Maritain, *Three Reformers* (1925), p. 24.
15. Ibid., p. 22.
16. Ludwig von Mises, *Liberalism in the Classical Tradition*, trans. Ralph Raico (Irvington-on-Hudson, New York: Foundation for Economic Education, 1985), pp. 7–8.
17. See Peter Berger, *The Capitalist Revolution* (New York: Basic Books, 1986).
18. Avowed socialists have begun to note the unpromising results of "worker democracy" in the much-touted experiments of Yugoslavia. See, e.g., Robert Heilbroner, "A Feasible Vision of Socialism," *Dissent*, Fall 1984; and Alec Nove, "Feasible Socialism?: Some Socio-Political Assumptions," *Dissent*, Summer 1985. Nove writes: "Reverting to labor's role in managerial decisions in socialized enterprises, one must recall two negative aspects of the Yugoslav experience. One is the interest of the workers in not expanding the labor force, at a time of serious unemployment, because to do so could reduce their incomes. The other is the workers' lack of long-term interest in 'their' enterprise, because it is in fact not theirs: they derive no benefit from working for it once they leave it, having no shares to sell" (p. 370; emphasis in original). Ludwig von Mises has argued that "a system in which the workers, as producers, and not the consumers themselves would decide what was to be produced and how," would be "as little democratic as, say, a political constitution under which the government officials and not the whole people decided how the state was to be governed. . . ." Von Mises, *Socialism: An Economic and Sociological Analysis*, trans. J. Kahane (Indianapolis, Indiana: Liberty Classics, 1981), p. 11. See also Freedom House, *Yugoslavia: The Failure of "Democratic" Communism* (New York: Freedom House, 1987).
19. Robert Heilbroner is a notable exception; he writes candidly about the tradeoffs between socialism and "bourgeois individualism": "A generation accustomed to the supporting discipline of socialism will not miss [the liberties] of bourgeois individualism. . . . Nor can we wriggle off this hook by asserting that, among its moral commitments, socialism will choose to include the rights of individuals to their Millian liberties. For that celebration of individualism is directly opposed to the basic socialist commitment to a deliberately embraced collective moral goal. . . . Because socialist society aspires to be a good society, all its decisions and opinions are inescapably invested with moral import. Every disagreement with them, every argument for alternative policies, every nay-saying voice therefore raises into question the moral validity of the

existing government. . . . Dissents and disagreements thereby smack of heresy in a manner lacking from societies in which expediency and not morality rules the roost." Heilbroner, "What Is Socialism?" *Dissent* 25 (Summer 1978):346–48.

20. J. Philip Wogaman, "The Common Good and Economic Life: A Protestant Perspective," in Williams and Houck, eds., *The Common Good and U.S. Capitalism*, pp. 89–90.

## Chapter Two: The New Order of the Ages

1. Hamilton warned: "the crisis at which we are arrived may with propriety be regarded as the era in which that decision is to be made; and a wrong election of the part we shall act may, in this view, deserve to be considered as the general misfortune of mankind." Alexander Hamilton, James Madison, and John Jay, *The Federalist Papers*, ed. Clinton Rossiter (New York: New American Library, 1961), No. 1, p. 33.

2. Ibid., No. 15, pp. 110–11.

3. Ibid., No. 41, pp. 255–6.

4. Michael Sandel, for example, has recently written that those who now call themselves liberals must not neglect the human need for community: "Here lies the lesson that American liberalism has still to learn: the themes that resonated most deeply [in Reagan's rhetoric] came from the second strand, the communal strand of conservative thought. For all Reagan's talk of individual liberty and market solutions, the most potent part of his appeal was his evocation of communal values—of family and neighborhood, religion and patriotism. What Reagan stirred was a yearning for a way of life that seems to be receding in recent times—a common life of larger meanings, on a smaller, less impersonal scale than the nation-state provides.

"To their political misfortune, Democrats in recent years have not spoken convincingly about self-government and community. More than a matter of rhetoric, the reason runs deep in liberal political theory. For, unlike conservatism, contemporary liberalism lacks a second voice, or communal strand. Its predominant impulse is individualistic." Today's "liberals" Sandel complains, misunderstand the nature of community: "When Democrats do speak of community, they usually mean the national community. . . .

"But the yearning for community can no longer be satisfied by depicting the nation as a family or a neighborhood. The metaphor is by now too strained to carry conviction. The nation is too vast to sustain more than a minimal commonality, too distant to permit more than occasional moments of participation.

"Local attachments can serve self-government by engaging citizens in a common life beyond their private pursuits, and by cultivating the habit of attending to public things. They can enable citizens, in Tocqueville's phrase, to 'practice the art of government in the small sphere within their reach.' " Sandel, "Democrats and Community: A Public Philosophy for American Liberalism," *The New Republic*, 22 February 1988, pp. 21–22. See also "Liberalism and 'Community': A Symposium," *The New Republic*, 9 May 1988; William A. Schambra, "The Quest for Community and the New Public Philosophy," *Catholicism in Crisis*, April and May 1984; and Michael Novak, *Freedom with Justice: Catholic Social Thought and Liberal Institutions* (San Francisco: Harper & Row, 1984), chap. 11, "The Communitarian Individual in Practice."

5. John Winthrop, "A Model of Christian Charity," in Perry Miller, ed., *The American Puritans: Their Prose and Poetry* (New York: Doubleday, 1956), pp. 78–83.

6. *The Federalist Papers*, No. 4, pp. 49–50.

7. *Summa Theologiae*, II–II, q. 66, a. 2, c.

8. *The Federalist Papers*, No. 51, p. 322.

9. Ibid.

10. Jonathan Elliot, ed., *Debates in the Several State Conventions on the Adoption of the Federal Constitution* (Philadelphia: Lippincott, 1907), Virginia, June 20, 1788.

11. *The Federalist Papers*, No. 51, p. 322.

12. Ibid.

13. Ibid., No. 10, p. 78.

14. Ibid. (emphasis added). The emphasized portion invokes the common good.

15. Ibid. (emphasis added).

16. Ibid., p. 79.

17. Ibid., pp. 80–81.

18. Ibid., p. 81.

19. Faction in popular governments leads to "the problem of the unjust majority. In societies relatively small and simple, the factional divisions reduce to two, . . . rich and poor. . . . Their encounters are massive, direct, violent, and often fatal to the commonwealth. . . . Enlarge the sphere of the republic, Madison argues, and embrace within one community all the various conditions of a spacious country, all the finely graded, closely mingled interests of a 'civilized' commercial society." As a result: "Sheer size and distance minimize the chances for a factious majority to discover their strength and concert plans of oppression. Thus in a broad American Union the sum of many small differences is more likely to be the principles of justice and general welfare on which the majority of a great society can unite. Liberty can be reconciled with order, democracy with equity, self-interest with patriotism." Marvin Meyers, Introduction to Meyers, ed., *The Mind of the Founder: Sources of the Political Thought of James Madison*, rev. ed. (Hanover, New

Hampshire: University Press of New England, 1981), p. xxix. See also Michael Novak, "The New Science," *National Review*, 17 July 1987.

20. Ibid., p. 77 (emphasis added).

21. See Martin Diamond, *The Founding of the Democratic Republic* (Itasca, Illinois: F. E. Peacock, 1981); Marvin Meyers, Introduction to Meyers, ed., *The Mind of the Founder;* Walter Berns, *Taking the Constitution Seriously* (New York: Simon and Schuster, 1987); and Ralph Lerner, *The Thinking Revolutionary: Principle and Practice in the New Republic* (Ithaca, New York: Cornell University Press, 1987).

22. Roy P. Basler, ed., *The Collected Works of Abraham Lincoln*, 8 vols. (New Brunswick, New Jersey: Rutgers University Press, 1953), 4:168–9.

23. Tocqueville wrote his work "with a mind constantly preoccupied by a single thought: the thought of the approaching irresistible and universal spread of democracy throughout the world." The fate of the world, he thought, depended upon the establishment of "democratic liberty," rather than "democratic tyranny," in France and the rest of Europe. "Indeed, one may say that it depends on us whether in the end republics will be established everywhere, or everywhere abolished. . . . This problem, newly posed for us, was solved in America sixty years ago. . . . Where else can we find greater cause of hope or more valuable lessons?" Alexis de Tocqueville, "Author's Preface to the Twelfth Edition," *Democracy in America*, ed. J. P. Mayer, trans. George Lawrence (Garden City, New York: Doubleday, 1969), pp. xiii–xiv.

24. Tocqueville entitles one chapter, "The Laws Contribute More to the Maintenance of the Democratic Republic in the United States Than Do the Physical Circumstances of the Country, and Mores Do More Than the Laws." He notes that Latin America is blessed with "more untouched and inexhaustible riches" than North America, "yet there are no nations on earth more miserable than those of South America." In short, "if in the course of this book I have not succeeded in making the reader feel the importance I attach to the practical experience of the Americans, to their habits, opinions, and, in a word, their mores, in maintaining their laws, I have failed in the main object of my work." Ibid., p. 308.

25. Tocqueville praises the American system of local government: "Local institutions are to liberty what primary schools are to science; they put it within the people's reach. . . . Without local institutions a nation may give itself a free government, but it has not got the spirit of liberty." No nation on the Continent "understand[s] communal liberty." But "the New Englander is attached to his township because it is strong and independent; he has an interest in it because he shares in its management; he loves it because he has no reason to complain of his lot; he invests his ambition and his future in it; in the restricted sphere within his scope, he learns to rule society; he gets to know those formalities without which freedom can advance only through revolutions,

and becoming imbued with their spirit, develops a taste for order, understands the harmony of powers, and in the end accumulates clear, practical ideas about the nature of his duties and the extent of his rights." Ibid., pp. 62–63, 70.

26. Ibid., pp. 237–8.
27. Ibid., p. 238.
28. Ibid., p. 509.
29. One sees this most clearly in vol. 2, bk. 2, chaps. 2–9.
30. "Among aristocratic nations," Tocqueville writes, "as families remain for centuries in the same condition, often on the same spot, all generations become, as it were, contemporaneous. A man almost always knows his forefathers and respects them; he thinks he already sees his remote descendents and he loves them. He willingly imposes duties on himself towards the former and the latter, and he will frequently sacrifice his personal gratifications to those who went before and to those who will come after him." Tocqueville, *Democracy in America*, pp. 506–7.
31. Ibid., p. 507.
32. Ibid., p. 506.
33. Ibid., pp. 507–8.
34. Ibid., p. 511.
35. Ibid.
36. Ibid., p. 512. Chesterton praised America's high regard for invention: "There is one real advantage that America has over England. . . . America does not think that stupidity is practical. It does not think that ideas are merely destructive things. It does not think that a genius is only a person to be told to go away and blow his brains out; rather, it would open all its machinery to the genius and beg him to blow his brains in." G. K. Chesterton, *What I Saw in America* (London:Hodder and Stoughton, 1922), p. 117.
37. "Our habit of speaking of 'Americanism' grates on the ears of other peoples, in part because, as the late Martin Diamond used to point out, no other country has an expression similar to it. . . . America is something in addition to a plot, an earth, a realm; something more than a place with a past; something, indeed, that was deliberately brought into being at a particular moment of time and for a specific purpose. At Gettysburg, our poet Abraham Lincoln defined it as a nation conceived in liberty and dedicated to a certain philosophical proposition, a nation brought into being by 'our fathers,' as Lincoln called them, who are related to us not necessarily or even essentially by blood but by a mutual dedication to that proposition. In principle, anyone can be Americanized, another term that has no analogue elsewhere; all that is required is a pledge of allegiance to the 'ism,' so to speak, to the flag of the United States, and, as Diamond emphasized, 'to the republic for which it stands.' " Walter Berns, *Taking the Constitution Seriously*, pp. 21–22. See also Martin Diamond, *The Founding of the Democratic Republic*, pp. 1–3.

38. Tocqueville, *Democracy in America*, p. 525. George Santayana also noted the American habit of helping others: "Everywhere cooperation is taken for granted, as something that no one would be so mean or so shortsighted to refuse. Together with the will to work and to prosper, it is of the essence of Americanism, and is accepted as such by all the unkempt polyglot peoples that turn to the new world with the pathetic but manly purpose of beginning life on a new principle. Every political body, every public meeting, every club, or college, or athletic team, is full of it. Out it comes whenever there is an accident in the street or a division in a church, or a great unexpected emergency. . . . The general instinct is to run and help, to assume direction, to pull through somehow by mutual adaptation, and by seizing on the readiest practical measures and working compromises. Each man joins in and gives a helping hand, without a preconceived plan or a prior motive." Santayana, *Character and Opinion in the United States* (New York: Charles Scribner's Sons, 1921), p. 196.

39. Tocqueville, *Democracy in America*, p. 525.

40. Ibid., p. 526.

41. Ibid.

42. Ibid., p. 527.

43. Ibid., p. 529.

44. "The fact is that [Mandeville's] *Fable*, so far from being representative of its time, profoundly shocked contemporaries, provoked a frenzy of attacks, and resulted in a presentment handed down by the grand jury of Middlesex condemning it as a 'public nuisance.' . . . Among his critics were . . . William Law, Francis Hutcheson, George Berkeley, Edward Gibbon, Lord Shaftesbury, Adam Smith. . . . And they attacked him as much for his attitude toward the poor as for his views on morality." Gertrude Himmelfarb, *The Idea of Poverty: England in the Early Industrial Age* (New York: Alfred A. Knopf, 1984), p. 30. In his *Theory of Moral Sentiments*, Adam Smith begins eight pages devoted to Mandeville's thought thus: "There is, however, another system which seems to take away altogether the distinction between vice and virtue, and of which the tendency is, upon that account, wholly pernicious; I mean the system of Dr. Mandeville . . . the notions of this author are in almost every respect erroneous. . . ." Smith, *The Theory of Moral Sentiments* (1853; reprint ed., Indianapolis, Indiana: Liberty Classics, 1976), Part VII, section ii, chap. 4, p. 487. On Mandeville, see also Friedrich A. Hayek, *Law, Legislation and Liberty*, 3 vols. (Chicago: University of Chicago Press, 1973–79).

45. Richard Hofstadter, "The Founding Fathers: An Age of Realism," in Robert H. Horwitz, ed., *The Moral Foundations of the American Republic*, 3rd ed. (Charlottesville, Virginia: University Press of Virginia, 1986), pp. 66–67.

46. *The Federalist Papers*, No. 37, p. 231.

47. Ibid.

48. Walter Berns writes of liberal societies: "We ought not to belittle that which has been attained. Man has indeed been provided with what he requires while he continues to be man and his estate on this earth has been relieved. This is true especially of the laboring poor who were of particular concern to Adam Smith. As Professor Himmelfarb recently wrote, the poor have a moral status in Smith's political economy:

[N]ot the special moral status they enjoyed in a fixed, hierarchic order, but that which adhered to them as individuals in a free society sharing a common human, which is to say, moral, nature.

Beyond that, our liberal, bourgeois democracies are free and tolerant. And it was on the basis of the liberal principles that slavery was abolished—no small achievement, that. . . . Finally, we owe it to mankind to emphasize that a defective solution to the human problem is preferable to any attempt to find a final solution." Berns, "The Constitution, Community, and Liberty," *Harvard Journal of Law and Public Policy* 8 (Spring 1985):284–5, quoting Gertrude Himmelfarb, *The Idea of Poverty: England in the Early Industrial Age*, p. 63.

# Chapter Three: Order Unplanned

1. Alexander Hamilton, James Madison, and John Jay, *The Federalist Papers*, ed. Clinton Rossiter (New York: New American Library, 1961), No. 55, p. 346.

2. Ibid., No. 57, p. 350.

3. What actually moves free persons "*as if* by an invisible hand" (to use Adam Smith's precise locution, used twice in thousands of words of his, once in each of two large works) is their own practical intelligence.

4. See Friedrich A. Hayek, *Law, Legislation and Liberty*, vol. 2: *The Mirage of Social Justice* (Chicago: University of Chicago Press, 1976), esp. chap. 11, "The Discipline of Abstract Rules and the Emotions of the Tribal Society"; and vol. 3: *The Political Order of a Free People* (Chicago: University of Chicago Press, 1979), "Epilogue."

5. Hayek acknowledges that "in some respects Lord Acton was not being altogether paradoxical when he described Thomas Aquinas as the first Whig." *The Constitution of Liberty* (Chicago: Henry Regnery, 1960), p. 457, n. 4.

6. Ludwig von Mises, *Liberalism in the Classical Tradition*, trans. Ralph Raico (Irvington-on-Hudson, New York: Foundation for Economic Education, 1985), p. 18.

7. "The discovery that by substituting abstract rules of conduct for obligatory concrete ends made it possible to extend the order of peace

beyond the small groups pursuing the same ends, because it enabled each individual to gain from the skill and knowledge of others whom he need not even know and whose aims could be wholly different from his own." Hayek, *The Mirage of Social Justice*, p. 109.

8. "In order that a good be common, it does not suffice that it should concern, in some way or other, several persons; it is necessary that it be of such nature as to cause, among those who pursue it and in so far as they pursue it, a common life of desire and action." Yves R. Simon, *Philosophy of Democratic Government* (Chicago: University of Chicago Press, 1951), p. 49.

9. "To the question whether the human will, in order to be good, must conform to the will of God *in volito*, Aquinas answers that the only conformity required is formal and that a formal conformity may well be compatible with material disagreement or even demand such disagreement. God, who takes care of the common good of the universe, holds me responsible for some particular goods and wants me to discharge my responsibility. God may want my father to die tomorrow, but he certainly wants me to do all I can to prolong the life of my father." Ibid., p. 42. See also Amitai Etzioni, *The Moral Dimension: Toward a New Economics* (New York: The Free Press, 1988).

10. "The American ought therefore to love this country much better than that wherein either he or his forefathers were born. Here the rewards of his industry follow with equal steps the progress of his labour; his labour is founded on the basis of nature, *self-interest;* can it want a stronger allurement? Wives and children, who before in vain demanded of him a morsel of bread, now, fat and frolicsome, gladly help their father to clear those fields whence exuberant crops are to arise to feed and to clothe them all; without any part being claimed, either by a despotic prince, a rich abbot, or a mighty lord." Hector St. John Crèvecoeur, *Letters from an American Farmer* (1782; reprint ed., New York: Fox, Duffield & Co., 1904), p. 55.

11. When Gabriel Marcel was at Harvard during the early 1960s, I had the privilege of talking with him several times in his rooms. On at least one occasion, he read one of his plays to me aloud. I remember him saying—or perhaps I remember reading from him—that he had early in his life learned the difference between a series of file cards describing a person and then actually coming to meet that person. He used this example to drive home the difference between knowledge by abstraction and knowledge by way of dialogue or participation. The second kind of knowledge leads to a sense of mystery, which in his Gifford Lectures he described as *The Mystery of Being*. I have not been able to find the exact passage in Marcel, such as I so vividly remember it, but he often makes allusion to the file cards for missing persons he dealt with when he served with the Red Cross during World War I, as for example in his Harvard Lectures, *The Existential Background of Human Dignity* (Cambridge:

Harvard University Press, 1963), p. 36; *Creative Fidelity*, trans. Robert Rosthal (New York: Farrar, Straus & Co., 1964), pp. 31–32; cf. *The Mystery of Being*, vol. 1: *Reflection and Mystery* (Chicago: Henry Regnery, 1960), p. 36.

12. For an extended treatment, see *Nicomachean Ethics*, Book I. For Aristotle, happiness is not a state of feeling; it lies in "acting well": "the man who does not rejoice in noble actions is not even good." Ibid., I, viii. "A virtuous life requires exertion. . . ." Ibid., X, vi. Aristotle avoided abstract rules for virtuous acts and concentrated instead on the practical living of the agent, who "must be in a certain condition when he does them; in the first place he must have knowledge, secondly he must choose the acts, and choose them for their own sakes, and thirdly his action must proceed from a firm and unchangeable character." *Nicomachean Ethics*, II, iv. Further, "it makes a great difference whether we conceive the Supreme Good to depend on possessing virtue or on displaying it—on disposition, or on the manifestation of a disposition in action. For a man may possess the disposition without its producing any good result, as for instance when he is asleep, or has ceased to function from some other cause; but virtue in active exercise cannot be inoperative—it will of necessity act, and act well. And just as at the Olympic games the wreaths of victory are not bestowed upon the handsomest and strongest persons present, but on men who enter for the competitions . . . so it is those who act rightly who carry off the prizes and good things of life." Ibid., I, viii. In a word, happiness lies not in feeling good but in acting well.

13. Aristotle writes of pleasure: "Again, it has grown up with us all from our infancy; that is why it is difficult to rub off this passion, engrained as it is in our life. . . ." Ibid., II, iii. "Argument and teaching . . . are not powerful with all men, but the soul of the student must first have been cultivated by means of habits for noble joy and noble hatred, like the earth which is to nourish the seed. . . . The character, then, must somehow be there already with a kinship to virtue, loving what is noble and hating what is base.

"But it is difficult to get from youth up a right training for virtue if one has not been brought up under right laws; for to live temperately and hardily is not pleasant to most people, when young." Ibid., X, ix.

14. "No one would choose to live with the intellect of a child throughout his life." Ibid., X, iii. "This is why the activities we exhibit must be of a certain kind; it is because the states of character correspond to the differences between these. It makes no small difference, then, whether we form habits of one kind or of another from our very youth. . . ." Ibid., II, i. The good man "gratifies the most authoritative element in himself and in all things obeys this; and just as a city or any other systematic whole is most properly identified with the most authoritative element in it, so is a man. . . . Besides, a man is said to have or not to

have self-control according as his reason has or has not the control, on the assumption that this is the man himself. . . ." Ibid., IX, viii. "That the irrational element [of the soul] is in some sense persuaded by a rational principle is indicated also by the giving of advice and by all reproof and exhortation." Ibid., I, xiii.

15. "While [arguments] seem to have power to encourage and stimulate the generous-minded among our youth, and to make a character which is gently born, and a true lover of what is noble, ready to be possessed by virtue, they are not able to encourage the many to nobility and goodness. For these do not by nature obey the sense of shame, but only fear, and do not abstain from bad acts because of their baseness but through fear of punishment; living by passion they pursue their own pleasures and the means to them, and avoid the opposite pains, and have not even a conception of what is noble and truly pleasant, since they have never tasted it. What argument would remold such people? It is hard, if not impossible, to remove by argument the traits that have long since been incorporated in the character; and perhaps we must be content if, when all the influences by which we are thought to become good are present, we get some tincture of virtue." Ibid., X, ix.

16. See Max Weber, *The City*, ed. and trans. Don Martindale and Gertrud Neuwirth (New York: The Free Press, 1958), esp. chap. 4, "The Plebeian City."

17. Maritain saw Christianity as "leaven in the social and political life of nations," the "bearer of the temporal hope of mankind": "Under the often misunderstood or disfigured but active inspiration of the Gospel, the secular conscience has awakened not only to the dignity of the human person, but also to the aspirations and the elan which are at work in his depths . . . in the realm of temporal life it is the natural aspiration of the person to liberation from misery, servitude, and the exploitation of man by man, that the repercussions of the Gospel's message were to stimulate. . . . What has been gained for the secular conscience, if it does not veer to barbarism, is the sense of freedom, and the conviction that the forward march of human societies is a march toward the conquest of a freedom consonant with the vocation of our nature." Jacques Maritain, *Christianity and Democracy*, trans. Doris C. Anson (New York: Charles Scribner's Sons, 1944), pp. 37, 53–54.

18. "Getting rich has never been regarded as being in any way sinful, degrading, or morally dubious within the Jewish religion, so long as such wealth is acquired legally and used responsibly. I was raised in a fairly Orthodox Jewish home, and everyone I knew was in business, including most of the rabbis. . . . It was generally assumed that the spirit of commerce is perfectly compatible with full religious faith and full religious practice. I think this is true within Islam as well, but it is not true in Christianity." Irving Kristol, "The Spiritual Roots of Capitalism and Socialism," in Michael Novak, ed., *Capitalism and Socialism: A*

*Theological Inquiry* (Washington, D.C.: American Enterprise Institute, 1979), pp. 1–2; reprinted as "Christianity, Judaism, and Socialism," in Kristol, *Reflections of a Neo-Conservative: Looking Back, Looking Ahead* (New York: Basic Books, 1983), p. 316.

19. See Alejandro Antonio Chafuen, *Christians for Freedom*, with an Introduction by Michael Novak (San Francisco, California: Ignatius Press, 1987), esp. chap. 12, "Late-Scholastic Economics in Comparison with Classical Liberal Economics."

20. See Alan Macfarlane, *The Origins of English Individualism* (New York: Cambridge University Press, 1979), esp. chap. 5, "Ownership in England from 1200 to 1344," and chap. 6, "English Economy in the Thirteenth to Fifteenth Centuries."

21. Jefferson devotes several pages to an outline for Virginians' education in his only book, *Notes on Virginia*, and his correspondence is replete with advice on the topic; see, e.g., his letter of 19 August 1785 to his nephew Peter Carr. For his epitaph, Jefferson chose the three achievements for which he wished "most to be remembered": "Author of the Declaration of American Independence, of the Statute of Virginia for Religious Freedom & Father of the University of Virginia."

22. Yves Simon, in an echo both of Aristotle and of Hayek, writes: "It is *good for the community* that military men be devoted with a passion to national defense, bridge builders to the building of bridges, foresters to the preservation of forests, physicians to public health, and classicists to the study of classics. The particularity of the function removes confusions and opens the way to the advantages of specialization." Simon reaches this conclusion after distinguishing between "two relations to the common good. The private person inasmuch as he is morally excellent, wills and intends the common good, and subordinates his private wishes to it. He may not know what action the common good demands, but he adheres to the common good formally understood, to the form of the common good, whatever may be the matter in which this form resides; as far as content or matter is concerned, it is his business to will and intend private goods. But the public person is defined by the duty of willing and intending the common good considered both in its form and in its matter. And because the service of the common good normally involves an arrangement of things private, and sometimes requires the sacrifice of private interests, the subject of the public capacity exercises authority over the private person, whose business it is to look after particular matters." Simon, *A General Theory of Authority* (Notre Dame, Indiana: University of Notre Dame Press, 1980), pp. 62, 55 (emphasis added).

23. See Friedrich A. Hayek, *Law, Legislation and Liberty*, vol. 1: *Rules and Order* (Chicago: University of Chicago Press, 1973), pp. 39ff, esp. p. 56.

24. Adam Smith, *An Inquiry into the Nature and Causes of the Wealth*

*of Nations*, ed. R. H. Campbell, A. S. Skinner, and W. B. Todd (Oxford: Clarendon Press, 1979; reprint ed., Indianapolis, Indiana: Liberty Classics, 1981), p. 456. Cf. Edmund Burke: "It is therefore the first and fundamental interest of the laborer, that the farmer should have a full incoming profit on the product of his labor. The proposition is self-evident; and nothing but the malignity, perverseness, and ill-governed passions of mankind, and particularly the envy they bear to each other's prosperity, could prevent their seeing and acknowledging it, with thankfulness to the benign and wise Disposer of all things, who obliges men, whether they will or not, in pursuing their own selfish interests, to connect the general good with their own individual success." "Thoughts and Details on Scarcity," in *The Writings and Speeches of Edmund Burke*, 12 vols. (Boston: Little, Brown, 1901), 5:140–141.

25. Smith, *Wealth of Nations*, p. 456. Reinhold Niebuhr makes a similar argument: Man "cannot count on inadvertence and the coincidence of private desires alone to achieve common ends. On the other hand, man is too immersed in the welter of interest and passion in history and his survey over the total process is too short-range and limited to justify the endowment of any group or institution of 'planners' with complete power. The 'purity' of their idealism and the pretensions of their science must always be suspect. Man simply does not have a 'pure' reason in human affairs." Niebuhr, *The Irony of American History* (New York: Charles Scribner's Sons, 1962), p. 108.

25a. Simon writes: "A society in which none intends, even materially, a particular good is like a dead world. . . . Far from being genuinely exalted, the common good has become a mere appearance. Common good cannot exist unless it does exist as the good of a multitude; but there is no good 'of a multitude' unless particular goods are intended by particular appetites and taken care of by particular agents." Simon, *Philosophy of Democratic Government*, p. 55.

26. Historian Oscar Handlin explains: "In the nineteenth century, planning would have been a straitjacket in the United States, because one would always have been planning for conditions that were out of date by the time the plan was implemented. . . .

"Most of the plans for railroads, for instance, envisioned railroads that would run from east to west, and in time, that is how the transcontinentals were built. A lot of that was very romantic; it looked interesting on the map. The most profitable single railroad in the history of railroading was probably the Illinois Central, which ran north and south from Chicago. From a planner's point of view, it had to compete with the Mississippi River and all its tributaries, and it did not make sense; but it did make money." "The Development of the Corporation," in Michael Novak and John W. Cooper, eds., *The Corporation: A Theological Inquiry* (Washington, D.C.: American Enterprise Institute, 1981), p. 16.

27. See Peter Berger, *The Capitalist Revolution* (New York: Basic Books, 1986), chap. 4, "Capitalism and Political Liberties."

28. "Since the early centuries of Christianity, the fathers of the Church, bishops and theologians have repeatedly pointed out that God, in His goodness, has distributed natural resources and the agricultural products unevenly among the various countries in order to stimulate nations to friendly exchange and to link them together in a peaceful manner. John Chrysostom (who died in 407) argued that it is God's will that not everything can grow and be produced everywhere on earth so as to link peoples closely together by an exchange of goods. . . . Heinrich Heinbuche von Langenstein (born in Hesse in 1325) took up this line of thought and argued that the task of foreign trade lay in joining together nations 'in friendship and love.' John Mayr, a Scotsman (died in 1550), observed that no country can exist without commerce." Joseph Cardinal Hoeffner, "The World Economy in the Light of Catholic Social Teaching," in Lothar Roos, ed., *Ordo Socialis*, May 1987, pp. 26–27.

29. "Rather than viewing each other suspiciously across class barriers, successful industrialists and struggling self-employed workers alike have begun discovering that their common enemy is the country's bureaucracy.

". . . Hampered and frustrated by rules, licenses, permits, taxes, bribes and state intervention in general, owners of large and small businesses [in Peru] have embarked on an experiment called the Union of Formals and Informals to campaign for across-the-board deregulation of society.

" 'This union is created because we know that, more than ever, Peru is torn between misery and violence, riddled with corruption and overwhelming economic injustice and paralyzed by statism,' its statement of objectives said. 'This country can no longer bear the privileges that the law grants to political power.' " Alan Riding, "Peruvians Combating Red Tape," *New York Times*, 24 July 1988. See also Mario Vargas Llosa, "Peru's Silent Revolution: Despite Government Regulation, Entrepreneurs Are Rolling Back a Feudal Economic Order," *Crisis*, July–August 1987.

## Chapter Four: Beyond Economics, Beyond Politics

1. Robert N. Bellah, "The Economics Pastoral, A Year Later," *Commonweal*, 18 December 1987, p. 740 (emphasis added).

2. Ibid. Bellah cites a recent essay by Robert Heilbroner where he "reminded us that it is unrealistic to expect any society to work well. The most is that we expect that it work well enough." See Heilbroner, "Realities and Appearances in Capitalism," in Robert B. Dickie and Leroy S. Rouner, eds., *Corporations and the Common Good* (Notre Dame, Indiana: University of Notre Dame Press, 1986).

3. Bellah, "The Economics Pastoral, A Year Later," p. 739 (emphasis added).

4. Ibid.

5. For a recent survey of how welfare efforts have fared in practice and what principles may aid welfare reform, see The Working Seminar on Family and American Welfare Policy, *The New Consensus on Family and Welfare: A Community of Self-Reliance* (Washington, D.C.: American Enterprise Institute, and Milwaukee, Wisconsin: Marquette University, 1987).

6. Friedrich A. Hayek, *Law, Legislation and Liberty*, vol. 3: *The Political Order of a Free People* (Chicago: University of Chicago Press, 1979), p. 165.

7. Bellah, "The Economics Pastoral, A Year Later," p. 738. Bellah writes (ibid., p. 741) that "it would seem that Christians even before the bishops' economic pastoral knew that 'the preferential option for the poor' is an obligation that impinges on all of us." As evidence, Bellah cites two quotations with which Gertrude Himmelfarb began *The Idea of Poverty* (New York: Alfred A. Knopf, 1983): "one from Samuel Johnson in 1770, 'A decent provision for the poor is the true test of civilization . . .,' and the second from R. H. Tawney in 1926, 'There is no touchstone, except for the treatment of childhood, which reveals the true character of a social philosophy more clearly than the spirit in which it regards the misfortunes of those of its members who fall by the way.' " *Toward the Future* (Lanham, Maryland: University Press of America, 1984), the lay letter on Catholic social teaching and the U.S. economy, inspired by Prof. Himmelfarb, made the same point at the beginning of its section on poverty and welfare (p. 58).

8. Daniel Bell writes of the difficulties of maintaining faith in socialism: "One might have thought that the Moscow Trials, with their gruesome execution of almost the entire cadre of old Bolshevik leaders such as Zinoviev, Kamenev, Bukharin, as well as hundreds of others; the revelations about the *Yezhovschina*—the sweeping elimination of hundreds of thousands of old party activists during the tenure of N. I. Yezhov as head of the secret police—and the imprisonment of millions in the labor camps . . .; and the Nazi-Soviet pact (when the swastika was hoisted on Moscow airport in honor of Ribbentrop's arrival and the Red Army band broke into the *Horst Wessel Lied*)—that all this would have ended the infatuation of intellectuals with the Soviet Union." Again: "Krushchev's 1956 revelations of the malign crimes of Stalin; the subsequent Polish October led by young intellectuals which forced out the old Moscow-imposed regime; and the Hungarian Revolution in 1956–57 . . . closed the book for another generation of believers." The phrase "the end of ideology" was devised by Albert Camus during "a debate within the French Socialist Party. . . . Camus wrote: 'The chief task of the last party congress was to reconcile the desire for a new morality superior to

murder with the determination to remain faithful to Marxism. But one cannot reconcile what is irreconcilable.' " Bell, "The End of Ideology Revisited," Afterword to *The End of Ideology: On the Exhaustion of Political Ideas in the Fifties*, 3rd ed. (Cambridge: Harvard University Press, 1988), pp. 410–11.

9. Hayek's famous warning is contained in *The Road to Serfdom* (Chicago: University of Chicago Press, 1944). Writing that text during World War II, Hayek praised Hilaire Belloc's *The Servile State* (1913): it "explains more of what has happened since in Germany than most works written after the event." See Belloc, *The Servile State* (1913; reprint edition, Indianapolis, Indiana: Liberty Classics, 1977). Yet Tocqueville himself was the first writer to warn of the possibilities of a new, "soft" despotism. He feared "an immense, protective power which is alone responsible for securing [citizens'] enjoyment and watching over their fate. That power is absolute, thoughtful of detail, orderly, provident, and gentle. It would resemble parental authority if, fatherlike, it tried to prepare its charges for a man's life, but on the contrary, it only tries to keep them in perpetual childhood. . . . It provides for their security, foresees and supplies their necessities, facilitates their pleasures, manages their principal concerns, directs their industry, makes rules for their testaments, and divides their inheritances.

". . . it daily makes the exercise of free choice less useful and rarer, restricts the activity of free will within a narrower compass, and little by little robs each citizen of the proper use of his own faculties." Alexis de Tocqueville, *Democracy in America*, ed. J. P. Mayer, trans. George Lawrence (Garden City, New York: Doubleday, 1969), p. 693.

10. See Robert N. Bellah et al., *Habits of the Heart: Individualism and Commitment in American Life* (Berkeley: University of California Press, 1985). For four penetrating reviews of *Habits*, see Richard John Neuhaus, "Habits of the (Academic) Mind," *The Public Interest*, Spring 1986; William A. Schambra, "Habits of the (Divided) Heart: The Schizophrenic Soul of American Liberalism," *Catholicism in Crisis*, October 1985; Robert Nisbet, "La Maladie Academique," *This World*, Spring/Summer 1985; and William Kristol, "Beyond Individualism," *Commentary*, July 1985. See also the interview with Robert N. Bellah and Walter Berns in *Public Opinion*, April/May 1985.

11. Lay Commission, *Toward the Future*, pp. x–xii.

12. Tocqueville, *Democracy in America*, p. 526.

13. The authors of *Habits* say of four of their interviewees: "They are responsible and, in many ways, admirable adults. Yet when each of them uses the moral discourse they share, what we call the first language of individualism, they have difficulty articulating the richness of their commitments. In the language they use, their lives sound more isolated and arbitrary than, as we have observed them, they actually are." Bellah et al., *Habits of the Heart*, pp. 20–21.

14. See Robert Nisbet, *The Quest for Community* (New York: Oxford University Press, 1953); *The Social Philosophers: Community and Conflict in Western Thought* (New York: Thomas Y. Crowell, 1973); *Twilight of Authority* (New York: Oxford University Press, 1975); and William A. Schambra, "The Quest for Community and the New Public Philosophy," *Catholicism in Crisis*, April and May 1984; "Progressive Liberalism and American 'Community,' " *The Public Interest*, Summer 1985.

15. See Peter L. Berger and Richard John Neuhaus, *To Empower People: The Role of Mediating Structures in Public Policy* (Washington, D.C.: American Enterprise Institute, 1977).

16. In a telephone conversation with the author to discuss an earlier draft of this chapter, Robert Bellah said that neoconservative works had purposefully been excluded from *Habits*, as had works by several leftists.

17. See Robert N. Bellah, *The Broken Covenant: American Civil Religion in a Time of Trial* (New York: Crossroad Books, 1975), esp. chap. 5, "The American Taboo on Socialism."

18. The "progressive" tradition has behind it, Schambra argues, a large "moral project: the creation of a genuine national community . . . there would have to be a 'subordination of the individual to the demand of a dominant and constructive national purpose'. . . .

"The catalyst of the national community, the articulator of the 'national purpose,' in the liberal view, was to be the president—the galvanizing, unifying voice of all the American people. . . .

"Every 'great' liberal president of the twentieth century following Wilson made the cultivation of the national community the central goal of his administration. . . . [Franklin] Roosevelt described the purpose of the New Deal as 'extending to our national life the old principle of the local community.' " Schambra, "Progressive Liberalism and American 'Community.' " Cf. Bellah et al., *Habits of the Heart:* "periodically presidents have been seen as rising above politics and expressing a sense of the national community. Franklin Delano Roosevelt . . . was superbly able to embody a sense of national purpose" (p. 202). What the authors of *Habits* most admire about the civil rights movement they hope to emulate is its explicit aim "at broadening and strengthening effective membership in the national community." Their biggest complaint with the contemporary social movement is that "it does not represent the kind of massive linkage of local to national concerns typical of earlier movements." The movement's main virtue is providing "some useful examples of how a renewal of democratic citizenship at the national level might be achieved" (p. 213).

19. "We shouldn't underestimate the lure of community for the sophists, rhetoricians, humanists, and philosophers of our day. They were shrewd in seizing upon the war community of 1917 as a motive force and future subject of nostalgia. Minds of the brilliance of Lippmann, Mumford, Croly, Sinclair Lewis, Edgar Lee Masters, Van Wyck

Brooks made the idea mesmeric in the circles of political intellectuals and mesmeric it remains today." Robert Nisbet, "The Present Age and the State of Community," *Reason*, June 1988.

20. Quoted in Bellah et al., *Habits of the Heart*, pp. 263–264, citing the *Los Angeles Times*, 6 February 1982.

21. "The impulse to acquisition, pursuit of gain, of money, of the greatest possible amount of money, has in itself nothing to do with capitalism. This impulse exists and has existed among waiters, physicians, coachmen, artists, prostitutes, dishonest officials, soldiers, nobles, crusaders, gamblers, and beggars. One may say that it has been common to all sorts and conditions of men at all times and in all countries of the earth, wherever the objective possibility of it is or has been given. It should be taught in the kindergarten of cultural history that this naive idea of capitalism must be given up once and for all. Unlimited greed for gain is not in the least identical with capitalism, and still less its spirit. Capitalism *may* even be identical with the restraint, or at least a rational tempering, of this irrational impulse." Max Weber, *The Protestant Ethic and the Spirit of Capitalism*, trans. Talcott Parsons (New York: Charles Scribner's Sons, 1958), p. 17 (emphasis in original).

22. See Paul Johnson, *Modern Times: The World from the Twenties to the Eighties* (New York: Harper & Row, 1983).

23. Bellah et al., *Habits of the Heart*, p. 263.

24. In 1978, as a Democrat asked for advice by the editors of the Republican Party's journal of opinion, I wrote: "My advice, then, is that Republican thinkers begin to concentrate their creative energies upon *mediating institutions* as the natural organisms of daily life, and in particular on the *family*, the *neighborhood* and the *work place*." "Prescription for Republicans," *Commonsense* 1 (Summer 1978):33 (emphasis in original). It was later reported that Richard Wirthlin tested this notion, and passed the results to candidate Reagan.

25. Thomas Jefferson, "First Inaugural Address, March 4, 1801," in Adrienne Koch and William Peden, eds., *The Life and Selected Writings of Thomas Jefferson* (New York: Modern Library, 1972), p. 323.

26. President Reagan continued: "We have every right to dream heroic dreams. Those who say that we're in a time when there are not heroes, they just don't know where to look. . . . They're individuals and families whose taxes support the government and whose voluntary gifts support church, charity, culture, art, and education. Their patriotism is quiet, but deep. Their values sustain our national life.

". . . We shall reflect the compassion that is so much a part of your makeup. How can we love our country and not love our countrymen; and loving them, reach out a hand when they fall, heal them when they're sick, and provide opportunity to make them self-sufficient so they will be equal in fact and not just in theory?

". . . if no one among us is capable of governing himself, then who among us has the capacity to govern someone else? All of us together, in and out of government, must bear the burden. The solutions we seek must be equitable, with no one group singled out to pay a higher price." U.S., President, *Public Papers of the Presidents of the United States* (Washington, D.C.: Office of the Federal Register, National Archives and Records Service, 1953–  ), Ronald Reagan, 1981, pp. 1, 2.

27. Bellah et al., *Habits of the Heart*, p. 263, citing Ronald Reagan, address to the Annual Concretes and Aggregates Convention, 31 January 1984, as quoted in the *Los Angeles Times*, 1 February 1984.

28. The authors of *Habits* repeatedly stress the role of the national government. E.g., they doubt that "neocapitalism" can provide "convincing and effective substitutes for active management of the political economy and 'compassionate government' " (p. 266).

29. "Among laws controlling human societies there is one more precise and clearer . . . than all the others. If men are to remain civilized or to become civilized, the art of association must develop and improve among them at the same speed as equality of conditions spreads." Tocqueville, *Democracy in America*, p. 517.

30. Bellah et al., *Habits of the Heart*, pp. 251–252. Also: "So a movement to transform our social ecology would, among other things, be the successor and fulfillment of the Civil Rights movement. Finally, such a social movement would lead to changes in the relationship between our government and our economy. This would not necessarily mean more direct control of the economy, certainly not nationalization. It would mean changing the climate in which business operates so as to encourage new initiatives in economic and social responsibility, whether from 'private' enterprise or autonomous small- and middle-scale public enterprises" (ibid., pp. 286–287).

31. Ibid., p. 250.

32. "I doubt if one can cite a single example of any people engaged in both manufacture and trade, from the men of Tyre to the Florentines and the English, who were not a free people. There must therefore be a close link and necessary relationship between these two things, that is, freedom and industry." And again: "An American will attend to his private interests as if he were alone in the world; the moment afterward, he will be deep in public business as if he had forgotten his own. Sometimes he seems to be animated by the most selfish greed and sometimes by the most lively patriotism. But a human heart cannot really be divided in this way. Americans alternately display passions so strong and so similar first for their own welfare and then for liberty that one must suppose these urges to be united and mingled in some part of their being. Americans in fact do regard their freedom as the best tool of and the firmest guarantee for their prosperity. They love them both for the sake of each other. . . . They are therefore by no means inclined to suppose that it is no business of theirs to meddle in public affairs." Tocqueville, *Democracy in America*, pp. 539, 541

33. Lerner quotes Montesquieu, one of the framers' principal teachers, on the value of commerce: " 'Commerce cures destructive prejudices'; it 'polishes and softens barbaric morals.' In making men more aware of both human variety and sameness, commerce made them less provincial and in a sense more humane." Ralph Lerner, "Commerce and Character: The Anglo-American as New-Model Man," in Michael Novak, ed., *Liberation South, Liberation North* (Washington, D.C.: American Enterprise Institute, 1981), p. 36.

34. Three of the most distinguished German commentators on Catholic social thought, Lothar Roos of Bonn, Johannes Stemmler of Cologne, and Franz Mueller of the United States, have pointed out in letters to the author (May 1988) that the Latin text, *ad propria incepta*, is translated in the official German text as "unternehmerische Initiative" or (in English) "entrepreneurial initiative." The Bund Katholischer Unternehmer e. V. (association of Catholic leaders of enterprise) in Cologne praised *Sollicitudo Rei Socialis* as follows: "No other social encyclical before has proclaimed the 'right to entrepreneurial initiative' with such clarity and provided it with an ethical foundation. This implies a clear rejection of any collectivistic order of economy and society, which has no room for entrepreneurial initiative. In other words: freedom is an essential element of a social order which is in compliance with Catholic Social Teaching."

35. John Paul II, *Sollicitudo Rei Socialis*, 15. For the English text, see *Origins*, 3 March 1988.

36. See Mikhail Gorbachev, *Perestroika* (New York: Harper & Row, 1987).

37. The authors of *Habits* depart from the realism of the framers in certain ways. For example, they write that the framers believed "men of vision and virtue" would reach national office and be "a national civic-minded elite" (p. 255). In *Federalist* 10, Madison writes: "It is vain to say that enlightened statesmen will be able to adjust these clashing interests and render them all subservient to the public good. Enlightened statesmen will not always be at the helm." The authors of *Habits* assert that the Revolution ironically "unleashed an egalitarian spirit and a drive for individual success that soon swamped this first, fragile pattern in a torrent of territorial and economic expansion." But the Revolution did not "unleash" a drive for "individual success." According to Madison, that drive exists in all regimes, equality in property is a "wicked project," and the protection of different and unequal faculties of acquiring property is "the first object of government." The framers explicitly intended to expand and "enlarge the orbit" of the diverse interests that result from this "diversity in the faculties of men." Flourishing commerce, they believed, would play an indispensable role in preventing the "tyranny of the majority." A close reading of the *Federalist* suggests a quite larger role for commerce than Bellah and his colleagues observe. See also

Walter Berns, *Taking the Constitution Seriously* (New York: Simon and Schuster, 1987), "The Commercial Republic," pp. 173–180.

38. John Paul II, Address to Workers in Melo, Uruguay (8 May 1988), in *Origins*, 26 May 1988, p. 26.

39. James Q. Wilson has noted the increasing attention being paid to character. See his "The Rediscovery of Character," *The Public Interest* 81 (Fall 1985). See also Michael Novak, *Character and Crime: An Inquiry into the Causes of the Virtue of Nations* (Notre Dame, Indiana: Brownson Institute, 1986); and "The Challenges of Adulthood for a Liberal Society," *The Christian Century*, August 27–September 3, 1986.

## Chapter Five: The Marriage of Two Traditions

1. See Jacques Maritain, *Integral Humanism: Temporal and Spiritual Problems of a New Christendom*, trans. Joseph W. Evans (New York: Charles Scribner's Sons, 1968), appendix: "The Structure of Action."

2. Maritain carefully distinguishes between state and society: "The *Body Politic* or the *Political Society* is the whole. The *State* is a part—the topmost part—of this whole." He adds: "The State is only that part of the body politic especially concerned with the maintenance of law, the promotion of the common welfare and public order, and the administration of public affairs. The State is a part which *specializes* in the interests of the *whole*." Again: "The state is inferior to the body politic as a whole. Is the State even the *head* of the body politic? Hardly, for in the human being the head is an instrument of such spiritual powers as the intellect and the will, which the whole body has to serve; whereas the functions exercised by the State are for the body politic, and not the body politic for them." Maritain, *Man and the State* (Chicago: University of Chicago Press, 1951), pp. 10, 12, 13. See also *The Person and the Common Good*, trans. John J. FitzGerald (Notre Dame, Indiana: University of Notre Dame Press, 1966), esp. chap. 4, "The Person and Society."

3. Some of the echoes of Locke in *Rerum Novarum:* "to say that God has given the earth to the use and enjoyment of the universal human race is not to deny that there can be private property . . . the limits of private possession have been left to be fixed by man's own industry and the laws of individual peoples" (7). "The soil which is tilled and cultivated with toil and skill utterly changes its condition; it was wild before, it is now fruitful; it was barren and now it brings forth in abundance. That which has thus altered and improved it becomes so truly a part of itself as to be in a great measure indistinguishable, inseparable from it . . . it is just and right that the results of labor should belong to him who has labored" (8). "The common opinion of mankind . . . has found in the study of nature, and in the law of nature herself, the foundations of the division

of property . . . as conducing in the most unmistakable manner to the peace and tranquillity of human life" (8). "To labor is to exert one's self for the sake of procuring what is necessary for the purposes of life, and most of all for self-preservation . . . it is *personal;* for the exertion of individual power belongs to the individual who puts it forth, employing this power for that personal profit for which it was given. Secondly, a man's labor is *necessary;* for without the results of labor a man cannot live; and self-conservation is a law of nature" (34). Leo XIII also repeated a central, Lockean theme of the *Federalist:* "There naturally exists among mankind innumerable differences of the most important kind; people differ in capability, in diligence, in health, and in strength; and unequal fortune is a necessary result of inequality in condition. Such inequality is far from being disadvantageous either to individuals or to the community; social and public life can only go on by the various kinds of capacity and the playing of many parts, and each man, as a rule, chooses the part which peculiarly suits his case" (14).

4. The bishops say they "write . . . first of all to provide guidance for members of our own church as they seek to form their consciences about economic matters. . . . At the same time, we want to add our voice to the public debate about the directions in which the U.S. economy should be moving. We seek the cooperation and support of those who do not share our faith or tradition. The common bond of humanity that links all persons is the source of our belief that the country can attain a renewed public moral vision.The questions are basic and the answers are often elusive, they challenge us to serious and sustained attention to economic justice." "Economic Justice for All," para. 27.

5. For texts of the successive drafts of the bishops' pastoral letter, see *Origins* 14 (15 November 1984); *Origins* 15 (10 October 1985); *Origins* 16 (5 June 1986). The final text is found in *Origins* 16 (27 November 1986).

6. *Mater et Magistra*, 65.

7. John XXIII gives the definition of the common good quoted by the bishops precisely because "public authorities" need to have "a correct understanding of the common good" in all its private aspects. The paragraph, with its echoes of Tocqueville and Madison, deserves quotation in full: "That these desired objectives [advances in "social organization"] be more readily obtained, it is necessary that public authorities have a correct understanding of the common good. This embraces the sum total of those conditions of social living, whereby men are enabled more fully and more readily to achieve their own perfection. Hence, we regard it as necessary that the various intermediate bodies and the numerous social undertakings wherein an expanded social structure primarily finds expression, be ruled by their own laws, and as the common good itself progresses, pursue this objective in a spirit of sincere concord among themselves. Nor is it less necessary that the above mentioned groups present the form and substance of a true community.

This they will do, only if individual members are considered and treated as persons, and are encouraged to participate in the affairs of the group." Ibid., 65. John XXIII adds that "two factors" must be "kept in balance: (1) the freedom of individual citizens and groups of citizens to act autonomously, while cooperating one with the other; (2) the activity of the State whereby the undertakings of private individuals and groups are suitably regulated and fostered." In short, "an appropriate structuring of the human community" requires that men and women "develop and perfect [their] natural talents." Ibid., 66, 67. "Experience . . . shows that where private initiative of individuals is lacking, political tyranny prevails. Moreover, much stagnation occurs in various sectors of the economy, and hence all sorts of consumer goods and services, closely connected with needs of the body and more especially of the spirit, are in short supply. Beyond doubt, the attainment of such goods and services provides remarkable opportunity and stimulus for individuals to exercise initiative and industry." "Precautionary activities of public authorities in the economic field," then, "although widespread and penetrating, should be such that they not only avoid restricting the freedom of private citizens, but also increase it, so long as the basic rights of each individual person are preserved inviolate. . . . This implies that whatever be the economic system, it allow and facilitate for every individual the opportunity to engage in productive activity." Ibid., 57, 55.

8. Joseph Hoeffner, *Fundamentals of Christian Sociology*, trans. Geoffrey Stevens (Westminster, Maryland: The Newman Press, 1965), p. 30.

9. For example, in para. 280, the bishops worry that "the ability of corporations to plan, operate and communicate across national borders without concern for domestic considerations" will make it "harder for governments to direct their activities toward the common good"; still, "the effort should be made." In a talk delivered in Italy as the pastoral letter was being drafted, Archbishop Weakland described what he saw as a "return in U.S. attitudes to an uninhibited freemarket thinking as a solution to problems. Two factors are evident here and are clear in the type of economics taught in our universities in both political science as well as economics courses. I am amazed at the strength of libertarian thinking, that is, the return of the philosophy of John Locke on less government but accompanied by the strong rugged individualism that was so much a part of the past in the U.S.A. The frontier days are over but not the attitude that accompanied them. With this rugged individualism there is a return to the free market philosophy with frequent citations from Adam Smith." Rembert G. Weakland, "The American Bishops and the Economy of the U.S.A.: Analysis and Suggestions," *Notes et Documents de l'Institut International "Jacques Maritain"*, July–December 1985, pp. 5–11.

10. "The church's teaching opposes collectivist and statist economic approaches," the bishops write. They also insist that securing the

economic justice they seek "depends heavily on the leadership of men and women in business and on wise investment by private enterprises. Pope John Paul II has pointed out, 'The degree of well-being which society today enjoys would be unthinkable without the dynamic figure of the business person. . . .' " "Economic Justice for All," paras. 115, 110.

11. "In order to protect basic justice government should undertake only those initiatives which exceed the capacity of individuals or private groups acting independently. Government should not replace or destroy smaller communities and individual initiative. Rather it should help them to contribute more effectively to social well-being and supplement their activity when the demands of justice exceed their capacities. This does not mean, however, that the government that governs least governs best. Rather it defines good government intervention as that which truly 'helps' other social groups contribute to the common good by directing, urging, restraining and regulating economic activity as 'the occasion requires and necessity demands.' This calls for cooperation and consensus building among the diverse agents in our economic life, including government." Ibid., para. 124, quoting *Quadragesimo Anno*, 80.

12. In its lay letter, the Lay Commission insists upon the same standard; see Lay Commission on Catholic Social Teaching and the U.S. Economy, *Toward the Future* (New York: Lay Commission, 1984), p. 58.

13. We wrote: "A just solicitude for the common good and a proper respect for law at times impels the political system to intervene in the economic system or in the moral-cultural order." Again: "The political system has many wholly legitimate and important economic roles, including care for the truly needy. . . . The young, the elderly, the disabled, those visited by sudden misfortune, and many others are permanently or for a time unable to work. In a good society, the moral system and the political system must come to the assistance of such persons in ways the economic system alone cannot. . . . Particularly in its welfare functions, as a last resort, the state is an indispensable institution of the good society." Lay Commission, *Toward the Future*, pp. 11, 32–33.

14. Walter Berns has warned against the U.S. Supreme Court's tendency to adopt the idea of "economic rights": "It is as if the Court is of the opinion that taking rights seriously requires it to accord to demands or wants the status of rights, as if, by natural right, a person consents to be governed on the condition that his wants be satisfied. But this is absurd because it is impossible, and it is impossible because not all wants can be satisfied. (For example, the wants of the pro and antiabortion groups cannot both be satisfied.) What government can promise, if it is organized properly, is that rights can be secured, by which I mean the natural right to be governed only with one's consent. Under the Constitution's system of representative government, this becomes the right to be part of a governing majority.

"To repeat: while rights, properly understood, can be secured, not all wants can be satisfied. As our history attests, however, when those rights are secured, many wants are satisfied. Their satisfaction depends on their not being seen as rights." Berns, "The Constitution as Bill of Rights," *In Defense of Liberal Democracy* (Chicago: Regnery Gateway, 1984), p. 28. See also Michael Novak, "Economic Rights: The Servile State," *Crisis*, October 1985; "Economic Rights," *National Catholic Register*, 16 February 1986; "The Rights and Wrongs of Economic Rights: A Debate Continued," *This World*, Spring 1987.

15. See *Survey*, August 1987.

16. To repeat, I learned this from Maritain: "man is by no means for the State. The State is for man." Jacques Maritain, *Man and the State*, p. 13. "Although man in his entirety is engaged as a part of political society (since he may have to give his life for it), he is not a part of political society *by reason of his entire self* and all that is in him. On the contrary, by reason of certain things in him, man in his entirety is elevated above political society." Maritain, *The Person and the Common Good*, p. 71. "By its liberty, the human person transcends the stars and all the world of nature." Ibid., p. 20.

17. Ludwig von Mises, *Liberalism in the Classical Tradition*, trans. Ralph Raico (Irvington-on-Hudson, New York: Foundation for Economic Education, 1985), p. 33.

18. David Hollenbach, "Liberalism, Communitarianism and the Bishops' Pastoral Letter on the Economy," *The Annual of the Society of Christian Ethics 1987* (Washington, D.C.: Georgetown University Press, 1987), pp. 19–20.

19. Ibid., p. 21.

20. Ibid., pp. 22–23.

21. Hollenbach writes that the bishops' letter incorporates "both a liberal emphasis on personal dignity and rights, and the communitarian stress on the common good. It links these polarities by insisting . . . that community is constitutive of selfhood. As the bishops put it: 'Human life is life in community' (no. 63)." Ibid., p. 26.

22. Ibid., p. 28.

23. For example, in an article generally favorable to the bishops' letter, Leon Wieseltier writes: "The document certainly leaves much to be desired. It seems satisfied to oppose the conventional wisdom of the '80s with the conventional wisdom of the '60s. By this late date, however, too many defects of the Great Society have been too well documented to allow for the more or less uncritical recidivism of social policy that the bishops seem to support." Wieseltier, "The Poor Perplex," *The New Republic*, January 7 and 14, 1985. See also Robert Royal, ed., *Challenge and Response: Critiques of the Catholic Bishops' Draft Letter on the U.S. Economy* (Washington, D.C.: Ethics and Public Policy Center, 1985); Michael Novak, "Toward Consensus: Suggestions for Revising the First Draft," *Catholicism in Crisis*, March 1985.

24. Thomas Jefferson, "First Inaugural Address, March 4, 1801," in Adrienne Koch and William Peden, eds., *The Life and Selected Writings of Thomas Jefferson* (New York: Modern Library, 1972), p. 323.

25. Hollenbach, "Liberalism, Communitarianism and the Bishops' Pastoral Letter on the Economy," p. 31, citing John Rawls, "Justice as Fairness: Political not Metaphysical," *Philosophy and Public Affairs* 14 (1985).

26. Hollenbach, "Liberalism, Communitarianism and the Bishops' Pastoral Letter on the Economy," p. 31.

27. Von Mises, *Liberalism in the Classical Tradition*, p. 24.

28. Hollenbach, "Liberalism, Communitarianism and the Bishops' Pastoral Letter on the Economy," p. 33.

29. I would like to take this opportunity to emphasize my pleasure in the bishops' attempt to reconcile "communitarian" and "liberal." Hollenbach begins his essay with a summary and a critique of my own book on Catholic social thought and liberal institutions, *Freedom with Justice* (San Francisco: Harper & Row, 1984), and my earlier essay "Free Persons and the Common Good" in *Crisis*, October 1986. The theme of communitarian liberalism has been central to my work for many years. A strong emphasis on family, neighborhood, and local associations— together with a sharp distinction between "family people" and those who see themselves primarily as autonomous individuals—appeared in *The Rise of the Unmeltable Ethnics* (New York: Macmillan, 1972). The theme of "the communitarian individual" runs through *The Spirit of Democratic Capitalism* (New York: Simon and Schuster, 1982), where it occupies all of chap. 7. The Lay Commission criticized the early drafts of the bishops' pastoral with arguments, focused on specific passages, that the bishops emphasized "solidarity," at the expense of the rights, duties, initiatives, creativity, and responsibility of individuals and their free associations. Both poles need to be respected; balance is required. Our lay letter, which appeared before any of the bishops' drafts had been made public, warned in its preamble:

> Today, that sense of balance is sometimes lacking in the language of those who either choose individual liberty over all other concerns, and hence embrace a kind of radical individualism, or seek to enlarge the power and scope of government, and hence embrace a kind of statist meddlesomeness. Catholic social thought has from the first sought to avoid the "double danger" (Pius XI) of individualism and collectivism. It holds firm three basic principles: the sacred dignity of the person, the social nature of human life, and the obligation to assign social decisions to the level of authority best suited to take them.

In short, I welcome strongly Hollenbach's emphasis on "the communitarian individual." If the efforts of the Lay Commission played even a modest role in helping the final draft of the pastoral to be more exact in its theory, our efforts were well spent. One can only thank the bishops for genuinely listening to their critics, as they rewrote and rewrote. This entire public dialogue was an exercise in (for the most part) "civil, reasoned argument."

30. See, e.g., the essays by Cardinal Ratzinger, Cardinal Hoeffner, and others in Lothar Roos, ed., "Church and Economy in Dialogue," *Ordo Socialis*, May 1987.  ·

31. See Kevin G. Long, "Natural Liberty and the Common Good: Statesmanship and Political Economy in Plato, Aristotle, and Adam Smith," (Ph.D. dissertation, Claremont Graduate School, 1986).

32. Von Mises, *Liberalism in the Classical Tradition*, p. 34.

33. Ibid.

34. See Friedrich A. Hayek, *Law, Legislation and Liberty*, 3 vols. (Chicago: University of Chicago Press, 1973–79).

35. See Hayek, *Law, Legislation and Liberty*, vol. 2: *The Mirage of Social Justice* (Chicago: University of Chicago Press, 1976), chap. 9, " 'Social' or Distributive Justice." Cf. Jean-Yves Calvez and Jacques Perrin, *The Church and Social Justice: The Social Teachings of the Popes from Leo XIII to Pius XII* (Chicago: Henry Regnery, 1961), chap. 6, "Justice." Calvez and Perrin argue that the term "social justice" was first used by Pius XI in order "to state more exactly the place of commutative and of distributive justice," but it "did not indicate a new demand or a newly discovered virtue." Ibid., p. 153.

36. Von Mises, *Liberalism in the Classical Tradition*, pp. 7–8.

37. Nathan Tarcov, "A 'NonLockean' Locke and the Character of Liberalism," in Douglas MacLean and Claudia Mills, eds., *Liberalism Reconsidered* (Totowa, New Jersey: Rowman & Allanheld, 1983), p. 131.

38. See John Locke, *Second Treatise*, 3, 89, 110, 130–31, 135, 137, 142–43, 156, 158–60, 162–167, 200, 215, 222, 239.

39. Locke, *First Treatise*, 93.

40. Locke, *Second Treatise*, 95–97.

41. Ibid., 212.

42. John Locke, "Some Thoughts Concerning Reading and Study for a Gentleman," in *The Educational Writings of John Locke*, ed. James L. Axthell (Cambridge: Cambridge University Press, 1968), Epistle Dedicatory.

43. Ibid., no. 70.

44. Tarcov, "A 'NonLockean' Locke and the Character of Liberalism," p. 135.

45. Locke, *First Treatise*, 92.

46. Von Mises, *Liberalism in the Classical Tradition*.

47. L. T. Hobhouse, *Liberalism* (1911; reprint ed., New York: Oxford University Press, 1964 and Westport, Connecticut: Greenwood Press, 1980), pp. 63–64.

48. Ibid., p. 66.
49. Ibid.
50. Ibid., p. 67.
51. Ibid.
52. Ibid., p. 68.
53. Ibid.
54. Ibid.
55. Ibid., pp. 68–69.
56. Ibid., p. 70.
57. Ibid.
58. Von Mises, *Liberalism in the Classical Tradition*, p. 5.
59. For example, Michael Walzer writes: "political power must always be twice-won. It must be won first with the help of the state. . . . Then it must be won again by new popular forces against the state." Walzer, *Radical Principles: Reflections of an Unreconstructed Democrat* (New York: Basic Books, 1980), p. 51. Similarly, Michael Harrington quotes with approval Jean-Jacques Servan-Schreiber: ". . . social justice is not only a moral objective but the condition of industrial growth. If that is what it means to be socialist, we should be socialist. But if, according to the dogmas and catechisms, proceeding toward the abolition of competition, authoritarian planification and the collectivist society are socialist, then we are not." Quoted in Harrington, *Socialism* (New York: Saturday Review Press, 1970), p. 207; see the entire chapter, "Socialist Capitalism."

## Appendix: Notes on Terminology

1. S. Iniobong Udoidem, *Authority and the Common Good in Social and Political Philosophy* (Lanham, Maryland: University Press of America, 1988), p. 87.
2. See Michael Novak, *A Time to Build* (New York: Macmillan, 1967), chap. 18, "Moral Society and Immoral Man"; and Novak, "Three Porcupines of Pluralism," *This World*, Fall 1987.
3. See Michael Novak, "A Key to Aristotle's Substance," *Philosophy and Phenomenological Research* 24 (September 1963): 1–19.
4. Jacques Maritain, *The Person and the Common Good*, trans. John J. FitzGerald (Notre Dame, Indiana: University of Notre Dame Press, 1966), pp. 52–53 (emphasis in original).
5. See Yves R. Simon, *Philosophy of Democratic Government* (Chicago: University of Chicago Press, 1951), pp. 39–42. Simon takes his examples from *Summa Theologiae*, I–II, q. 19, a. 10. See also chap. 3, n. 9, *supra*.
6. Simon, *Philosophy of Democratic Government*, p. 48 (emphasis in original).
7. The points at which Simon's emphasis differs from mine should

perhaps be stated as succinctly and clearly as space allows. Simon explicitly recognizes that liberalism has many strands and many diverse positions, e.g., in *A General Theory of Authority* (Notre Dame, Indiana: University of Notre Dame Press, 1980), p. 101. But sometimes he criticizes one or more strands of liberal thought, while leaving aside the strands of which he approves. I count five positions within the strands of liberalism he rejected. He sometimes emphasized what he rejected; I try to emphasize, by contrast, the strands to be welcomed. In Simon's eyes:

(1) liberalism defined the common good merely as *sum* of individual goods, rather than as a holistic, organic unity of spirits (as in a team); and in this respect he sometimes ignored such definitions of an organic liberalism as that of Hobhouse (pp. 165–169, above);

(2) liberalism stressed mere *contract*, as in a business partnership, rather than a truly community-inspiring sense of common purpose, public service, and willing self-sacrifice; but here he sometimes overlooked the pledge of "lives, liberty, and sacred honor" with which the American republic began, as well as its self-understanding as expressed in its patriotic hymns and founding "covenants";

(3) liberalism conceived of humans as *individuals*, rather than as *persons* (Maritain's distinction); here Simon at times ignored the American emphasis upon virtue, civic spirit, public duty, association, education, and "biblical republicanism";

(4) liberalism imagined that every human individual is equal in *strength and ability*, and thus overlooked the inequalities of nature and human weakness that inspire conscience to reach out to the *weak and vulnerable;* and here Simon sometimes ignored, e.g., the differences between Adam Smith and Thomas Malthus that Bellah (above, pp. 115–116) praises Himmelfarb for stressing;

(5) liberalism thinks of the state in Hobbesian terms, founding it upon human *evil*, rather than upon the moral goodness of the human being, who is a social and political animal in his very nature; but here Simon at times ignores evidences to the contrary, as in the *Federalist* (see pp. 42–55, above).

In a word, Simon's interpretation of liberal ideas does not fix attention upon the *American* form of the liberal society, and often passes over many texts in Madison, Jefferson, Tocqueville, Lincoln, and others, including important aspects of the Progressive movement (from Theodore Roosevelt to Franklin Delano Roosevelt). Simon misses, too, the influence of Burke's "little platoons" upon the classic American understanding of family, neighborhood, local associations, and small communities of shared living and shared concern. Clearly, Simon drew upon and embraced the positive values of such sources as these. The point is, rather, that he gave too little credit to the "whig," "progressive," and "liberal" convictions from which they emanated. He did not stress, as Maritain (and Walter Lippmann) did, the continuity of the *philosophia perennis* in American thought and institutions. Simon frequently used certain strands of liberalism as a polemical target, while hardly emphasizing its sounder strands. My own judgment, by contrast, is that, even precisely as Thomists and as Catholics, we ought to give the liberal tradition in America (and elsewhere) considerable credit for awakening Catholics from our own slumbers, and for leading us where *we* might have led, had we been more faithful to our own inspirations and more inventive concerning their institutional embodiments. Alas, we did not offer such leadership when it was needed, and must now work double-time to make up lost ground, and to offer our own fresh perspectives (some of them rooted in Simon's work) to the common human project.

# INDEX OF NAMES

# INDEX OF SUBJECTS